Pioneers, Hidden Champions, Changemakers, and Underdogs

Pioneers, Hidden Champions, Changemakers, and Underdogs

Lessons from China's Innovators

Mark J. Greeven, George S. Yip, and Wei Wei

The MIT Press
Cambridge, Massachusetts
London, England

This book was set in Sabon by Toppan Best-set Premedia Limited.

Library of Congress Cataloging-in-Publication Data

Names: Greeven, Mark J., author. | Yip, George S., author.
Title: Pioneers, hidden champions, changemakers, and underdogs : lessons from China's innovators / Mark J. Greeven, George S. Yip, and Wei Wei.
Description: Cambridge, MA : MIT Press, [2019] | Includes bibliographical references and index.
Identifiers: LCCN 2018030556 | ISBN 9780262039697 (hardcover : alk. paper) ISBN 9780262547895 (paperback)
Subjects: LCSH: Technological innovations--Economic aspects--China. | New business enterprises--China. | New products--China. | Entrepreneurship--China.
Classification: LCC HC430.T4 G74 2019 | DDC 338/.0640951--dc23 LC record available at https://lccn.loc.gov/2018030556

Mark J. Greeven dedicates this book to Irene Greeven-de Gruil and Harry Greeven.

George S. Yip dedicates this book to Lucas Yip and Ellie Yip.

Wei Wei dedicates this book to Chen Jingmin.

Contents

Acknowledgments

Mark J. Greeven thanks Zhejiang University (ZJU) School of Management, ZJU alumni, and the many Chinese entrepreneurs for enabling most of this research. George S. Yip thanks the Centre on China Innovation (CCI) at China Europe International Business School (CEIBS) and CCI's corporate sponsors (Akzo Nobel, Bosch, DSM, Philips, and Shell) for their previous support of his research about innovation in China and Imperial College Business School for its current support. Wei Wei thanks the alumni of Tsinghua University and the participants of our executive workshops with companies such as Bosch, DSM, Philips, Sanofi, Vanderlande, and others that have provided critical and reflective perspectives on our ideas and helped to develop the key insights from a business and professional perspective.

We thank Emily Taber, editor in economics, finance, and business at the MIT Press, for signing this book and for sharing her insights and encouragement. We also thank the anonymous reviewers who have helped to improve this book. We thank the manuscript editor, Rosemary Winfield, for her meticulous work.

1

Introduction: China's Emerging Innovators

The time is long gone when tech unicorns, digital disruptors, and celebrity entrepreneurs came exclusively from Silicon Valley. A new generation of Chinese entrepreneurs includes the many elite entrepreneurs who return from overseas studies and establish technology ventures as well as young digital natives who are disrupting the world of industry incumbents, creating hero entrepreneur identities, and relentlessly pursuing growth. In addition, hundreds of global market leaders from China appear to be hidden from the broader global public's view. This book is about the rise of these emerging Chinese innovators.

What Is This Book About?

This book is about who is innovating in China and how they are doing it. Although corporate professionals and academic observers have praised the innovators behind companies such as Alibaba, Haier, and Huawei, there is more to come. Dozens if not hundreds of "hidden champions" (a term first used by Hermann Simon to describe small and medium-sized enterprises that are highly successful but inconspicuous) already occupy global leadership positions in various industrial niches, and an enormous number of Chinese innovators are operating under the radar. Moreover, a new generation of changemakers in China is looking beyond boundaries and cultivating a disruptive business mind set. If one Alibaba can shock international stock markets and disrupt traditional industries, we can only imagine what tens of thousands under-the-radar technology entrepreneurs, global hidden champions, and young changemakers will accomplish. This book is about Chinese innovators—not only the large domestic incumbents but those next-generation changemakers who are operating under the radar.

We take a strategic perspective and focus on managerial questions to explore the opportunities and challenges that Chinese innovators pose for Chinese and global markets. This is a remarkable opportunity for small and large companies inside and outside of China. Business observers have announced that we live in turbulent, hypercompetitive, and uncertain times, but Chinese innovators have never known otherwise. They have proven to be well equipped to deal with and embrace widespread technological, market, and regulatory uncertainties to better their competitive positions.

This book is organized around the "why," "who," "what," "how," and "what's next" questions about innovation in China. The "why" question asks what makes innovation in China a long-term necessity. The remainder of chapter 1 outlines the drivers of innovation, including encouragement by the government, increases in the cost of labor, intensifying competition, and the rise of a demanding middle class. We briefly review the key conditions that are facilitating and inhibiting innovation in China, such as manufacturing capability, venture capital, standardization, the management and protection of intellectual property, and innovation islands.

In chapters 2 to 5, in a search for an answer to the question of "who" is innovating in China, we go beyond the traditional business-school emphasis on large successful companies, which typically are domestic market leaders and global companies. We also do not focus exclusively on what economists call "small businesses," a term that usually refers to the small ventures that are run by "mom-and-pop" entrepreneurs and are drivers of any economy. The book also does not focus only on student or nascent entrepreneurs or "born-global companies" (companies that from inception use resources from and sell products in many countries). The purpose of the book is to identify and assess all types of entrepreneurial innovators, regardless of size and visibility. Drawing on our decade-long in-depth study and the extant innovation literature, we define "innovators" as companies that successfully develop and commercialize new offerings that bring new value to customers. New offerings may include new products and services, new business processes, new business models, new ways to organize the value chain, or new organizational arrangements. The key is that innovation brings new value to customers (whether they are existing or new customers or are consumer, business, or government customers) and that the innovation might be new to the world, new to the industry, or new to the country and region.

Table 1.1
Emerging innovators framework

	Mass market	Niche market
Incumbent	Pioneer	Hidden champion
Newcomer	Changemaker	Underdog

We distinguish four types of innovators in China (pioneer, hidden champion, underdog and changemaker) according to two dimensions (mass market and niche market) (table 1.1). We distinguish incumbent innovators from newcomers, and we distinguish mass markets from niche markets.

The first type (chapter 2), pioneer, is a leading innovator in its respective industries with revenues well over $10 billion (USD), national top three market share, and international awareness. We distinguish manufacturing champions (such as Haier, Huawei, Lenovo, and Sany) from Internet pioneers (such as Alibaba, Baidu, Tencent, and Xiaomi). The second type (chapter 3), hidden champion, is a midsize but leading innovator with revenues smaller than $5 billion, national top three market share, and a low level of public awareness. We discuss hidden champions such as Goldwind, Hikvision, and Mindray, which are market leaders in their niches. The third type (chapter 4), underdog, is a technology venture that is under the radar, was generally established after 2000, is technology driven, and has significant intellectual property. We discuss innovative underdog ventures in science- and technology-intensive industries such as biotechnology, flexible display, nanotechnology, and photovoltaic devices. The fourth type (chapter 5), changemaker, is a technology venture that was generally established after 2007 and is characterized by cross-industry innovations and digital disruption. We discuss changemakers such as Didi Chuxing, Ele.me, Mobike, and Toutiao. Many have grown into the world's largest unicorns in just five years.

In chapters 2 to 5, we use a comparative assessment model of innovation to look at the types of innovations that Chinese companies develop. We assess the type of innovation, ranging from a product and process model to an organizational and business model. Second, we investigate the type of competitive strategy that is followed. Finally, we identify the key drivers of innovation for Chinese innovators, including efficiency, customers, science, and technology. This book provides accounts of varieties of innovation that go beyond process and efficiency improvements that improve, sustain, and disrupt industrial and consumer markets.

Chapter 6 examines how Chinese innovators innovate. Our inductive research with Chinese companies has identified at least six underlying elements of the innovative capability of Chinese firms. Although some critics claim that any one of these methods is not unique to China, their combination has fostered a distinctive style of Chinese innovation. Our studies have consistently found these ways of innovation regardless of firm size, experience, or sector and have questioned the assumption that companies from developing economies can catch up only slowly. The rise of a middle class and an entrepreneurial class has created an unexpected acceleration of innovation.[1] Our findings suggest that multinational corporations or companies (MNCs) and other innovating companies may have a lot to learn from Chinese innovation.

Finally, chapters 7 and 8 focus on the future and what might come next. In chapter 7, we discuss the ways by which Chinese innovators are going global, including globalizing sales and market, globalizing R&D, creating innovation networks, expanding digital ecosystems abroad, and exporting disruptive business models. The challenges of growing into a global innovator are also discussed. We illustrate these with a variety of examples such as Baidu, Damon, Envision, Hikvision, Huawei, Mobike, and Weihua. Chapter 8 concludes the book by summarizing the four types of innovators, discussing important implications for developed economy companies and proposing areas for future investigation. We explore the applicability of the Chinese innovators' way in other developed and emerging markets. Our main argument is that innovators in China are not only the visible champions but are also the hidden champions that are under the radar and the young changemakers who innovate beyond process and efficiency and improve, sustain, and disrupt markets.

Our focus is on Chinese innovators and their rapidly developing innovative competences. Although we outline the drivers and conditions of Chinese innovators in chapter 1, we take these conditions mostly as a fact of business life. We focus on Chinese innovators operating within the currently existing economic and political system. We identify and assess challenges to Chinese innovators, but our focus is on the who, what, and how of successful innovation by Chinese companies. Although this also includes the management of government relations and we acknowledge the wider economic context and political economy of China, our focus is strategic and managerial rather than economic and political.

For the academic reader, we recommend recently published academic edited volumes such as *China's Innovation Challenge: Overcoming the Middle-Income Trap* by Arie Y. Lewin, Martin Kenney, and Johann P. Murmann; *China as an Innovation Nation* by Yu Zhou, William Lazonick, and Yifei Sun; and the excellent academic perspective by Xiaolan Fu in *China's Path to Innovation*, which lays out the challenges and achievements in the transition toward an innovation nation.[2] For a focus on the emergence of global innovators from China, we recommend *Created in China* by George Haour and Max von Zedtwitz.[3] For readers interested in the macroeconomic and political economy of China's technological development and innovation, we suggest the critical assessments in *Paper Tigers, Hidden Dragons* by Douglas Fuller and *Run of the Red Queen: Government, Innovation, Globalization, and Economic Growth in China* by Dan Breznitz and Michael Murphee.[4] Contributions from a more strategic perspective are George S. Yip and Bruce McKern's *China's Next Strategic Advantage: From Imitation to Innovation* and Ming Zeng and Peter J. Williamson's *Dragons at Your Door: How Chinese Cost Innovation Is Disrupting Global Competition*.[5] Popular books include Shaun Rein's *The End of Copycat China: The Rise of Creativity, Innovation and Individualism in Asia* and Yinglan Tan's *Chinnovation: How Chinese Innovators Are Changing the World*, among others.[6] In the last few years, there has been a steep increase in the number of publications on innovation in China. A quick search of the top academic journals in business shows that over a hundred articles have been published in the last five years. The number of business articles in the *Economist*, the *Financial Times*, the *New York Times*, and other periodicals is enormous. We contribute to the ongoing debate on the sustainability of China's innovation by focusing on a large number of unknown or relatively hidden innovative companies. We claim that most of the current arguments in the debate about sustainability miss most of the innovative companies in and from China.

For university instructors, teaching cases have been published on Alibaba, Baidu, Didi Chuxing, Ele.me, Goldwind, Haier, Huawei, Sany, Tencent, and Xiaomi. Books have been published on Alibaba, Baidu, Haier, Huawei, Tencent, and Xiaomi, and recently a comparative case study of business ecosystems appears in Mark J. Greeven and Wei Wei's *Business Ecosystems in China: Alibaba and Competing Baidu, Tencent, Xiaomi, and LeEco*.[7] However, no teaching cases or books have been published on most of the companies discussed in our book, such as Ease Power, GeneChem, Hailide, Han's Laser, Magnity, Ringpu, Shining 3D, Uninano,

Weihua, and Zongmu. This book provides rich material and discussion insights for instructors in university courses on innovation, international business, and strategic management.

This book provides a uniquely comprehensive account of who the Chinese innovators are—pioneers, hidden champions, underdogs, and changemakers—rather than focusing only on a handful of large incumbents. We include at least three groups of companies that frequently are ignored in other studies. Second, we assess the varieties of innovation in the Chinese context and conclude that innovations in China go beyond process, cost, and efficiency and include sustaining and disruptive consequences for competition.

Third, we look at the output of the innovation process, a variety of innovations, and also the innovation process itself. Based on our own in-depth research, we propose a Chinese innovator's way that reflects the competence for innovation found in Chinese companies. Throughout the book, a deeper look at Chinese companies' competence for innovation is provided through rich illustrations and thick descriptions.

Fourth, we adopt a strategic perspective on innovation in China as we document the competitive consequences for domestic and global companies. Although knowledge about the pioneers is readily available, we provide insights through a comparative perspective. Insights and knowledge that we have gained about the large group of hidden champions and under-the-radar underdogs could have great competitive consequences for multinationals that are active in China or seeking to expand further into China's markets. A deeper understanding of the changemakers may lead to unexpected opportunities from hidden corners in existing or emerging new industries.

Fifth, we contribute to the debate on the sustainability of innovation in and from China by providing evidence of a large number of Chinese innovators that up until now have been largely ignored. Moreover, the approach to innovation that these innovators follow indicates a capability to thrive in highly uncertain business environments. We argue that with such a large group of innovating companies, the long-term sustainability of innovation coming from China is guaranteed.

Sixth, although most publications on China focus on a handful of champions, our book features over forty cases and many more illustrative examples. This comparative case perspective includes pioneers, hidden champions, underdogs, and changemakers and is valuable for executives, professionals, students, and academics in the field of innovation. This book is intended for the business reader rather than the academic one, but we hope that our decade-long in-depth research on Chinese innovators will be a source for hypotheses and insights for researchers.

The Rise of Innovative Companies in China: Countering the Copycat View

Are Chinese companies capable of innovating?[8] Many people argue that Chinese companies are copycats and that the successful Chinese companies have received significant government protection. An example often used is Baidu's search engine or the so-called Goodapple smartphone. In early 2015, *Harvard Business Review* published an article entitled "Why China Can't Innovate," and many thought leaders have supported a copycat view of Chinese innovation.[9] On the other hand, many other authors have proposed an alternative view of an innovative, sometimes disruptive China. In its December 2017 issue, *Fortune* highlights China's innovators; the February 2018 *Time* cover features Robin Li, the founder of Baidu; in its March 2015 issue, *Wired* claims that it is "time to copy China"; and in its February 2018 issue, the *Economist* suggests that "Silicon Valley may not hold onto its global superiority for much longer." Yip and McKern's *China's Next Strategic Advantage* summarizes the key arguments in this debate.[10] In this book, we identify a group of Chinese innovators that were previously left out of the discussion and highlight the unique ways in which Chinese innovators approach innovation. Rather than just investing and exporting, Chinese innovators have already started to globalize innovation. In what follows, we discuss the evolution and rise of innovative companies in China.

China's economic growth, expansion of markets, and increasing consumer income are clear drivers of innovation, and competition is forcing Chinese innovators to accelerate.[11] In less than forty years, China has transformed itself from imitation to innovation in an evolution that goes hand in hand with the development of China's entrepreneurial private sector.

Not long ago, private entrepreneurs in China were seen as signs of unwanted capitalism. In 1978 to 1992, during the early phase of the economy's opening up, private companies were seen as supplements and had a dubious semi-illegal status. This is the period when Zhang Ruimin's Haier, Zong Qinghou's Wahaha, and Liu Chuanzhi's Lenovo were founded and later transformed from government organizations to semiprivately run companies. China was building its manufacturing capability, and original equipment manufacturers (OEMs)—such as Lu

Guanqiu's Wanxiang Group in Zhejiang and many industrial manufacturers of mechanical components and electronics—were under enormous cost pressures. The first attempts at incremental innovation, rather than imitation, focused on cost-driven innovations such as employing abundant and low-cost labor and introducing new ideas in various parts of the production process.

In 1992, Deng Xiaoping's famous speech in Shenzhen endorsed the legal status of private firms, and from 1992 to 2000, elite entrepreneurs who previously worked for the government (such as Feng Lun' s Vantone Group and Chen Dongsheng's Taikang Life Insurance) saw that private companies provided many opportunities. With the public endorsement of private enterprise, competition also increased for the first-generation enterprises. Leveraging the skills acquired for cost reduction, companies started to adapt and improve their technological capabilities. Companies such as Haier and Huawei started to develop and produce new products. Their innovations were mostly market driven and tapped into growing markets, which increasingly allowed them to compete with foreign entrants.

Since 2000, China has fully endorsed and promoted private entrepreneurship and given it a status that is equal to the state sector. At around the same time, digital technologies started to drive innovation in China.[12] At the end of 1990s, during the Internet boom when companies like Alibaba, Baidu, and Tencent were benchmarking Western Internet businesses, the patterns began to change to digital disruption. Chinese Internet technology companies are disrupting nontech traditional industries and leading in global ecommerce and recently financial technology innovations. High growth and competition forced companies to innovate new products and technologies. In this phase, incumbents started to produce intellectual property (IP) in research and development (R&D) centers, while at the same time a boom in new technology ventures after 2000 was fueled by overseas returnees, well-educated domestic entrepreneurs, and growing venture capital firms that were aiming to commercialize knowledge-driven innovation.

More recently, a new wave of technology changemakers has been innovating across industry boundaries.[13] The new generation of Chinese entrepreneurs has produced true changemakers. Their mindset is different from first-wave predecessors such as Haier's Zhang Ruimin, Lenovo's Liu Chuanzhi, and Huawei's Ren Zhengfei. The new entrepreneurs have embraced digital technologies to rethink product offerings in various traditional industries. Not afraid of and perhaps unaware of the complexities and legacy of traditional industries, these young changemakers have been innovating across industry boundaries. Moreover, this new generation of entrepreneurs is digital savvy and has shown strong public identities and excellent marketing capabilities. They are not afraid of the spotlight, unlike older entrepreneurs like Ren Zhengfei, Lu Guanqiu, and Zong Qinghou, who are known for their modesty and low public profiles.

In the latest phase, the globalization of innovation goes hand in hand with the significant increase of Chinese outward foreign investment. Companies like Haier and Huawei have established R&D centers abroad, where they connect with foreign research and talent and look for markets, resources, knowledge, and technology. Companies like Damon, Envision, and Weihua are setting up either innovation bases or technology outposts. Although digital giants like Alibaba, Baidu, and Tencent have been globalizing their digital ecosystems for years, changemakers like Didi Chuxing and Mobike are also exporting their disruptive business models. This is an era of Chinese innovation for both China and the world.

China's Innovation Ecosystem

Whether or not innovation is there to stay depends on two things—the need to innovate and the capacity and conditions for innovating. As with many things in China, the overall public rhetoric of the government is strong and supports innovation. For instance, a recent major policy initiative is Made in China 2025, which focuses on making China a global leader of smart manufacturing. China's strong manufacturing base, more than adequate capital, army of entrepreneurs, scalability in the domestic market, and science and engineering tradition have allowed the country to be well positioned to achieve this goal. Chinese companies are going to drive information technology (IT) transformations such as the Internet of things, big data, and the cloud. China's new changemakers are increasingly attracting investors and entrepreneurs from Silicon Valley to fund projects in China. However, enterprises must have a grassroots need and a sense of urgency because they are the carriers of innovation and often the locale of innovation. Even if they have the drive, they also need supportive conditions in China. In what follows, we provide evidence of the sustainability of the drivers and conditions for innovation to show that China's innovation ecosystem provides long-term and fertile conditions for innovation in China.

The Need for Innovation

China has two special characteristics that apply to the innovation ecosystem as well as most aspects of the country. The first is that most things in China change very quickly, mostly in an upward direction in recent decades. The second is that the country has great regional diversity in geography and in economic and institutional development. These differences in rate of development have been driven by geography (such as distance from the coast and from the central government), the speed of reform embraced by provincial and other local government entities, and the individual actions taken by local government officials. The central government has an unspoken policy of allowing regional governments to experiment with reforms and other activities that are not explicitly legitimate. If successful, these reforms will be legitimized later.

These two characteristics—rapid change and also geographical and developmental diversity—have two consequences. First, the changes in China have pushed companies to develop new products, improve processes, and explore new business models and services. Change in China arises from many sources, including government regulations, consumer behavior, competition, and technologies. These continuous changes require companies to adapt and try to stay in front of regulatory changes. According to the Global Entrepreneurship Monitor, entrepreneurs rate China's internal market dynamics as an average 40 percent higher than global or regional averages.[14] Rapid change drives innovation by Chinese enterprises and is unlikely to change anytime soon.

Second, China's wide local diversity has a similar effect, although across geographies rather than time. If China's inequality is considered in terms of gross regional products and associated levels of income, customers in fourth-tier cities can be seen to have structurally different requirements and behavior than customers in first-tier cities. Moreover, according to the World Bank's Doing Business in China data,[15] the investment and regulatory climates across Chinese cities are distinctly different. Doing business in different areas requires delivering different value propositions to local customers and also developing a different business model. Again, local companies operating across China need to be innovative and often produce new products and design new business models for different areas. Geographical and developmental diversity in China drives innovation.

China's rapid change and geographical and developmental diversity combined with governmental encouragement, increased labor costs, intensifying competition, and a rising middle class create a strong sense of urgency in Chinese enterprises to innovate.

The Conditions for Innovation

In the most basic sense, the conditions for innovation should include input and output factors—from capital, knowledge, and human resources to organizations—for executing and commercializing innovation and a governance mechanism for connecting and managing the relevant stakeholders. In this section, we discuss the following critical conditions:

- An education system that produces graduates in science, technology, engineering, and mathematics (STEM),
- Government support for research and innovation,
- The protection of intellectual property rights,
- Many entrepreneurial startups, and
- A financing system for startups that includes access to venture capital.

Education: A "China plus" approach In education, China depends on its own university graduates and on returning graduates who have been trained in developed markets—a "China plus" approach. China has one of the world's largest percentages of university classes devoted to STEM subjects and the largest number of bachelor-, master- and doctoral-level graduates in STEM (over 3 million STEM students were enrolled in 2017).[16] But it is widely accepted that these graduates are not as well trained as those coming out of universities in developed markets, with the exception of the graduates from China's top twenty elite universities. More than any other country, however, China attracts citizens who attended schools in other countries. Since 1978, 4 million students have studied abroad, 2.8 million students have graduated, and 80 percent of those overseas graduates (2.2 million graduates) have returned to China.[17] These returnees or *haigui* (sea turtles) form a critical and distinctive part of China's innovation ecosystem. In this way, China combines its quantitative advantage of large numbers of less well-trained STEM staff members who have studied in Chinese schools with world-class returnees who have studied in developed countries.

China's education system is often regarded as suppressing creativity, and there is some truth in that stereotype. However, China's culture of creativity has been developing. First, the single-child generation is much less accepting of authority. Second, the Chinese government has recognized the problem and is supporting the stakeholders (such as schools, parents, and companies) to find solutions. And third, large numbers of Chinese students now earn their first university degrees in developed markets, where they are exposed to creative ways of thinking. As they return to China, these foreign-educated students are steadily changing the local culture. Our research uncovered increasing levels of creativity and innovation—many technology-based ventures that were established after 2000 and a new generation of changemakers who are establishing ventures with disruptive business models.

Government support and Communist Party influence: Ambition and indirect guidance China's government pursues innovation with great determination and planning in a typically Chinese way that results in more support than is seen in many developed markets. Innovation has now reached the top position on the list of priority focus areas in China's latest Five-Year Plan (2016 to 2020). The Chinese Academy of Sciences has designated twenty-two strategic science and technology initiatives to be of strategic importance in China's modernization.[18] The Made in China 2025 policy is equally ambitious. It focuses on ten priority sectors and leverages China's advantages in Internet, data, and cloud technologies.[19] Government subsidies have gone to technologies such as three-dimensional (3D) printing, semiconductors, electric vehicles, and precision medicine (the latter has been funded at $9.2 billion, in contrast with a little over $100 million in funding in the United States).[20] The Global Entrepreneurship Monitor's 2017 report indicates that China's government policies are more supportive and relevant than both the global and regional averages.[21]

China has many components to its government-controlled innovation system. The highest-ranking body for managing science and technology is the State Council, which is chaired by the prime minister and takes the lead responsibility for China's science and technology (S&T) strategic plan.[22] Although most other countries also have multifaceted structures to support S&T and innovation, China has a unique integrating mechanism—the Communist Party of China (CPC) and a single-party national government via the CPC. In this way, the government can successfully push large-scale national R&D programs (such as the Torch, 863, and 973 programs since the 1990s and the Made in China 2025 programs in since 2015). China also has many partially state-owned firms that are directly or indirectly controlled by the state.[23] Hence, the national government has powerful instruments for implementing innovation policies.

China's innovation ecosystem is characterized by local autonomy and consequent regional diversity. Some observers refer to this as China's "dual innovation system."[24] The national-level innovation system includes most of the features of a developed market's innovation system and focuses on advanced technologies. However, the regional innovation system (RIS) is deeply embedded in local industries and markets that have different strategic priorities and, in many provinces, are related to agriculture and traditional technology fields. Our research with Chinese companies and MNCs confirms that there are many "innovation islands" where linkages among actors, synergies, and spillovers are limited.

China, like most emerging countries, pushes for technology transfers from MNCs in return for market access, and its centralization and determination have made it very effective at forcing foreign companies to share technology with Chinese companies and research institutions. This was prevalent especially in the 1990s. This transfer of technology can be viewed as part of the Chinese innovation ecosystem. Nevertheless, limited evidence indicates that foreign companies are not transferring new technologies to Chinese counterparts to the extent that might be expected from the extensive presence of their local R&D centers. In 2014, foreign sources provided only 1.3 percent of the total funding for R&D and accounted for 18 percent of local patent applications.[25] The policy of technology transfer has been largely abandoned.

Last, but not least, the role of the Communist Party and its influence, albeit indirectly, in the business world in China cannot be ignored.[26] Private businesses with more than fifty employees need to install a party secretary, and companies such as Baidu, Tencent, and Xiaomi have members of parliament in their ranks.[27] Contrary to popular belief, however, the role played by party officials and party secretaries in private business is guiding rather than directing. On the one hand, this arm's-length monitoring allows the party to be aware and informed of private-sector activities, but on the other hand, this is a channel for private business to reach out to and lobby the political system. Moreover, China's government system, based on a central government power structure, can be best characterized as a de facto federalist state with high levels of local autonomy at the provincial level. Such a system prevents ultimate centralized party power and limits its direct influence in day-to-day business operations.[28]

Intellectual property rights: Lowering innovation risks Intellectual property rights (IPR) have been acknowledged and protected in China since 1979. The legal framework for this protection is built on national and local laws that protect intellectual property. However, although the laws are no less complete than those in the United States, there are many deficiencies in their implementation.

The risks of innovation in China include the risk of imitation. According to the 2014 China Innovation Survey, more Chinese companies were concerned about protection of intellectual property than Western companies surveyed.[29] Such concerns are warranted because of the limited effectiveness of China's IP policies. There is an abundance of junk patent applications and junk patents granted, for example, because patenting activities are motivated by incentives rather than market demand. In other words, many patents have limited market value. Junk patents in themselves are harmless and do not affect market competition, but they are a signal of an unhealthy IPR protection mechanism. In response, companies carefully assess their technological needs, firm-level factors, and alternative methods for protecting IP in China.[30] As is shown in later chapters, speed to market is a method that is often used to lower the risk of not being able to appropriate the innovation rent by legal patent protection.

This concern applies even more when it comes to innovating or conducting R&D in China. But there is encouraging news for foreign MNCs on this front: the framework for IP protection in China is improving, and more and more firms have successfully taken legal action. China's government has made several recent announcements about IP protection and taken several actions, including increasing the number of IP courts. In 2016, more IPR lawsuits were filed by Chinese companies against other Chinese than were filed by foreign companies.[31]

Entrepreneurial startups In the 2017 Global Entrepreneurship Monitor survey, the total early-stage entrepreneurial activity (TEA) of China is similar to that in India, Israel, and the United States but lower than the global and regional average.[32] From 2010 to 2014, the number of startups in China doubled and reached 1,609,700, which was almost twice the number of startups in the United Kingdom and India. The startups in China are booming especially in the technology sector; and small and medium-sized enterprises (SMEs) are increasingly embracing digital technology. According to Chinese national statistics, fifteen thousand new companies registered every day in 2016, up three thousand per day compared to 2015, which led to a total of over 5.4 million newly registered companies in 2016.[33]

Startups in China are booming, especially in the technology sector due to many government initiatives, including newly promoted university courses, incubators, and science parks. In 2016, seven thousand new venture projects entered one of the regional competitions in Shanghai, and seventeen hundred projects remained after two rounds of selection.[34] A true cohort of entrepreneurs has emerged and become a force that cannot be ignored. Entrepreneurs are the focus of this book, and chapters 2, 3, 4, and 5 examine four groups of innovating entrepreneurs.

Venture capital: Taking off A recent account by Douglas Fuller that focuses on the challenges of technology development in China reveals an inefficient financial support system for the private sector.[35] But a deeper look into the source of capital for new ventures reveals that private capital, not public capital, is fueling new ventures. The 2017 Global Entrepreneurship Monitor report reveals that Chinese entrepreneurs' access to entrepreneurial finance is 27 percent better than the global average and 32 percent better than the regional average.[36]

The availability of private risk capital has increased immensely over the last decade, both in terms of number of deals and total investment value. This was a necessary condition for China to start developing as an innovation economy. Before this period, most private enterprises encountered great difficulties in gaining access to capital. Although the types of investments—such as angel investment, venture capital, private equity, and corporate venture capital—tend to lack clear definition in China, a growing number of investors are focusing on early stage companies and accepting angel investment by the affluent class. Figure 1.1 illustrates the growth of venture capital in China.

Before China's investment industry started to take off in 2010, several important regulations were created to promote private investment—the first foreign venture capital (VC) provision in 2001, the launch of the Shenzhen SME capital market in 2004, the measures for the administration of VC investment enterprises in 2005, the relaunch of China's initial public offering (IPO) application in 2006, and the launch of ChiNext (China's NASDAQ) in 2009. In concordance with the twelfth Five-Year Plan, the government issued opinions on encouraging and guiding the development of private investment and policies on the taxation of equity investment funds. The positive signals from the government and the

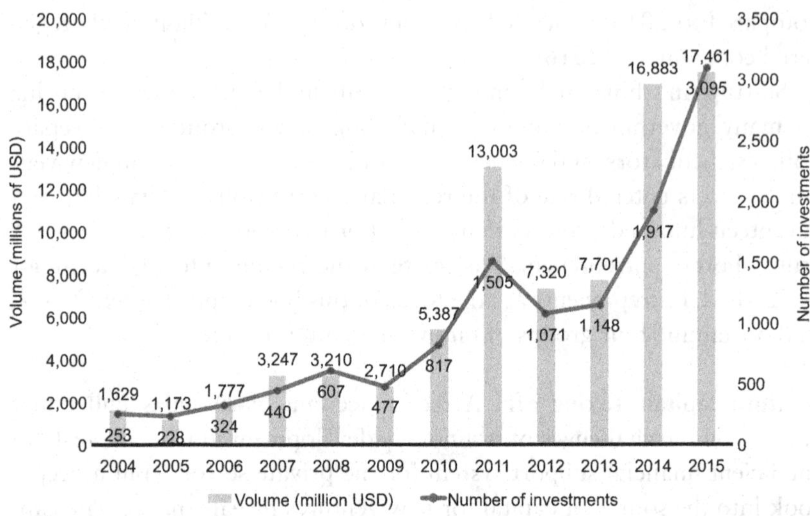

Figure 1.1
The rise of venture capital in China, 2004 to 2015
Source: "China VC/PE Market Review 2015," *Zero2IPO*, accessed December 12, 2016, https://free.pedata.cn/1440998436833724.html.

prosperity of the domestic capital market encouraged the equity investment industry.

China's VC environment is still immature and relatively unprofessional. In late 2014, the scale of private investment (private equity and venture capital) in the United States was ten times that of China.[37] In the United States in 2014, pension organizations were the largest player in the private equity (PE) market, accounting for 25.3 percent of the capital, and private capital accounted for 13.9 percent. In China's PE market, however, the main player was private capital, and social insurance funds allowed into the PE market until 2008. Moreover, there are only limited ways for PE to exit in China, and over the counter (OTC) and IPO are the main methods. China's PE market lacks professional investors and investing organizations. Most of them follow market trends to invest instead of relying on knowledge and experience to judge the value of a company independently. Professional investors and observers often refer to a VC bubble in China, where second-rate startups can relatively easily receive venture capital investment. Nevertheless, the overall flow of private capital to startups is good.

Our Research: Multi-industry Cross-Case Comparisons

This book is based on over a decade of research, teaching, and advisory experiences in China with over two hundred Chinese companies, and its fundamentals are based on four strands of empirical research. One strand is a research program that ran from 2011 to 2015 and that included interviews with hundreds of executives at dozens of Chinese firms. Those interviewed were involved with R&D and innovation or were top senior executives, mostly in companies based in China but also companies that are headquartered in Europe.[38] The second strand is a long research program that ran from 2005 to 2017 and that included interviews with hundreds of local Chinese entrepreneurs, investors, and executives in large Chinese firms, focusing on the status and development of innovation competence by local Chinese firms. The third strand of research was a program based at Zhejiang University that focused on the growth of China's digital ecosystems. It is summarized in *Business Ecosystems in China: Alibaba and Competing Baidu, Tencent, Xiaomi, and LeEco* by Mark J. Greeven and Wei Wei.[39] The fourth strand of research includes the greatly beneficial discussions that the authors have had with peers in the China Europe International Business School (CEIBS), Zhejiang University, and the various forums and conferences organized around the topic of innovation in China. Our frequent discussions with and presentations to executives and innovation professionals from Fortune 500 companies have helped us to reflect on our research findings and refine the validity of our findings and insights.

The companies examined in our emerging innovators framework come from a wide variety of sectors. The manufacturing sector is represented by the pioneers, hidden champions, and underdogs in chapters 2, 3, and 4. The service sector is discussed with pioneers such as Alibaba, Baidu, and Tencent in chapter 2 and changemakers such as Didi Chuxing, Meituan Dianping, Mobike, Pinduoduo, and Toutiao in chapter 5. The financial technology (fintech) space, which has been attracting a lot of attention in China, is represented by Ant Financial in chapter 2 and the changemaker 51 Credit Card in chapter 5. Table 1.2 summarizes the economic sectors covered in this book.

Reading Guide

The book is organized around four questions—why (chapter 1), who and what (chapters 2, 3, 4, and 5), how (chapter 6), and what's next

Table 1.2
Economic sectors covered in this book

Manufacturing	Service
Telecommunications	Ecommerce
Equipment manufacturing	Agritechnology
Household appliances	Digital communication
Heavy machinery manufacturing	Data services
Consumer electronics	Online gaming
Security electronics	Media
Medical devices	Catering
New energy (wind, solar)	Financial technology
Chemicals	Mobility
Pharmaceuticals	Location-based services
Biotechnology	Digital healthcare
3D printing	
Electronic parts and components	
Automotive	
Internet of things	
Precision instruments	
Flat-panel display	
Integrated circuit chips design	
Unmanned aerial vehicles	
New materials	

(chapter 7). Concluding remarks are presented in chapter 8. Chapters 2, 3, 4, and 5 introduce the pioneers, hidden champions, underdogs, and changemakers. Chapter 6 summarizes the six ways in which Chinese companies innovate. The global activities of Chinese innovators are examined in chapter 7.

When anyone writes about dynamic businesses like Chinese innovators, change is the only constant. Although we have gone to great lengths to continue updating the information presented here until the book's publication, the future of our Chinese innovators is constantly changing.

We hope that the readers of this book will be inspired by the unique features and methods of Chinese innovators, which allow them to adapt and improve constantly. Innovation is the driver of China's future.

Notes to the Reader

We follow the Chinese pinyin description of Chinese names by putting the family name first and given name second (i.e., Ma Huateng). Although many Chinese people have English names, we use only full Chinese names.

We generally use the local currency (renminbi) instead of conversions to U.S. dollars. We try to stay as close as possible to the original data and also note that 2017's fluctuation of the USD-RMB exchange rate was significant. As a rough guideline, we recommend 1 USD equals approximately 7 RMB.

We use the Chinese pinyin system, not Chinese characters, when referring to Chinese terms.

2

Pioneers: Giants from the East

Who Are the Pioneers?

The pioneers are enterprises that were founded by visionary entrepreneurs who introduced products and technologies in their industries in China. These first movers have made their way from zero to global enterprises with revenues exceeding $10 billion (USD) and international public awareness as market leaders. From the twenty-five to thirty enterprises that are at the top of the heap of Chinese innovators,[1] we selected eight exemplary innovators that represent both traditional and newly emerging industries. Our empirical research reveals that these pioneering innovators excel at innovating not only products or technology but also organization, marketing, and business models. Our research also reveals that the pioneers have particular noteworthy innovations that warrant rethinking innovation under uncertainty. In this chapter, we discuss the following themes:

- Huawei as a global R&D leader,
- Haier's decades of organizational experimentation,
- Sany as China's good enough answer to Caterpillar,
- Lenovo's rise to global computer leadership,
- The BAT business ecosystems in the Internet era, and
- Xiaomi's social marketing revolution in smart hardware.

Executives, academics, media members, and nonprofessional observers generally would include the eight cases summarized in table 2.1 as the most innovative Chinese companies. The first four in the table (Haier, Huawei, Lenovo, and Sany) represent the first wave of China's emerging global pioneers. China has become (and will continue for a while to be) the main producer of products for the rest of the world. However,

Table 2.1
Eight Chinese pioneers: Giants from the East

Case	Location	Year	Technology field
First wave:			
Haier	Shandong	1984	Household appliances
Huawei	Shenzhen	1987	Telecom and consumer electronics
Lenovo	Beijing	1984	Consumer electronics
Sany	Hunan	1989	Heavy machinery manufacturing
Second wave:			
Alibaba	Zhejiang	1999	Ecommerce
Baidu	Beijing	2000	Search engines
Tencent	Shenzhen	1998	Digital communication
Xiaomi	Beijing	2010	Consumer electronics

Source: Authors' research.

Chinese companies are no longer just original equipment manufacturers for multinationals but have become multinationals themselves with increasingly strong brand names. The second group of four in the table (Alibaba, Baidu, Tencent, and Xiaomi) have been hailed as the second wave of China's emerging pioneers—this time as global digital technology giants.[2] The rapid rise of the Internet in China and the leapfrogging of its entrepreneurs to mobile Internet and digital commerce suggests that Chinese innovators may soon lead global developments. In this chapter, we discuss these eight cases and analyze their advantages as innovators. We discuss Baidu, Alibaba, and Tencent (the BAT companies) as a single case and focus on their innovative organizational structure—a business ecosystem.

Huawei as a Global R&D Leader

Huawei is probably China's most famous and successful global enterprise. It is the largest telecommunication equipment manufacturer in the world, and smartphones are the most visible part of its business.[3] With a market presence in 170 countries and twenty-eight joint innovation centers with fourteen leading telecom operators worldwide, Huawei's overseas markets represent over half of its global revenue.[4] The company is a global innovation leader in telecommunications and plays a role in setting global technology standards.[5]

Huawei, founded in 1987 in Shenzhen by Ren Zhengfei, started by manufacturing telephone exchange switches.[6] The initial objective of the company was to reduce the country's reliance on imported technology and create a domestic telecommunication company. By 1990, it had about six hundred R&D staff members and had begun to commercialize the private branch exchange switches that serve private organizations and concentrate central office lines. The company's first international deal came ten years after its founding, with a contract for providing fixed-line network products to Hutchison Whampoa. As the overseas expansion continued, Huawei needed to make a larger R&D commitment. This was underscored by Cisco's 2003 patent lawsuit. Since 2013, Huawei has become the world's largest patent filer. In 2016, it spent $9.2 billion on R&D, and its staff was over 60 percent engineers. Huawei's grassroots approach has allowed it to build a global innovation system with sixteen R&D centers in countries like India, Japan, Sweden, and the United States.

Customer-Driven Technology

Huawei has a track record of developing new technologies such as SingleRAN (in 2008) and long-term evolution (LTE) technologies (in 2011). SingleRAN is a radio access network (RAN) technology that allows mobile telecommunication operators to support multiple mobile communications standards and wireless telephone services on a single network. LTE is a standard for high-speed wireless communication for mobile phones and data terminals. In 2009, its first commercial application was with Huawei's SingleRAN technology infrastructure in Stockholm and Oslo. Later, the 4G (fourth-generation broadband cellular network technology) variant LTE-TDD was developed by a global consortium that had Huawei and Datang Telecom at the forefront. In 2011, Huawei's second worldwide 4G deployment was in collaboration with China Mobile Communications Corporation. To date, Huawei has deployed hundreds of SingleRAN commercial networks, which are capable of evolving into LTE. Huawei has become a global technology leader in the field of telecommunication technology.

In 2011, Huawei began to move into the mobile phone business. As an equipment provider, Huawei was building tunnels for carriers and saw opportunities in the mobile phone business because the 3G operators at that time did not have enough mobile phones. According to our interviews, this customer-driven innovation approach is a key principle for Huawei. New businesses (like the photovoltaic inverter business) are still generated with this approach. As an equipment manufacturer, Huawei had a strong technological advantage. For instance, Huawei is one of the few mobile phone producers that can make its own integrated circuit chips, significantly lowering costs and guaranteeing smooth inventory operations. Huawei's December 2016 release of 5G technology in collaboration with dozens of foreign operators is part of its goal of developing the next standard for mobile phones. Another feature of the company's innovative approach can be seen in how Huawei started in the telecommunication equipment business: begin at the low end, but keep upgrading. Because the company's first overseas markets were in low-income countries, customers needed low prices. This positioning initially gave Huawei a weak reputation and low profit margins, but the company quickly changed perceptions and launched the high-end Mate9 at Electronica 2016 in Munich and the P9 at the 2017 Consumer Electronics Show in Las Vegas. Huawei has become the top-selling producer in developed markets such as the Netherlands and Portugal and has achieved annual sales growth of 40 percent in the United States.

Organizational Innovation

Technology is not the only thing that is innovative about Huawei. Table 2.2 summarizes Huawei's approach to innovation. The first is wolf culture. From the beginning, Huawei's founder Ren Zhengfei embedded ideas about self-discipline and decisive execution in the organization. Many popular business observers in China admire Ren Zhengfei's embrace of military-style organization. The company's wolf culture embraces a sharp sense of market needs, a high-pressure work environment, and collective heroism. The devotion and loyalty of its employees to the company was made explicit in, for instance, its 2015 annual report. The second is

Table 2.2
What is innovative about Huawei?

Customer-driven technology	Organizational innovations
R&D commitment	Wolf culture
Lower-end market entry	Employee ownership
Quick upgrades	Rotating CEO (shared leadership)

Source: Authors' research.

employee ownership. Huawei is not listed on any stock exchange and is not supported by external funds. It is more or less owned by its employees. Ren Zhengfei owns about 1 percent of the equity in the company, and over eighty thousand employees own the rest. The employees have a standing committee of sixty representatives. This employee ownership arrangement includes incentives such as bonuses and dividends. However, the employee ownership is actually virtual—that is, the shares are mostly rights for dividends and must be bought back by the company at the employee's resignation. Governance seems to be a bit fuzzy, but the standing committee has the right to select the company's top management team, including the rotating CEO. Three vice chairmen take six-month turns as CEO, which is also the third organizational innovation of Huawei. Huawei's philosophy is that a company should not depend on one person to run a large and complex organization. A strategic decision committee, led by the current rotating CEO, reports to Ren Zhengfei, and Ren Zhengfei keeps a veto right on all decisions. This rotation creates a sense of shared leadership because executive perspective periodically changes from business and technology to strategy.

Haier's Decades of Organizational Experimentation

Haier Group is the world's leading brand of major household appliances. Since 2009, it has been the top supplier of large appliances with 10 percent global market share. In 2016, it had over 78,000 employees, and the World Brand Lab ranked Haier at the top of its global list of large appliances. By leveraging its global R&D network across four continents, a widespread online and offline sales and service network in over a hundred countries, and the open innovation and entrepreneurship platform, Haier reached a historic revenue of over 200 billion renminbi (RMB) in 2016. The immense success of the company led *Fortune* magazine to name Haier's founder Zhang Ruimin to its 2017 list of the world's fifty greatest leaders.[7] In 2016, Haier acquired GE's appliance division for $5.4 billion, a feat that would have been unimaginable three decades ago.

In 1984, Zhang Ruimin took the helm of Qingdao General Refrigerator Factory, which was close to bankruptcy. In the same year, a refrigerator production line was imported from Liebherr in Germany, and the German company's name later became the root of the company's new name—Haier. In 1985, Zhang Ruimin smashed seventy-six new Haier refrigerators that had minor defects. At that time, Haier's first priority was building a domestic brand with a good reputation. The company describes its development phase as a typical step-by-step approach that is followed by many Chinese companies—domestic brand building (1984–1991), diversification (1991–1998), international expansion (1998–2005), global brand strategy (2005–2012), and platform strategy (from 2012 onward). Observing Haier's development and transformation, two approaches to innovation stand out—market-driven product diversification and platform organization.

Market-Driven Product Innovation

Haier was one of the earliest Chinese companies to bring new products to the market continuously, mostly with incremental improvements and different versions. Many of Haier's products satisfy special needs in China. For instance, washing machines have quick washing cycles—fifteen minutes of nonstop washing. A failed but interesting local China example is a washing machine that washes both clothes and vegetables. This model, targeting rural areas, was developed after Haier's repairmen reported back to the company that people in rural China were using their washing machines to clean vegetables as well as clothes. The focus on niches and positioning, rather than on low cost, also extended abroad. For instance, Haier's initial focus on the compact refrigerator market in the United States allowed Haier to fight U.S. incumbents such as GE. A refrigerator model with a foldout table was aimed at students after product designers who visited cramped dormitory rooms discovered that students put boards across two refrigerators to create a makeshift desk. In France and Italy, the company first sold air conditioners before entering other niches based on local consumer studies. Haier still does not sell small household appliances in any overseas markets that market the same appliances.

Ideas for new products come from engineers and managers, but many product ideas come from the front end of the company, such as repairmen and salespeople. Haier's Crystal washing machines series is the outcome of several series of user observations, surveys, and innovations in terms of spin speed and operating noise. Haier has always visited people's homes to observe consumer behavior rather than trusting only focus groups and market studies. Moreover, Haier has developed a pioneering online platform to sourcing ideas globally—Haier Open Partnership Ecosystem (HOPE).[8] Since 2013, Haier has employed the HOPE initiative to tap into an online community of thousands of external experts and hundreds of thousands of users for finding ideas and for sourcing solutions. For instance, an air conditioning kitchen ventilator was developed based on a requirement first proposed by users on the HOPE platform. Haier started a bidding request for the technology and finally developed the product together with a university within four months after the requirement was accepted.

To meet the demands of new product development, Haier combined product diversification, product upgrades, and internationalization with a strategy for technology acquisition. Although Haier has built five global R&D centers and works on ambitious innovative projects (such as low water consumption and a noise-free washing machine), a major component of its development has been acquiring available technologies from abroad either through direct purchases or strategic alliances with leading global firms. In the early phase, technology was acquired by importing it from Liebherr, buying the Qingdao Freezer General Plant and Qingdao Air Conditioner Plant, buying the Red Star Electric Appliance Factory, and entering a joint venture with the Shandong Laiyang Household Appliance General Plant.[9] When the private economy took off and domestic markets started to grow, companies began to adapt and improve their technological capabilities while leveraging the skills acquired for cost reduction. Haier began to produce new products with its own brands, focus on market-driven product innovation, and compete with foreign entrants. To improve technological capabilities in the later phase, Haier collaborated with international partners such as Mitsubishi, Philips, Sanyo, and Toshiba. The quick-cycle washing machines required important technology such as high-powered motors. This was developed in a collaboration with New Zealand's Fisher & Paykel, which Haier later acquired. These partnerships were instrumental in allowing Haier to deliver better-quality products or new products after acquiring domestic firms in fields such as air conditioners and washing machines, which were at the time outside its core expertise.

Platform Organization ("De-Haierization")

Haier implemented two major innovations—market-driven product innovation and organizational innovation. Since 1998, the company has experimented with new organizational forms to reduce hierarchy and control and increase autonomy with self-organizing work units and internal labor markets. But it was not until 2010 that Haier established a platform organization (an organization with an open architecture, together with a governance model, designed to facilitate and commercialize interactions) throughout the company.

To eliminate the distance between the company and the users of its products, it got rid of strategic business units and managerial hierarchies

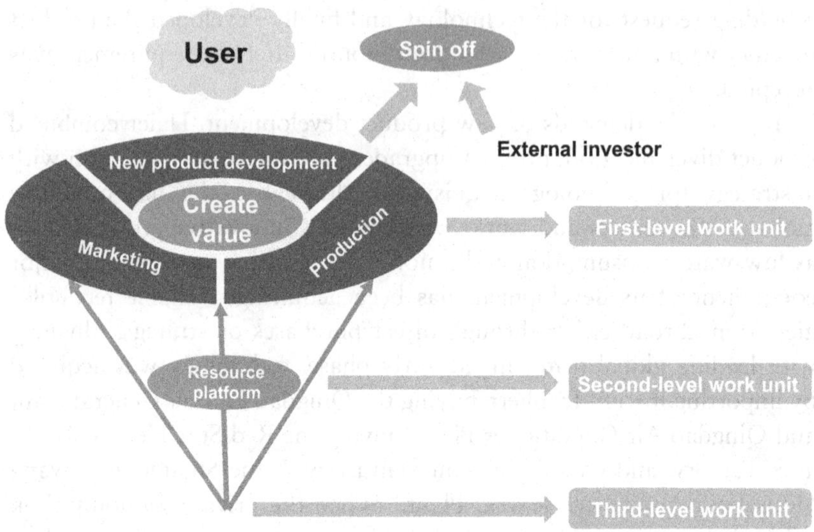

Figure 2.1
Haier's platform of micro-enterprises
Source: Based on Bill Fisher, Umberto Lago, and Fang Liu, *Reinventing Giants: How Chinese Global Competitor Haier Has Changed the Way Big Companies Transform* (San Francisco: Jossey-Bass, 2013), and extended with the authors' research.

(figure 2.1). The company was reorganized in work units called *zi zhu jing ying ti* (ZZJYT) that each included around twenty people. These later were called micro- enterprises. Initially, three types of work units were designed: first-level work units communicated directly with users, second-level work units fulfilled corporate support functions (like human resources, accounting, and legal), and third-level work units (the executive team) supported the other units.

The first-level work unit currently consists of three types—new product development, production, and marketing and sales. The second-level work unit has been transformed into a resource platform. The role of middle management (functional expertise such as HR, legal, and accounting) has been mostly abolished, and the second-level work units have mostly ceased to exist. The functional specialists were assigned to specific work units where they served as consultants. The third-level work unit is the smallest and is positioned at the top of the inverted pyramid. Its role has been redefined as a support function for the customer-facing, self-organizing work units.

The three-door fridge illustrates how this system works. After Haier decided that it needed a three-door refrigerator model, it asked for bids from individuals inside the company. Anybody in the organization could develop a proposal for a new work unit that would develop this product, and a committee consisting of relevant representatives selected the best proposal. The writer of the winning proposal was given an opportunity to start the new work unit as a micro-enterprise. From that moment on, the new work unit made all decisions concerning the product. It created its own profit and loss statement, set its own objectives, and acquired all necessary resources (including hiring contract employees for the work unit). Organization-wide performance appraisal systems were abolished, and performance was assessed completely by the performance of the work unit. Employee compensation was a small basic salary plus a highly flexible performance bonus, depending on the performance of the work unit. There is no up and down reporting and no peer or supervisor review. Full autonomy and responsibility exists at the work unit level, like a micro-enterprise. After a product is developed, the work unit needs to produce. The three-door refrigeration work unit, for example, entered into contracts with the production work unit it works with, and its contracts stipulated how much it was going to cost to produce the unit. It also entered into contracts with the marketing and sales work units, whose performance was determined by whether it lived up to the contracts as well.

Haier is now made up of thousands of work units, and more than a hundred of them have over 100 million RMB in annual revenues. More recently, the platform has evolved further to allow work units of non-core products to spin off. After 2014, external investors were allowed to invest in promising new products jointly with Haier's investment fund. For instance, a furniture maker invested in one of the ecommerce platforms (youzhu.com) that a Haier work unit developed for house decoration. Forty-one of such spinoffs have received venture capital funding, and sixteen of these received in excess of 100 million RMB. Another recent development is a deeper transformation of work units into open platforms where Haier creates platform advantages for multiple brands. A good example is Goodaymart, which originally was a distribution platform for delivering Haier's electric appliances within twenty-four hours in China.[10] This used to be an advantage exclusively for Haier. After it was opened up as a platform consisting of three work units (marketing, logistics, and services), however, any players in the market could leverage this advantage. Now the platform accepts products from domestic and international players (including competitors) and also has extended into a service platform. For instance, Black & Decker uses this platform to distribute in China, and Haier also helps Black & Decker in design, quality control, and manufacturing.[11] Through measures such as decentralization, disintermediation, and elimination of internal communication barriers, Haier has decreased employment by 45 percent from its peak but has created more than 1.6 million job opportunities.

Sany as China's Good Enough Answer to Caterpillar

Sany is a heavy machinery manufacturing group that is located in Changsha in Hunan province. With 70 billion RMB revenues in 2016 and ninety thousand employees, it is one of the top ten global construction companies. Sany has seen immense growth—a 70 percent compound annual growth rate (CAGR) over more than two decades—and it is the first Chinese company in its industry to enter the *Financial Times*'s list of the global top five hundred, ranked by market capitalization. Sany has been on *Forbes*'s list of one hundred most innovative companies for several years, one of just five global construction equipment manufacturers that have made the ranking.[12] Within China, the reputation of Sany as an innovator is even better. *Fortune China* has ranked Sany as one of the three most innovative companies in China.[13] Although it began as a grassroots enterprise, Sany has entered the global stage with thirty subsidiaries outside China, three hundred offices, and over 40 percent of total revenues overseas.

The predecessor of Sany was established in 1989 by four cofounders who came from Liangyuan in Hunan province and had just 60,000 RMB to invest. The lead founder was Liang Wengen, a graduate in material science from Central South University with several years' working experience for a defense contractor. By 1991, the predecessor company (a welding material factory) was renamed Sany Group. In 1994, the founders initiated a double development strategy by changing the company business from welding materials to heavy machinery construction and relocating the company from Lianyuan to Changsha, the capital of the province, where it would have access to many more resources. In 2002, the company started to export products (first to Morocco in North Africa), and in 2006, it established its first overseas factory in India. In the following years, it entered markets in developed economies such as the United States and Germany, where it also established an R&D center and acquired Putzmeister, a leading concrete pump manufacturer. In recent years, Sany has diversified into manufacturing products for the wind energy infrastructure, with most projects located in the United States.

Rapid Product Development

Sany has pursued speed at any price when developing new products, and this approach is reflected in how the company organizes the new product development (NPD) process. For several decades, speed and short lead times have been competitive advantages for the booming construction equipment market. One interviewee from Sany indicated that its average time to market is about twelve months, which is half the time that many competitors take. For Sany, being first to market is more important than being the best in the market, so good enough designs seem to be a reasonable choice, but Sany also has succeeded in introducing new products.

A key feature of Sany's new product development process is the truncated process model rather than a traditional stage gate model (a technique that divides a project into stages, separated by distinct decision-making moments). The Sany NPD process has been divided into smaller and overlapping but iterative steps—create a good enough design, launch good enough quality products, test, and improve—that speed up the innovation process and increase customer responsiveness. On average, less time is spent on market analysis, business case development, and feasibility studies. Customer requirements and improvements are often verified on site with the customer rather than in advance. The acute demand in the booming market for construction equipment in China and other emerging markets often means that customers are willing to accept a process that allows them to improve and tinker on site with products that are good enough. This process also stems from China's special and diverse land and weather features. Sany often has had to make small adjustments on site to address local land or weather features, such as soft or dry land, altitude, and humidity.

"New to the World" Technologies

After failing to receive technology transfers from foreign companies in its early development phase, Sany decided to develop its own core technology instead of importing technology, which most Chinese companies were doing. To develop and manufacture quality and industry-leading products, Sany has reinvested 5 percent to 7 percent of its annual sales revenue in R&D. After years of learning, Sany now can innovate many core enabling technologies based on the needs of the Chinese market.

Because of its ability to develop its own technology, Sany has introduced many "new to the world" products globally. In 2007, while building the Shanghai Global Financial Center, it used a single pump to transport concrete up to 492 meters, winning a reputation as China's pump king. Its 86 meter pump car has the world's longest boom, has the largest number of arms, and pumps the largest displacement. Since 2009, Sany also has been the world's largest concrete pump manufacturer and has brought to market the first full hydraulic motor grader, a third-level concrete pump (during China's famous Three Gorges Project), and a bitumen cement mortar mixer. In 2011, it was the first to lift a 96 ton 2 megawatt (MW) wind power cabin up to 80 meters in altitude. In the same year, it developed the world's most powerful crawler crane. The crawler crane has a maximum lifting capacity of 3,600 tons. Among its thirty patents are two main chord tube arm technologies and a double super car-lifting technology.

Embracing Digital Industrial Platforms

Sany has embraced digital technology and developed a large data storage and analysis platform that it calls an enterprise control center (ECC) customer service platform. This industrial platform allows two-way interaction, the remote control of equipment, and the collection of real-time operation data from clients' devices. The daily monitoring collects operation information like location, working hours, speed of revolution, main pressure, and fuel consumption. It has collected 40 terabytes of data on about five thousand dimensions. The platform is open and available for agents, operators, excavators, owners, and R&D personnel.

Sany's industrial platform has four main functions. First, it is used to predict the macroenvironment. Sany and Tsinghua University launched the excavator index, which uses the construction time and operating rate of the equipment to predict the fixed assets investment and to a certain extent the China macroeconomic trends as well.[14] Based on data from each province, Sany can identify the trend of the fixed assets investment in different provinces, analyze the changes of the regional market in real time, and use this information to guide the company's marketing tactics. Second, with the intelligent service platform and data intelligence analysis, Sany has developed energy-saving technology that greatly improves the fuel efficiency of excavators and reduces the fuel cost. Third, the company's industrial platform allows for the analysis of Sany's product mix. Based on the data analysis model, Sany can identify its most popular models and use this information to help plan future product development. Fourth, the platform helps Sany predict equipment failure and forecast the demand for spare parts. The platform can predict about 50 percent of warnings of equipment failure and early maintenance, which can be used to forecast the demand for spare parts, reduce relevant costs, and reduce customer losses significantly. By breaking through the bottleneck of the safety and controllable core technology of construction machinery and equipment, the company has also promoted its financing and leasing business and improved service efficiency.

As a spinoff product, in 2016, Sany and its partners established Jiulong Insurance, which was the first domestic specialty insurance company based on the Internet of things. Few insurance companies venture deep into the equipment insurance field because of the complexities of the risk. Relying on the Internet of things and big data, Jiulong Insurance can more accurately identify risk and pricing and therefore customize insurance products and services according to the customer's risk characteristics. Overall, Sany has been continuously innovating and going outside its comfort zone of hardware manufacturing.

Lenovo's Rise to Global Computer Leadership

Lenovo is a multinational technology company with headquarters in Beijing and Morrisville, North Carolina. It has operations in more than sixty countries and sells its products in around 160 countries. As the world's largest personal computer (PC) and service provider and second-largest smartphone and tablet producer, the company had $40 billion in revenues in 2016 and sixty thousand employees. It is the only company that is in the global top three of all key IT technologies—tablets, phones, and computers and servers. Among the company's three main lines of business—data centers, mobile devices, and personal computers and smart devices (PCSD)—revenue from its PCSD business accounted for around 70 percent of its total revenue for 2016.

In 1984, Liu Chuanzhi and ten other engineers founded Lenovo (as Legend) in Beijing with 200,000 RMB in initial capital. Because the new company was a carveout from a state institution, the Chinese Academy of Sciences provided Lenovo with technological support and business connections. Initially, Lenovo was a distributor for AST computers in mainland China and Hong Kong and then expanded to distribute the products of other multinationals, such as Hewlett-Packard and IBM.

Using the strong science background of its team, Legend soon developed a circuit board that allowed IBM-compatible personal computers to process Chinese characters. This product was the company's first major success, and in 1990, Legend started to manufacture and market computers under its own brand. In 1994, Legend became publicly traded on the Hong Kong Stock Exchange with an initial public offering (IPO) that raised nearly $30 million (but still disappointed traders' overly high expectations). By 1996, Legend reached the leading market position in China and launched its own laptop. By 1998, it had sold about a million computers, which was a 43 percent domestic market share of a computer market that was still in its infancy. During the 2002 Legend World Conference, the company launched its high-performance computer called DeepComp 1800 and expanded into the mobile phone business through a joint venture with Xoceco, a local consumer electronics manufacturer. In 2003, Legend rebranded itself as Lenovo and started a wave of innovations via large-scale international acquisitions.

Innovating by Acquisition

In 2005, when Lenovo purchased IBM's personal computer division, Liu Chuanzhi said, "We benefited in three ways from the IBM acquisition. We got the ThinkPad brand, IBM's more advanced PC manufacturing technology, and the company's international resources, such as its global sales channels and operation teams. These three elements have shored up our sales revenue in the past several years." With this eye-catching acquisition, Lenovo was the top global computer producer. In 2011, it developed a joint venture with NEC for the Japanese market and acquired Medion, a German consumer electronics company that produced computers, tablets, digital cameras, and phones. The following year, it established a joint venture with EMC for developing network storage products; acquired Digibras, a Brazil-based electronics company; and started a local factory to expand in Brazil. It also expanded its software capability by acquiring the U.S. software company Stoneware to improve and expand its cloud computing services. By 2014, the deal with IBM to acquire the IBM x86 server business was finalized, and Lenovo was suddenly also one of the global top three server businesses. In the same year, Lenovo acquired Motorola Mobility from Google, making Lenovo one of the largest smartphone brands in terms of shipments and the only PC producer (other than Apple) that successfully expanded into phones and tablets.[15] Lenovo has shown a remarkable ability to integrate the acquired companies and keep alive the top brands of IBM and Motorola under the Lenovo umbrella. But in addition to these accomplishments, Lenovo also has developed a range of design product innovations.

Product Design Innovation

Lenovo has been at the forefront of exploring new PC designs, such as the Yoga notebook (which can emulate tablets with a screen that flips around and folds back and a completely flat keyboard that transforms into a writing pad that can be used with a real pen) and the Horizon tabletop (a design that can be put on a table and used like an electronic game board). Lenovo has developed a phone (the Moto Z) that allows users to add new modules and functions via an ingenious magnetic system. Lenovo has developed an augmented reality (AR) phone that leverages Google's Tango depth-sensing technology, and a tablet with a cylindrical handle that packs extra battery power was recognized for an Edison innovation award. The company has achieved a leading market position by continuously innovating on the basis of its acquired technologies. The final feature of Lenovo's innovation approach is its highly successful corporate venturing.

Corporate Venturing

Lenovo has a mature strategic investment approach consisting of three core funds—strategic investment, venture capital, and artificial intelligence, robotics, and cloud computing. The strategic investment areas include IT, financial services, innovative consumption and service, agriculture and food products, and new materials. The goal is to spot and invest in upcoming technologies that are strategically complementary to Lenovo's businesses. With the successful acquisition of a range of large companies (including IBM, Medion, and Motorola), Lenovo has developed into one of the most professional venture capital organizations in China.

The venture capital fund was already established in 2001 when Liu Chuanzhi set up a team led by Zhu Linan and Lenovo contributed $35 million as the first phase of the fund. Currently, the fund invests in USD and RMB totaling 30 billion RMB. The fund has invested in over three hundred companies of which fifty were listed and forty already exited via merger or acquisition. In 2003, Lenovo established its private equity fund, Hony Capital. Hony manages eight equity funds and two mezzanine funds, totaling 68 billion RMB. Investors include CAS Holdings, China Life Insurance, Goldman Sachs, Lenovo Holdings, Temasek, and other pension funds. The key investment areas are urbanization and consumption related—culture, healthcare, manufacturing, media, and new energy. Hony Capital has invested in over a hundred companies, including CIMC, PizzaExpress, Suning, WeWork, and Zoomlion. Hony also is known as an expert in restructuring state-owned enterprises (SOEs) and has actively participated in the restructuring of over thirty state-owned enterprises and other mixed-ownership reforms. Furthermore, Hony is active in cross-border transactions and was the first, in 2013, to invest in the Shanghai Free Trade Zone. Except for the venture capital and private equity arms mentioned above, the angel investment fund of Lenovo is Legend Star, established in 2008 with a 1.5 billion RMB fund.

In 2016, Lenovo established a $500 million startup fund that is managed internally by Lenovo Group and focuses on artificial intelligence, robotics, and cloud computing industries.[16] In 2017, Lenovo announced a four-year plan to invest over $1.2 billion in artificial intelligence, the Internet of things, and big data as part of its efforts to diversify its operations amid the stalled growth of its PC and smartphone businesses.[17]

The BAT Business Ecosystems in the Internet Era

Leading Chinese Internet companies Alibaba, Baidu, and Tencent (BAT) are showing unprecedented growth with a combined market capitalization of close to $800 billion, an average annual growth of over 50 percent, and over five hundred new ventures incubated. Of the sixty-four Chinese unicorns in 2015, 50 percent are either spinoffs or have equity investment relationships with the BAT companies.[18] In 2015, Alibaba, Tencent, and Xiaomi reported that 10 percent of their total revenues (billions of USD) came from abroad, which makes them truly international Internet giants. Unsurprisingly, Fast Company's list of the global top fifty most innovative companies for 2017 includes Alibaba (number 11) and Tencent (number 12), and Baidu is included in the China and AI/machine learning global ranking.[19]

Originally, these three leading digital ecosystems were considered to be copycats of foreign business models—Baidu a copycat of Google, Alibaba a copycat of eBay, and Tencent a copycat of ICQ messaging and many foreign computer games. These companies were not considered to be innovative, and they were seen to have owed their success to government protections and the Chinese firewall. Nevertheless, the BAT companies have not only grown out of the foreign imported business models but have outgrown many of their competitors worldwide. Alibaba's ecommerce businesses are larger than Amazon and eBay combined, Tencent is Asia's highest-valued company, and Baidu is a worldwide leader in big data and machine learning technology. It also should be noted that Alibaba's C2C platform Taobao was launched before eBay entered the Chinese market and that Taobao's localized strategy, free listing, and deep market understanding outcompeted its billion-dollar competitor eBay within a year.[20] Baidu's Li Yanhong, who was a search algorithm technologist in

Silicon Valley in the 1990s, is said to have been consulted by the founders of Google at the end of that decade. Well before the Chinese government started to control the Internet in China and block Google services in 2010, Baidu already outcompeted Google in China in 2002 with a superior Chinese search engine.[21] Finally, in the early 2000s, Tencent's QQ developed beyond a popular instant messenger into a fully functioning social community. Its later product WeChat disrupted China's mobile Internet without copying anyone. Our research shows that the source of the successes of the BAT companies lies in their innovative approach to organizing, rather than their imitation of foreign business models and government protection.

Innovative Business Ecosystems

A key feature of BAT's business approach is the way the three enterprises organize their many businesses. The BAT companies adopted a business ecosystem approach to lead but also create and disrupt markets. A business ecosystem is "a new organizational form where the businesses are interdependent through a variety of equity relationships combining product and service offerings into a customer centric offering."[22] Business ecosystems have five key features:

- The business ecosystems are enabled by digital technology. The digital-enabled business allows for convenient communication and sharing of information across the ecosystem rather than between just two actors.
- Each business ecosystem has one focal player as the gravity provider and network orchestrator in its ecosystem. For instance, Alibaba's core is comprised of four ecommerce platforms (Alibaba.com, 1688.com, Taobao.com, and Tmall.com).
- The actors in business ecosystems appear to be strongly interdependent. A prerequisite to this interdependence between the actors is financial and equity connections. But the interdependence also is found in growth strategies, investment approaches, and complementarities between offerings, business synergies, and resource sharing.
- The transformation of the business ecosystem is not just a response to internal or external forces but a proactive transformation. These business ecosystems first organically fit themselves into the business context to meet the demands of the market and then at a later stage proactively orchestrate the transformation of the business context by

experimenting and exploring technology, product, or business model innovations and opening up new markets.

- Cross-industry diversification is a key feature and the source of a competitive advantage of the business ecosystems. The scope of business activities within the ecosystem is wide. The BAT companies have diversified their core business. Alibaba, for example, moved from B2B to C2C, B2C markets, then to cross-border ecommerce, and later to group buying, online payment, and logistics that support the ecommerce core. It also diversified beyond its core and original industry. In particular, Alibaba surprised many incumbents in traditional industries such as finance, healthcare, education, catering, and entertainment by entering these industries with new and often disruptive service offerings.

The ecosystem approaches taken by the BAT companies share similarities—a core of the ecosystem developed and fully owned by the company, a second layer of a variety of businesses and companies that support the core, and a third layer of invested companies and service providers that participate and facilitate the whole ecosystem. Moreover, the innovation strategies are also similar. In the first decade, BAT organically and internally developed products with a process that is characterized by modularization, reducing the time and cost required to develop a product that offers greater value for customers. A strong pragmatism in decision making in the R&D process facilitated speed and responsiveness to existing and new customer requirements.[23] Since 2012, the BAT companies have aggressively bought and invested in technology ventures and innovative startups, inside and outside their core business. Finally, each of the three ecosystems has an important "glue" that keeps it together, like a shared user base, cloud services, and online payment systems (such as Baidu's Baidu Wallet, Alibaba's Alipay, and Tencent's WeChat Pay).[24] The BAT business ecosystems are highly diversified businesses and grow by extensive entry into newly emerging sectors in China and around the world.

Cross-Industry Innovation

Alibaba is known for its ecommerce empire, Tencent is famous for its gaming and communication platforms, and Baidu is often considered to be China's Google. But these are no longer fair representations of these ecosystems' businesses. As a fertile ground for innovation, new ventures, and disruptive business models, the BAT companies have surprised many multinationals and incumbents in traditional industries. Through their cross-industry innovations and expansion into newly emerging industries, the BAT companies now operate in at least twenty different industries. Their main expansion approach has been investment and acquisition, both domestically and internationally, and they jointly invested in over three hundred companies in the last five years. Their investments include angel investments in small startups as well as billion-dollar investments in large companies.

Since 2013, Alibaba has moved from organic growth to high-speed growth by investing in and acquiring companies in different sectors like ecommerce, logistics, location-based services (LBS), finance, healthcare, travel, and entertainment. Investment in such a significant number of companies suggests an overall boost in the growth of the business ecosystem, where about 180 new participants entered in just five years' time. In our research, we identify at least twenty-three distinct sectors of investment. We can identify several sectors of particular interest, such as culture and entertainment, ecommerce, location-based services, finance, and enterprise services. Recent investments include new important strategic areas such as digital healthcare and logistics.

A case in point, with significant market impact, is Ant Financial. In October 2014, Alibaba established Ant Financial, a comprehensive financial services company that positioned itself as inclusive finance to serve individuals and small and medium-sized enterprises (SMEs). Alipay and Yu'ebao are both part of Ant Financial. Ant Financial has brought to market many new financial products—such as Huabei for online consumer loans, Ant Dake for crowdfunding, Ant Fortune for wealth management, and Ant Financial Cloud for cloud services for financial institutions. Ant Financial and the affiliated Alipay have been active investors both domestically and in nearby Asian markets such as India, the Philippines, South Korea, and Thailand. In July 2015, Ant Financial received funding from eight investment institutions, including China's National Social Insurance Fund and CDB Capital, with a super unicorn valuation of $45 billion, and in April 2016, Ant Financial raised $4.5 billion with a valuation of $60 billion. By April 2018, Ant Financial's estimated market value was $150 billion.[25] Giving its current valuation and prospects, an historic IPO is expected.

Baidu employed three mechanisms to diversify into different sectors successfully. First, it initiated several innovative products and services, like Dulife (a smart health device platform) and the Apollo driverless car. These have been developed mostly by Baidu. Second, Baidu invested significantly in new companies and technologies like Pixellot (AR/VR) and Velodyne Lidar (laser detection and measuring). Third, Baidu initiated an incubation strategy called the Baidu Entrepreneurship Center for Internet entrepreneurs in 2013. So far, five cities in China have the Baidu Entrepreneurship Centers, and over one hundred venture teams have participated in the incubation program. So far, Baidu has significantly diversified into four business areas—digital healthcare, online education, Internet finance, and location-based services.

Baidu is emphasizing its technology advantage in artificial intelligence (AI) to expand into new industries. In May 2014, the company attracted Andrew Ng, a founder of Google AI and an associate professor at Stanford University, as the key scientist to lead the Baidu Research Academy—AI Lab (Silicon Valley), Deep Learning Lab (Beijing), and Big Data Lab (Beijing). By the end of 2015, the Baidu driverless car, another application of its AI technology, finished its road tests. In March 2018, Beijing city gave the first licenses for open-road testing of Baidu's autonomous cars. Baidu will test its Apollo autonomous driving technology in Beijing, where vehicles can take full control under certain conditions. Baidu received its license from Beijing one month after Shanghai issued licenses for road tests of driverless vehicles to NIO, a Chinese electric vehicle startup, and the state-owned automaker SAIC Motor.

Similar to Baidu, Tencent also employed three mechanisms to diversify into different fields. First, Tencent initiated several innovative products and services. As has been shown with its development of WeChat, Tencent is adept at developing new products with an approach that allows parallel product development. Second, Tencent has invested significantly in new companies and technologies. As will be shown in chapter 7, Tencent has the most proactive strategy for diversification: over two hundred companies in a wide variety of sectors and phases have joined the Tencent business ecosystem. Third, in January 2015, Tencent initiated an incubation strategy called the Double Hundred Plan, which aims to invest 10 billion RMB by 2018 to support a hundred startups in mobile Internet, including smart hardware. In 2013, the company initiated a plan called Entrepreneurship Bases, and by 2017, it had over twenty locations in China. Tencent's business ecosystem includes five major business areas—ecommerce, digital healthcare, culture and entertainment, Internet finance, and location-based services. Table 2.3 summarizes the top five investment sectors for Baidu, Alibaba, and Tencent.

Table 2.3
The top five investment sectors for Baidu, Alibaba, and Tencent (BAT)

Ecosystem	Top five investment sectors
Baidu	Location-based services, culture and entertainment, ecommerce, education, enterprise services
Alibaba	Culture and entertainment, ecommerce, location-based services, finance, enterprise services
Tencent	Game, culture and entertainment, ecommerce, healthcare, location-based services

Source: Mark J. Greeven and Wei Wei, *Business Ecosystems in China: Alibaba and Competing Baidu, Tencent, Xiaomi, and LeEco* (Abington, UK: Routledge 2018).

Xiaomi's Social Marketing Revolution in Smart Hardware

Xiaomi is a Chinese electronics company that focuses on smart hardware and electronics. It was established in 2010 by an all-star team of seasoned entrepreneurs and business executives. In 2014, three years after launching its smartphone, Xiaomi overcame Apple and became the top smartphone seller in China. By the end of 2017, Xiaomi had sold over 300 million smartphones and expanded its electronics portfolio to over thirty product categories, such as air purifiers, televisions, earphones, wearables, self-balancing scooters, and even rice cookers. The total revenues of Xiaomi in 2017 reached $17.6 billion, and the company has seen an impressive compound annual growth rate of 80 percent since its founding. Xiaomi is one of the most valuable Chinese unicorns, with a market capitalization of close to $100 billion and second on the *MIT Technology Review*'s list of fifty smartest companies of 2015. In April 2016, the company's cofounder, Lei Jun, was on the cover of *Wired* magazine, which quoted him saying, "Don't call me China's Steve Jobs" and "It's time to copy China." Xiaomi is planning an initial public offering at the time of this writing.

Lei Jun is a seasoned entrepreneur—the former CEO of a Chinese-listed software company called Kingsoft and a well-known angel investor as well. Together with six senior professionals and two angel investors, Lei Jun cofounded Xiaomi in Beijing. In August 2010, Xiaomi launched MIUI, which is an Android-based operating system (OS) for smartphones. At that time, the public did not know who developed MIUI. The goal was to create a user-friendly OS by means of iterated development with quick updates based on the real-time feedback of users and the open source developer community. Within one year after the launch, MIUI had gained a following of half a million fans in twenty-four countries. It was crucial for Xiaomi to create a strong and large loyal user base before launching any commercial product. In August 2011, after contracting with suppliers and having secured half a million MIUI fans, Xiaomi launched its first smartphone.

An Asset-Light Business Model

Xiaomi's business model is different from traditional electronics and smartphone producers. Rather than building up an R&D and production capability, Xiaomi decided to outsource as much as possible. An asset-light business model was the result. Hardware development, production, and hardcore R&D are outsourced. The company focuses on the operation system software and service, where its competitive advantage lies. Xiaomi's business model has the following features:[26]

- *A limited product range and a high price-to-quality ratio:* Xiaomi is similar to Apple in terms of its limited product range, high configuration, and high performance, but it sells for one third of the iPhone's price. The quality of the core technologies of Xiaomi's products are as good as most competitors, such as Huawei and Apple.
- *Fan marketing:* The company uses social media rather than paid media to promote the product. The result is a base of fans that follow the social media of Xiaomi and take active part in the Xiaomi's community on a daily basis. The overall culture is one of "just for fans," which speeds up market penetration at a limited cost.
- *Iterated software R&D and product design:* Xiaomi uses a new product development approach that focuses on getting prototypes to the market as soon as possible with "almost" good enough products and on actively involving users in the fine tuning and updating of the technology and design. For example, every Friday evening, a new round of software updates is released. Within hours, fans provide feedback, and Xiaomi's staff follows up rigorously. The result is a product that is to a large extent codeveloped with the user (fan) community, is closer to the market's needs, and has a more cost-efficient R&D process.
- *Online sales:* It uses online sales channels and social media platforms instead of heavy asset retail shops and distributors. Considering the

narrow target market of young engineering-focused and tech-savvy men, the online sales channel meets the expectations of this market. The result is a low-cost sales channel that meet the demands of the initial target group of customers. However, Xiaomi has been willing to modify this business model in response to market trends and its strong emerging competitors Oppo and Vivo. By 2017, the company had expanded offline sales channels for third- and fourth-tier markets that are less tech savvy and prefer to buy offline rather than online.

- *Outsourced components, production, and delivery:* Xiaomi has used the best-qualified suppliers for components and focused on integration and design rather than production and hardware R&D. The key competencies of Xiaomi include its business model, marketing and promotion, and design rather than manufacturing. These have allowed it to deliver similar-quality products without the heavy investments and time-consuming capability formation in production and R&D of it competitors.

Fan Organization

Lei Jun and Xiaomi are probably best known for innovations in marketing. Often popularly termed "Internet thinking," this approach refers mostly to creating online word of mouth and a fan following. However, fan marketing does not quite capture the essence of this innovative organizational approach. In fact, only one aspect is related to marketing. Table 2.4 summarizes the fan organization approach taken by Xiaomi. One of the core principles of Xiaomi is to create friendships between customers and employees. Many of its eight thousand employees, especially engineers, are fans of Xiaomi. In fact, employees and their families are

Table 2.4
Fan organization

Components	Fans, employees, owners
Core concept	Zero distance to market
Social media tools	Weibo, WeChat, QQ Space, Xiaomi forum
Fan marketing	Word of mouth Hunger marketing Topic plus strategy Social retainer strategy

Source: Authors' research.

required to be fans. A third type of fan is the engaged user. The Xiaomi forum and various social media platforms are the main tools that Xiaomi uses to interact with fans. Discussions can go beyond Xiaomi's products and services to hobbies and daily life conversations as well.

The company itself has a fairly flat organizational structure in which the seven cofounders are only one line of management away from the engineers. The cofounders are required to be involved with new product development directly, participate in user interactions (such as on Xiaomi's platform), and keep up to date about the product. Lei Jun acts as a role model, and his social media account (a Weibo account) has over 4 million followers. This direct communication with users is not only for the cofounders, sales representatives, and service employees. All employees have to take turns in answering questions from users. The user feedback system gives more technical questions directly to the engineers who worked on specific features. In this way, there is a direct pressure on employees to respond to the market.

Fan marketing is a core aspect of the fan organization. A core concept is Xiaomi's decision to rely on word-of-mouth recommendations to drive traffic to online sales channels. This has cut marketing costs by an estimated 30 percent. Low marketing costs and strong negotiation and innovation in the value chain have brought down the overall cost structure of Xiaomi's products. A second feature is hunger marketing. After every much-anticipated sales event, the phones are sold in limited batches, so an artificial sense of competition among fans boosts demand. Third, Xiaomi uses a topic plus activities strategy. Xiaomi carefully selects topics that are close to the fans' interests and creates activities around these topics, both online and offline. For instance, the puzzle My 150 Grams, which was a prelude to the launch of Xiaomi's Youth smartphone, was a classic example of Xiaomi's topic marketing, and it immediately generated a lot of debate among fans. Several possible puzzle answers spread throughout social media, curiosity was generated among fans, and increased enthusiasm led more fans to join the group. Finally, Xiaomi has developed a mature and systematic social media strategy to retain fans. Weibo is the platform mostly for attracting new users, Xiaomi forum is for experienced users and plays a crucial role in the iterated product development, QQ Space is for organizing fan events, and WeChat is the home for customer service. To make the most out of the involvement of fans, Xiaomi established Popcorn awards to recognize, on a weekly basis, the most popular feature of the week.

The Innovation Advantages of the Pioneers

As the first movers, the pioneers have made their way from zero to international recognition as market leaders. They are an exclusive group of around twenty-five to thirty innovative enterprises in traditional and newly emerging industries. Table 2.5 summarizes the innovation advantages of the pioneers discussed in this book. Although the entrepreneurs who founded the pioneers came from a variety of backgrounds and are established in different eras and industries, they share a relentless approach to innovation. In fact, contrary to popular opinion, these companies have been aware of the importance of innovation since their founding. These pioneers emerged as market leaders because they have had an innovation mindset from day one.

Our research highlights several themes that characterize the innovation advantages of the pioneers:

- *Self-reliance:* When most Chinese companies imported foreign technology, the pioneers developed their own technology. The BAT

Table 2.5
The innovation advantages of the pioneers

First wave:	
Haier	Market-driven product innovations Agile platform organization
Huawei	Customer-driven technology innovations Organizational innovations
Lenovo	Innovation by acquisition Product design innovation Corporate venturing
Sany	Rapid product development "New to the world" technologies An embrace of digital industrial platforms
Second wave:	
BAT	Innovative business ecosystems Cross-industry innovations
Xiaomi	An asset-light business model Fan organization

Source: Authors' research.

companies did not really import technology, but in the first phase of benchmarking foreign business models, the three companies were quick to catch up and innovate.

- *Boundaryless:* The pioneers accepted and pursued resources from outside their organizational boundaries. Although Haier, Huawei, Lenovo, and Sany have developed extensive partnerships and made significant investments and acquisitions to mobilize and absorb resources, BAT and Xiaomi have built business ecosystems to orchestrate resources without directly absorbing them. Haier also has been evolving from using resource integration to building a resource ecosystem or platform.
- *Digitization:* With the arrival of the Internet and subsequent digital technology revolution, the pioneers have been quick to adapt, to the surprise of many international enterprises. The digital natives (such as the BAT companies and Xiaomi) and also traditional manufacturers (such as Sany and Haier) have embraced digital technologies and created competitive advantages in the new era.
- *Entrepreneurial:* To a large extent, the innovation advantage of the pioneers lies in their entrepreneurial approach to business. Even though these companies are all large, their advantages are not just in innovating new technologies and products but also in consistently innovating new ways of organizing and renewing business models.

3

Hidden Champions: Unknown Global Market Leaders

Who Are the Hidden Champions?

The hidden champions are highly specialized market leaders (the top three nationally) that have a low level of public awareness and revenues of less than $5 billion (USD). They are driven by long-term growth and continuous innovation to add value for existing loyal customers in niche markets. Our empirical research reveals five distinguishing features of the hidden champions:

- *Rapid growth from divergent roots:* Within less than three decades, these Chinese companies made their way from being domestic emerging players to outcompeting international suppliers and becoming global niche market leaders. Their roots lay in transformed state-owned enterprises but also grassroots new ventures.
- *Strong R&D capability:* The hidden champions have quickly developed strong R&D capabilities in their niche segments. They have done this by hiring more R&D employees, increasing investment in R&D, and making R&D their strategic priority.
- *Continuous product innovation:* The hidden champions excel at continuous product innovation. Innovation's sole purpose is to add more value for customers and lower the cost of production, increasing margin and loyalty rather than price.
- *Leveraging the advantage of being hidden:* Chinese hidden champions try to stay out of the spotlight and shield themselves from competition and the entry of newcomers. In this way, their product life cycles can be extended, influence from outside can be limited, and time can be spent on managing and independent decision making.
- *Global innovators:* Considering their narrow business customer market focus, these companies need to cross geographic boundaries

in order to grow. These companies can be considered early globalizers, especially considering their age.

Although both business and academic observers tend to praise the large well-known companies, our studies indicate that China has a significant number of hidden champions. The world's largest producers of a variety of industrial and electronics products are from China, including radio producer Tecsun Radio, smart surveillance camera innovator Hikvision, port machinery producer ZPMC (with 70 percent global market share), container producer CIMC (with over 50 percent global market share), and Chongqing Changyuan Group (which produces 55 percent of the world's potassium permanganate, which is used as an inorganic chemical compound and has medicinal uses in cleaning wounds). The majority of the hidden innovation champions are in a select set of industrial sectors. According to a recent sample of hidden champions listed by Sino Manager, a Chinese professional management publication, 36 percent of hidden champions are in machinery and equipment, 26 percent in chemicals and materials, and 17 percent in electronics—that is, about 80 percent of hidden champions are in these three sectors.[1] The rest of the sectors include packaging, printing, textile, medical equipment, and veterinary medicine.

In this chapter, we present seven illustrative cases of hidden champions (table 3.1). Because the nature of hidden champions is that they are not visible, data availability is limited. Nevertheless, based on published sources and incomplete lists of the largest hidden champions, we have selected cases that are more or less representative of the total population. Moreover, the seven cases we draw on are highly innovative hidden champions. Although there are many more hidden champions than we can discuss here, our main message is to draw attention to these innovative and competitive global market leaders that are mostly ignored by the media and other global businesses.

Rapid Growth from Divergent Roots

After China's economy started to open up in the 1980s, most midpriced and high-end technology products were imported from abroad. Technologies such as medical devices, electronics, and new energy often were imported from Japan, Taiwan, the United States, and Western Europe. This first period was characterized by pioneering entrepreneurs who operated in a hostile business environment. There was no company law,

Table 3.1
Seven of China's hidden champions: Unknown global market leaders

Case	Location	Year	Technology field	Global position	Domestic position
Goldwind	Xinjiang	1998	Wind energy	1	1
Hailide	Zhejiang	2001	Synthetic resins	1	1
Han's Laser	Shenzhen	1996	Laser equipment	Top 3	1
Hikvision	Zhejiang	2001	Security camera	1	1
Lens	Hunan	2003	Electronic components	Top 3	1
Mindray	Shenzhen	1991	Medical device	Top 3	1
Ringpu	Tianjin	1998	Veterinary medicine	1	1

Source: Authors' research.

and ownership rights were at best fuzzily defined. However, in the 1990s, especially after the 1994 company law was passed, the era of business and entrepreneurs arrived in China. Although many state-owned companies and institutions were transformed and privatized, there was a boom in grassroots entrepreneurs and enterprises established by former government officials. The latter led to the establishment of over 100,000 new companies in 1992 alone.[2] In the 1990s and early 2000, most future champions started to emerge. During this period, entrepreneurs had specialized backgrounds, professional skills, and a willingness to take entrepreneurial risks. Two types of roots of hidden champions can be distinguished—grassroots enterprises and existing organizations that are transformed with hybrid ownership.

The first type of hidden champion emerged from already existing organizations. For instance, Hikvision, a supplier of video surveillance products and solutions based in Hangzhou, is an example of a hidden champion with hybrid ownership. The origin of Hikvision is the Number 52 Research Institute of the China Electronics Technology (CET) Group. CET Group is a state-owned enterprise that is supervised by the state-owned Assets Supervision and Administration Commission of the State Council. The chairperson of Hikvision, Chen Zongnian, was the head of the research institute at that time. CET's Research Institute was established in 1962 and focuses on computer storage technology, which is also the technological root of Hikvision. In 2001, Chen Zongnian, Hu Yangzhong (chief engineer of the institute), and twenty-eight researchers from the institute started a new initiative, Hikvision Digital Technology, which was domestically listed in 2011. By 2017, China Electronics Technology HIK Group (CET HIK), a wholly owned subsidiary of CET Group, owned 40 percent of Hikvision Digital. The second largest shareholder of Hikvision Digital was Gong Hongjia, whose private equity fund owned 18 percent shares. Gong Hongjia also invested in Tecsun Radio, another hidden champion. The third largest shareholder of Hikvision Digital was a management shareholder private equity fund that had a 7 percent share. These shareholders included core members of the management team.

Another example is Goldwind, a wind power equipment manufacturer headquartered in Beijing. The origin of Goldwind was Xinjiang New Wind Company, a company established in 1988 to operate a wind field in Xinjiang province. The company is owned by the provincial government and receives less monitoring and support than a central state-owned company receives. In 1999, Xinjiang New Wind Company started R&D in wind generation equipment. After only one year, the company launched its first product—a 600 kilowatt wind generator. The transformation started in 2001, when New Wind incorporated as Goldwind. By 2007, the company was domestically listed, and by 2010, it was on the Hong Kong Stock Exchange. The company's largest shareholder is Xinjiang Wind Power, a provincial state-owned company, which holds 14 percent of the shares. The second largest shareholder is also a state-owned company, Three Gorges New Energy, which holds 11 percent of the shares. The chairperson of Goldwind, Wu Gang, owns 1.5 percent of the shares. Wu Gang used to be a teacher in a local engineering specialized school and became a wind field manager at Xinjiang Wind Power before becoming a vice president of the company until 1998. Then, similar to Chen Zongnian, he initiated the Goldwind initiative.

Another type of hidden champion was founded by grassroots entrepreneurs. For instance, Mindray, a medical equipment producer, was established by the entrepreneur Xu Hang. Born in 1962, he graduated from Tsinghua University's Computer Science and Bioengineering School in 1987. His first job was at Shenzhen Anke Medical Equipment as an engineer. There he successfully led the R&D development of color B type ultrasound diagnosis equipment until 1991. Then the twenty-nine-year-old engineer established Mindray. Originally, the company functioned mostly as a sales agent for foreign medical equipment in China, providing the initial capital for the company's R&D activities. Xu Hang always felt that to succeed in the medical equipment market he needed to develop his own technology capability. The company's global champion product was launched in 2001—a portable digital black and white ultrasound diagnosis device. Mindray was listed on the New York Stock Exchange in 2006 and currently is China's largest medical equipment producer of a variety of medical devices and one of the global top three in patient monitoring devices.

Another example is Lens Technology, one of the world's top three producers (and China's largest producer) of lens products such as touch panel cover glass and touch sensor modules. The company was established by the world's richest woman, whose self-made fortune had a net worth of $7 billion after her company went public on the Shenzhen ChiNext market in 2015. Originally from a poor family in Hunan province, she is a high-school dropout and became a migrant worker at age sixteen in Shenzhen while taking part-time courses in Shenzhen University.[3] She took a job with a local family-run firm that made watches, and after this company went bankrupt in 1993, she started her own company producing watch lenses with her brother, sister, and their families. By 2001, Lens Technology signed its first contract for mobile phone screens with TCL, which allowed her to enter a new industry and proved to be the turning point for the company. In 2003, after she received a request from Motorola to develop glass screens for the Razr V3, she formally established the touch-screen maker Lens Technology. Her major innovation was to adopt watch glass technology to smartphone screens, which at that time were transitioning from plastic to glass screens. She is the sole founder and majority shareholder with 88 percent of the company's shares. By 2017, her company was a true hidden champion whose clients included Apple, Huawei, Samsung, and other large cell phone brands.

Although the hidden champions come from different backgrounds and show different growth strategies, they have one thing in common—rapid growth. Compared to the German hidden champions, the Chinese hidden champions took much less time to grow into domestic and global market leaders—just a little over a decade.[4] The German hidden champions are on average a hundred years old, are family-owned, and grew slowly into market leadership. Stability and survival came before speed of growth. For instance, Hikvision became the top global supplier for video surveillance equipment in ten years. By 2010, it had a market share of around 20 percent. In the last decade, it has seen a compound annual growth rate (CAGR) of 44 percent. Goldwind took only eight years to become China's market leader by 2006 and seventeen years to be the global number one, maintaining a CAGR of 24 percent for the past five years. Mindray's best-selling ultrasound device was the top global seller by early 2000, around ten years after the company's founding, with a CAGR of 30 percent since 2003. Lens Technology became a dominant player in the industry (it had a 30 percent market share in 2015) after producing the touch screens for Apple's iPhone during its 2007 market entry. From 2005 to 2015, it had a CAGR of 40 percent, and by 2017, it employed seventy thousand people and manufactured over a billion glass screens per year. Han's Laser, China's leading laser equipment manufacturer, saw an average annual growth rate of 50 percent during the last decade as well. Clearly, Chinese hidden champions prioritize speed and growth and rapidly emerged from humble roots.

Strong R&D Capability

Hidden champions gave R&D a strategic priority in the early stages of their founding, unlike most of their manufacturing peers in that period. A case in point is Hikvision and cofounder Hu Yangzhong's vision for developing intellectual property. Established in 2001, Hikvision became the global leader in a decade in an industry that is technology intensive and mostly dominated by a handful of foreign incumbents such as Bosch. Hikvision is also an example of staying ahead of copycats. Immediately after it was established, it faced a surge of copycats that were responding to the large demand and growth of this industry. Hu Yangzhong realized that Hikvision's technology advantages could quickly erode, so early on the company focused on quickly upgrading technology. Moreover, starting in 2002, it filed intellectual property (IP) infringement cases against all copycats, when most Chinese companies had not started to notice IP, clearly showing a commitment to develop and own IP. Table 3.2 summarizes the R&D capabilities of the seven companies discussed in this chapter in terms of number of R&D employees, R&D expenditures, number of R&D centers, and domestic patents.

Overall, the hidden champions in our sample of illustrative cases spend an average of around 8 percent of their total revenues on R&D across their diverse industries and often multiple R&D sites. Some of them (such as Goldwind, Hikvision, and Mindray) also have international R&D centers. The hidden champions have on average at least 25 percent of their total staff in R&D functions. Han's Laser has over three thousand R&D personnel, which is 30 percent of its total staff, and claims that the

Table 3.2
The strong R&D capability of seven hidden champions

Case	Technology field	R&D employees (% of total)	R&D expenditures (% of revenues)	Number of R&D centers	Patents in China[a]
Goldwind	Wind energy	1,200 (21%)	5%	4	551
Hailide	Synthetic resins	270 (13%)	5%	1	397
Han's Laser	Laser equipment	3,000 (31%)	8%	3	280
Hikvision	Security camera	9,300 (47%)	7% to 8%	7	1,222
Lens	Electronic components	8,700 (12%)	9%	1	554
Mindray	Medical device	2,000 (20%)	10%	10	3,500
Ringpu	Veterinary medicine	300 (15%)	8% to 10%	9	120

Note: a. Number of patents both approved by and filed in the Chinese Patent Office.
Source: Authors' research.

company employs 50 percent of China's national laser talents, including famous academics in the laser engineering science field. Close to half of Hikvision's employees are in R&D, reaching over nine thousand in 2017, which means that it has the world's largest R&D capability in terms of engineers in its segment. In terms of patents, Hikvision was one of the earliest companies to focus on developing and protecting IP in China. Han's Laser owns 50 percent of all laser-related patents in China. Similarly, Mindray also has a strong IP base and a strong strategic commitment to investing in R&D, where it assigns over 10 percent of its revenue.

The R&D capability of the hidden champions is impressive, and international executives often show surprise and feel a sense of urgency when they are presented with the quantitative evidence. Although industries differ in their R&D intensity and their need for R&D, the overall picture is one of strong commitment to developing an indigenous R&D capability that gives them a sustainable competitive advantage to compete in China and in the rest of the world.

Continuous Product Innovation for Niche Markets

In China, there are increasingly more product innovations, but many remain incremental rather than radical. According to a National Bureau of Statistics survey, 19 percent of large Chinese manufacturing companies reported that they invested in significantly improving existing products or developing new products (that is, product innovation).[5] For companies in the top five provinces (Beijing, Guangdong, Jiangsu, Tianjin, and Zhejiang), this was over 40 percent. Leveraging their strong R&D capability allows the hidden champions to excel at continuous product innovation for niche markets. It is one of their competitive advantages.

The hidden champions quickly increase their product range without diversifying into new segments. For instance, although Mindray initially was a trader for medical equipment, in 1992, it developed its first self-made product, which was a single parameter blood oxygen saturation monitor. In 1993, it developed a multiple parameter version, and later it developed a transcranial Doppler cerebral blood flow diagnostic device and a range of other new-to-China medical equipment devices (such as a portable color Doppler ultrasound system and an automatic biochemical analyzer). Until 1997, the company developed slowly and built up R&D capability. In that year, it successfully raised foreign venture capital from Walden International. In 2001, it launched its global champion product—a portable digital black and white ultrasound diagnosis machine. After this success, it launched ten new products every year, and each used at least ten of its own patents. Mindray stayed within its segment of medical monitoring equipment and successfully brought many global champion products to the market.

Similarly, Ringpu launched its first product in 1998—Tai Ling, which was a chemical-based medicine for poultry. As the first product of this type in China, it was a large success domestically. In 2001, the company entered biology-based veterinary medicine. It now produces 170 different chemical-based medicines and over fifty different types of biology-based medicines. In 2014, it developed a new vaccine for avian influenza, a third-generation vaccine that is produced only in China and the United States. In a different industry, glass screens for electronic products, Lens Technology follows a similar approach of increasing product range within its niche segment. The company started with glass screens for watches, innovated the glass screen for touch applications on smartphones and pads, and expanded into applications for laptops, digital cameras, and GPS navigators. Most recently, it developed glass screens for new consumer products such as wearables and smart watches. Expanding its screen technology, in 2011, the company started to develop precision ceramics application and sapphire-related technology for applications such as infrared optical components and high-durability windows. Pioneering products (such as touch screen modules, fingerprint-recognition glass, and iris scanner modules) are currently being developed by Lens for clients such as Apple, Huawei, Lenovo, LG, Microsoft, OPPO, Samsung, and Xiaomi.

Another example is Han's Laser. Leveraging an immense R&D capability and occupying the majority of laser-related resources in China, the company has been continuously upgrading its product offering. Its first product was a relatively low-end laser labeling device for small products like buttons or leather products. In 2004, it signed a deal with Motorola and started to develop a laser product that can light sculpture products. The company then expanded its products to include laser welding machines and printed circuit board laser driller machines, and it marketed them to cell phone producers. New clients like Samsung and Apple approached Han's Laser. The company's next step was to expand to high-voltage laser applications like light cable-cutting machines. Applications include products for aerospace, automotive, and solar industries. The company's laser-cutting machine has been used for making large parts on the automatic production lines of the China Commercial Aircraft Corporation. It has developed over two hundred industrial laser devices that are used in all kinds of industries.

Hailide's case is interesting because it illustrates that Chinese hidden champions are starting to move up the value chain. Hailide is a Shenzhen-listed company that was established in 2001 in Zhejiang. Its main products are highly niche and include industrial polyester yarn, plastic materials, and tire cord fabric. The main application for polyester yarn is in car airbags, and Hailide holds 90 percent of the global market for this material. The manufacturing method for industrial polyester airbag yarn is the first that was developed in China. Hailide is one of the companies that successfully realized the development and commercial production of industrial polyester airbag yarn, and it is a national key new product. Breakthrough progress also has been made in tire cord fabric, which has been accredited by Michelin and Sumitomo. The company's high-end digital printing materials and movie screens are also in a leading position in the industry. Hailide's niche market focus and market leader position leave little room for growth, however. Since 2011, Hailide has had no revenue growth and has not expanded. However, the company significantly increased its margin from 16 percent in 2011 to 25 percent in 2016. Although its product range is still limited, the company has improved its products and production process to lower costs and improve performance.

Overall, Chinese hidden champions excel at continuous product innovation by increasing the types of products produced or improving the product for niche markets. The hidden champions leverage a strong R&D capability and rapid growth in the domestic market. Moreover, as is shown in the next sections, they leverage their hidden status and global innovation opportunities.

Leveraging the Advantage of Being Hidden

These hidden champions remain out of view for four main reasons: they have low-profile founders, they seek limited media visibility, they are geographically hidden, and they have a strategic intention to remain hidden. Unlike many family-owned German companies that shy away from investment and especially stock market listings, Chinese hidden champions look to raise capital, and many (such as Goldwind, Hailide, Han's Laser, Hikvision, Lens, and Ringpu) are listed on domestic and sometimes international stock markets. Mindray used to be listed on the New York Stock Exchange but privatized in 2016.

The founders of the hidden champions generally maintain a low profile, are not eager to appear in media, and prefer to stay out of the spotlight. In contrast to people like Ma Yun and Zhang Ruimin, who like to promote their companies and their management approaches in various media, the founders of hidden champions prefer to focus on business and operations. In hidden champions from emerging economies, external financing is used mostly to fuel growth. Despite the public nature of these companies, the hidden champions remain largely invisible for consumers and the international audience.

Our research on their media visibility, as summarized in figure 3.1, reveals their hidden status. We looked at three features—number of employees, appearances in international mainstream and financial/investment media (Google; *Fast Company* magazine, which is a leading investment outlet; and *Financial Times*, which is a leading financial news portal), and appearances in domestic mainstream and financial/investment media (Baidu; *PEdaily* magazine, which is a leading investment media outlet; and *Caijing* magazine, which is a leading financial

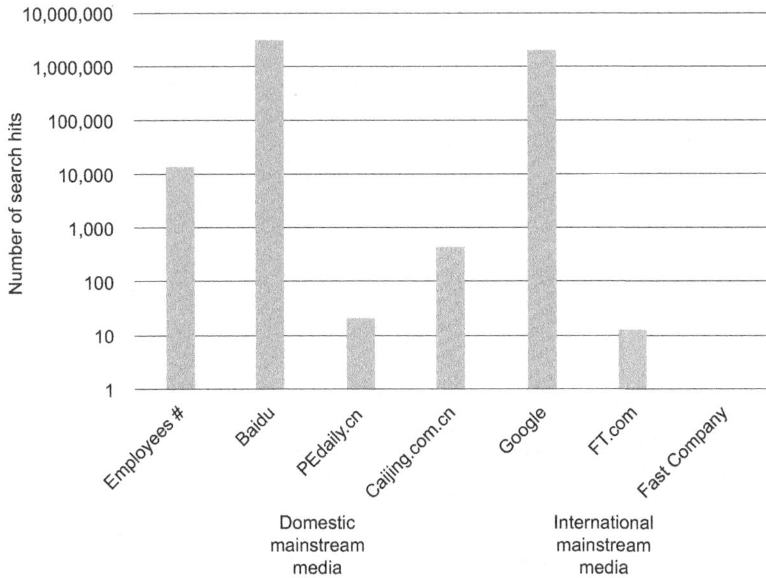

Figure 3.1
The media exposure of hidden champions
Source: Authors' database, search date May 10, 2017.

news portal). The scale in the figure is logarithmic, and the figure refers to number of search hits on the various platforms.

The hidden champions in our sample have an average of fourteen thousand employees, but compared to pioneers, their visibility is low. They have an average of a few hundred appearances in domestic specialized media and are mostly invisible internationally. Even on broad search media like Baidu and Google, they receive only 2 to 3 million hits, which is just 3 percent to 5 percent of the pioneers, even though their ages do not differ much. The most visible hidden champion is Hikvision, probably because of its consumer market development in the recent years. Despite their public nature, the least visible are companies like Hailide and Ringpu.

Another way that these companies are hidden is in terms of location. When the locations of fifty-three known hidden champions are examined, an interesting pattern emerges.[6] Figure 3.2 illustrates the locations of the top fifty-three hidden champions. Three features stand out. First, the hidden champions are dispersed throughout China—north, southeast coast, internal provinces (such as Henan, Hubei, and Hunan), the more

Figure 3.2
The geographic distribution of the top fifty-three hidden champions in China
Source: Authors' research; "2016 Chinese Manufacturing Hidden Champion List" (in Chinese), *Sino Manager*, accessed December 12, 2016, http://www.sino-manager.com/22140.html.

developed regions (such as Jiangsu and Zhejiang), and also the less developed regions (such as Henan and Liaoning). Second, most hidden champions are not founded in first-tier cities such as Beijing and Shanghai. Of the nine hidden champions in Zhejiang, only one is in the prosperous provincial capital city of Hangzhou, and in Guangdong province, only one hidden champion is in the capital Guangzhou. Third, Shenzhen and Zhejiang stand out as locations that traditionally are strong in entrepreneurship and private-sector development.

Finally, the strategic intention of many of hidden champions is to stay hidden. As our research with Chinese hidden champions suggests, the Chinese hidden champions strongly prefer to be a big fish in a small pool than a small fish in an ocean surrounded by a lot of sharks.[7] They intentionally avoid massive expansion but focus on their niche and specialized products. They focus but keep innovating, not necessarily in terms of higher performance but by adding more value for their customers. Innovation often lowers the cost of a product and thereby increases the margin. In addition, most of the hidden champions are cautious about strategic collaboration, mergers and acquisitions (M&A), outsourcing, and franchising. They prefer to do everything themselves, as is evidenced by their early development of R&D capability and a pool of intellectual property.

They go mostly unnoticed by consumers but have a strong brand reputation with their direct customers. In fact, these companies do promote themselves but mostly only with direct customers. In this way, they avoid drawing attention and unnecessary disturbances from outsiders. Considering their focus on continuous product innovation and building up their own R&D capability, being hidden is also more or less a necessity: it takes longer for companies in a product niche to emerge as champions compared to companies competing in a mass market. The lower the direct competitive pressure and need to build a public profile, the greater the energy and effort that are available to build a sustainable competitive advantage. This is significantly different than quick-growth consumer-oriented companies such as Didi Chuxing and Toutiao (the changemakers of chapter 5), which grew rapidly in a short time. Although the low-profile features of the founders and the rather inconvenient locations of their companies limits visibility, to some extent it is also a strategic choice that makes business sense for the global market leaders in niche markets.

Global Innovators

Chinese companies are increasingly innovating abroad. Survey results from Strategy& show that over 80 percent of responding Chinese firms intend to expand abroad in the next ten years.[8] This result fits the overall trend of strongly increasing outward foreign direct investment (OFDI) from China. China's OFDI has risen sharply since 2003 with an average annual growth rate of over 80 percent. In 2014, OFDI in terms of flow from China was already 10 percent of global FDI flow compared with 8 percent of global inward FDI flow.[9] China's pioneers have started to go global, and companies such Huawei and Haier are taking the lead.

In addition to the expansion of Chinese innovation champions abroad, the 2014 China Innovation Survey shows that over two-thirds of responding Chinese firms intend to expand both their markets and R&D presence abroad.[10] Hidden champions are globalizing. In our research, we have assessed the globalization of seven hidden champions, summarized in table 3.3.

First, most hidden champions expand internationally relatively quickly after founding, usually within five to ten years. Their need to internationalize is significant because they are operating mostly in niche markets. Nevertheless, Chinese companies have a relatively large home market advantage, and our study shows that hidden champions first quickly capture the market. Second, most hidden champions have multiple subsidiaries overseas ranging from a handful to over forty. In addition, many hidden champions have a strong overseas agent and distributor network in place. Third, although these companies are on average still young (less than two decades old), many earn most of their revenue from international markets. Companies such as Hailide, Lens, and Mindray are predominantly active in overseas markets, while Goldwind, Han's Laser, and Hikvision still have a strong domestic focus but also have a fast-growing overseas revenue contribution. Fourth, hidden champions invest and acquire companies overseas, as is illustrated with Mindray and Hikvision below. Fifth, hidden champions cast a wide international net and are active in most regions, including Africa, the Middle East, and South America.

Hidden champions differ in their approaches to international expansion. Some are more greenfield, and others are more cautious. For instance, Mindray and Hikvision have expanded aggressively overseas with dozens of subsidiaries and 30 percent to 50 percent of their total revenues from overseas markets. Their approach to internationalizing is similar. For instance, they both started with exporting their products via trade exhibitions before quickly establishing subsidiaries. Hikvision built its first subsidiary in the Netherlands in 2007, and ten years later, it had twenty-eight subsidies in over a hundred country markets, including two R&D centers in North America. Mindray's first subsidiaries were in the United States in the early 2000s, and now it has forty-two subsidiaries covering most of the world's markets. The first subsidiary in the United States initially targeted mostly Latin American markets before it entered the U.S. market. Both Mindray and Hikvision acquired an overseas company. In 2016, Hikvision acquired a British company, Secure Holdings Limited, that had mature sensor and detection technology, an

Table 3.3
The globalization of seven hidden champions

	Goldwind	Hailide	Han's Laser	Hikvision	Lens	Mindray	Ringpu
Year of establishment	1998	2001	1996	2001	2003	1991	1998
Year of entry in a foreign market	2004	2005	2011	2007	2003	2000	Not available
Number of overseas subsidiaries	4	2 and agents	13 (12 agents)	28	3	42	Agents
Revenue from overseas markets	8%	70%	11%	29%	85%	50%	Limited
Investments overseas?	Yes	No	Yes	Yes	Yes	Yes	No
Countries and regions	Global except Southeast Asia	Global	Global	Global (100 countries)	Europe, Japan, Korea, United States	Global	Egypt, Jordan, Pakistan, Philippines

Source: Authors' research.

alarm system product line, and a brand (Pyronix) that was well-known in European markets. In 2008, Mindray spent $200 million to acquire Datascope, a U.S. patient monitoring equipment company, with the goal of expanding outside the China market.

Unlike Mindray and Hikvision, Goldwind followed a more careful approach to internationalization. First, in 2004, the company took a preliminary step abroad—not with a subsidiary or agent but with a research collaboration with Vensys, a German wind energy manufacturer. They jointly researched pioneering technology called the permanent magnet direct drive (PMDD) wind turbine generator. In 2016, after the first prototype was successfully developed, Goldwind registered a new company in Germany, Goldwind Wind Energy. A year later, Goldwind acquired a 70 percent share of Vensys and thereby also acquired this core technology.

Second, in 2009, Goldwind started its first project in the United States. In 2010, it set up a subsidiary, Goldwind Americas, a wholly owned company of Xinjiang Goldwind Science and Technology, based in Chicago. The next year, it entered markets in Africa and South America and later Australia and Thailand. In South America, the company also established a new team while the Chile and Panama markets were served directly from Goldwind Americas in Chicago. Recently, Goldwind acquired two Texas projects whose combined capacity is 300 megawatts. In 2017, Goldwind obtained $140 million in tax equity financing commitments from a unit of Berkshire Hathaway Energy and Citigroup. After they are constructed, these two projects will be Goldwind's largest U.S. projects to date.

Third, because Goldwind strongly believes in internationalizing its talent base, the next step in its internationalization is about talent. For instance, the company's current human resources director is Malaysian, and the chief technical officer is German. The general managers of its overseas subsidiaries are all local hires. Goldwind's next step is to open up more subsidiaries all over the world. In sum, Goldwind's approach is first to internationalize its technology and products instead of making heavy investments in subsidiaries as Hikvision and Mindray have done.

Insights into the Hidden Champions

Chinese hidden innovation champions are unknown to most of the business world. Although they come from diverging roots, their growth, R&D capability, and product innovation capability are strong. In most cases, the hidden champions leverage their anonymity and quietly but significantly become global innovators. Five insights stand out:

- *Rapid growth from divergent roots:* Regardless of their different roots and growth strategies, hidden champions have one thing in common—rapid growth. If they are compared to the German hidden champions,[11] the Chinese hidden champions have taken much less time (a little over a decade) to grow into domestic and global market leaders. German hidden champions are on average a hundred years old, are family-owned, and grew slowly into market leadership. They value stability and survival more than speed of growth, whereas Chinese hidden champions prioritize speed and growth and rapidly emerged from humble roots.
- *Strong R&D capability:* Hidden champions in China have given R&D a strategic priority. The impressive R&D capability of these hidden champions often surprises international executives, who feel a sense of urgency when they are presented with the quantitative evidence. Although industries differ in their R&D intensity and their need for it, the overall picture is one of a strong commitment to develop an indigenous R&D capability for creating a sustainable competitive advantage for competing in China and in the rest of the world.
- *Continuous product innovation:* Chinese hidden champions excel at continuous product innovation while increasing the types of products or improving the product for niche markets. The hidden champions leverage a strong R&D capability and rapid growth in the domestic market. Compared to the German hidden champions, they place less pressure on cost control due to a cheap labor supply and their third- or fourth-tier city locations in China. In contrast with the German hidden champions, the Chinese hidden champions do not focus on high-end consumer niches but are upgrading at the middle. Therefore, they show less process innovation than the Germans show but more product innovation.
- *The advantages of being hidden:* There are four reasons that these hidden champions have remained hidden: their founders remain low profile, they seek limited media visibility, they are geographically hidden, and their strategic intention is to remain hidden. They do not operate the same as the many family-owned German companies that shy away from investment and especially stock market listings. The Chinese hidden champions do look to raise capital, and many of them are listed on domestic and sometimes international stock markets. External financing is used mostly to fuel their growth ambitions and also probably is specific to emerging economies.

Table 3.4
A comparison of Chinese and German hidden champions

	Chinese hidden champions	German hidden champions
Average age	25 years	100 years
Ownership	Mostly listed	Mostly family owned
Positioning	Middle end	High end
Talent development	Self-developed practitioners	Apprenticeship
Management team	Founding team	Professional managers
Primary objective	Growth and speed	Survival and stability
Home market size	Large	Small

- *Global innovators:* Chinese hidden champions are globalizing. Despite the large home market, most of the hidden champions expand internationally relatively quickly after founding, usually within five to ten years. But they approach international expansion differently. For instance, Goldwind's approach is first to internationalize its technology and products instead of expanding in heavy investments in subsidiaries as Hikvision and Mindray have done. Nevertheless, the Chinese hidden champions are still not as global as the German hidden champions. Table 3.4 summarizes differences between Chinese and German hidden champions.

The Chinese hidden champions are also remarkable from an innovation talent perspective. First, although the German apprenticeship system has always guaranteed talent development, China has no such legacy. Therefore, China's most talented workers are either educated in a small group of elite universities or overseas. Second, the educational resources in China are highly concentrated in the first-tier cities and around the top twenty universities. However, most Chinese hidden champions are not located in first-tier cities. Third, because hidden champions are mostly invisible to the larger public and student community, they have difficulty attracting top talent.

Their rapid rise to market leaders is difficult to explain from a traditional management and talent perspective. The hidden champions have a differentiated strategy when it comes to talent development. On the one hand, top talents are not attracted by an invisible, incremental, and distant company with an ordinary profile. On the other hand, hidden champions do not hire top talents but instead focus on hiring practical, loyal, and skilled employees who can be internally developed. Instead of disruptive and elite thinkers, they are looking to hire people who are similar to the founders and the company itself and who are willing to work long term on incrementally improving product value for customers. This approach creates cost advantages over competitors and clearly differentiates them from other companies.

4

Underdogs: Technology Ventures under the Radar

Who Are the Underdogs?

In China, the underdogs are small and medium-sized enterprises—smaller than \$60 million (USD) revenues or a thousand employees, according to the standard set by Ministry of Industry and Information Technology (MIIT) of China—that are driven by innovative technology, have significant intellectual property, and were established after 2000. Our empirical research reveals five distinguishing features of these Chinese underdogs:

- *Elite entrepreneurs:* Underdogs are often ventures established by overseas returnee entrepreneurs who have top educational backgrounds in science and technology.
- *Early international exposure:* Underdogs are often internationalizing early with export and technology partners abroad, international markets, and overseas facilities.
- *Under the radar:* The market visibility of the underdogs is limited, and most of these companies are young and small.
- *Cutting-edge technology:* Underdogs compete on cutting-edge technology and often are driven by technological and scientific advances rather than customers and engineering solutions.
- *Niche innovators:* Underdogs often innovate in niches (although of global market size) in business-to-business markets by combining new products with new processes and business models.

Although both business and academic observers tend to praise the large incumbent companies (such as Alibaba, BYD, Haier, and Huawei), our studies indicate that they are only the tip of the iceberg. Our extensive research—many interviews with representatives of Chinese companies, comments by executives of Western companies about their Chinese competitors, our study of the extant literature, media reports, and comments and critiques received during presentations to managerial and academic audiences—confirm that this third group (the underdogs) poses a competitive threat. The difficulty of identifying, let alone assessing, the enormous quantity and force of Chinese innovators who are operating under the radar poses a great challenge for the future of many multinational and domestic firms alike.

In this chapter, we draw on twelve illustrative cases (table 4.1) of under-the-radar technology ventures in a large variety of technology fields and industries. Although not a complete and exhaustive list, these cases reflect our experiences of the last decade. These technologies reflect government-supported industries, investor attention, and market trends. We do not engage in technology forecasting but report on current status and potential. The key message is that there is an ocean of interesting technology enterprises in China, some more successful than others, and that is bound to make a difference.

Table 4.1
Twelve Chinese underdogs: Technology ventures under the radar

Case	Location	Year	Technology field	New to the world?
Ease Power	Suzhou	2011	Integrated circuit design	No
Gago	Beijing	2015	Big data	No
GeneChem	Shanghai	2002	Biotechnology	No
Juzix	Shanghai	2014	Block chain	Yes
Magnity	Shanghai	2008	Infrared imaging	No
Malong	Shenzhen	2014	Artificial intelligence	Yes
Rejoin	Hangzhou	2006	Healthcare	No
Royole	Shenzhen	2012	Flexible display	Yes
Shining 3D	Hangzhou	2004	3D printing	No
Uninano	Shenzhen	2008	Nano technology	Yes
Weihua	Xiamen	2010	Photovoltaic	Yes
Zongmu	Shanghai	2013	Automotive	No

Source: Authors' research.

Elite Entrepreneurs

In the twenty-first century, a new type of technology enterprise emerged in China that was built around elite entrepreneurs who returned from overseas studies.[1] More than any other country, China attracts back citizens who have studied in other countries. Since 1978, 4 million Chinese students have studied abroad, 2.8 million students have graduated, and 80 percent of these 2.8 million overseas graduates have returned to China. Because all returnee alumni are not necessarily highly talented, in 2008, the government introduced a program to attract the best talents back to China.

Since 2008, more than forty thousand high-level talents have returned to China and have found jobs. In that time, the number of returnees working at a professor level has been more than twenty times than that of the total number between 1978 and 2008, forming the biggest overseas returning wave since the founding of the People's Republic of China. According to official statistics, more than 70 percent of project leaders working at key national research projects are overseas returnees.[2] A large number of academicians at the Chinese Academy of Sciences and the China Academy of Engineering are overseas returnees. Currently, there are more than three hundred overseas returnees' pioneer parks and 24,000 enterprises in the parks across the country, where about 24,000 overseas returnees are employed.

China leverages these returnees by placing them at the top of large pyramids of locally trained graduates (whether trained in universities or companies). Unsurprisingly, many of these returnees come back to become entrepreneurs and seize the opportunities of China's emerging economy and booming middle class. For instance, Fan Bin, the founder of Weihua Solar, graduated from Tsinghua University before pursuing a doctoral degree at Switzerland's École Polytechnique Fédérale de Lausanne (EPFL).[3] After studying chemistry at Jilin University, Richard Luan also pursued his doctorate in Europe, in combinatorial materials chemistry in the University of Edinburgh in the United Kingdom. However, most high-level talents come back from the United States. For instance, Zhang Gong, the founder of Gago, started at Nanjing University and Beijing University in the field of geography and then continued with a doctoral degree in ecology at Utah State University in the United States. His other three cofounders (Wang Yungang, Zhang Wenpeng, and Gu Zhu) all received their higher education in the United States. Royole's Liu Zihong obtained his degrees from one of China's top institutions,

Tsinghua University, in electronic engineering before studying at Stanford University in California. Also a Tsinghua University alumni, Shen Chongfei, the founder of Magnity, went to Princeton University to pursue his doctoral degree in electrical engineering.

Although they have similar international education experience, the roads that these men have taken to entrepreneurship are quite different. For instance, Fan Bin established Xiamen Weihua Solar after returning to China, and Liu Zihong first worked for IBM in the United States. Similar to Liu Zihong, Zhang Gong also first worked in the United States as a researcher for the National Aeronautics and Space Administration (NASA). His cofounder Wang Yungang is a former researcher for the U.S. Energy Department National Laboratory. Shen Chongfei not only first worked in the United States (at Agere Systems and Brion Technologies, owned by ASML) but also founded his first venture in Silicon Valley in California, Transvision Microsystems (2005 to 2007). This company develops novel imaging systems with micro-electro-mechanical systems (MEMS) technology that can provide clear images for night vision, thermography, security, firefighting, and automotive applications. A year after his return to China, while working as a professor at Tsinghua University, he founded Magnity Electronics. After his return, Richard Luan worked in Shenzhen for the British firm Sciford, a device maker for chemical compounds applications, before he established his own venture (Uninano) in 2008.

But not all underdog talent is groomed abroad. China has 2,529 universities of which 39 are considered top universities and "985" program universities. The universities in China have an elite ranking system, and students enter based on their college entrance exam scores. On average, 9 million students take this exam annually, but only roughly 0.3 percent end up in the top ten universities. In terms of global reach, these universities are included in lists of the world's top hundred universities, although they generally have very few international students.

For instance, GeneChem's founder Cao Yueqiong received her degree in life sciences from Fudan University in Shanghai. Ease Power's founder Wu Yuchun graduated in microelectronics from Tsinghua University in Beijing in 2007. The founder of Zongmu, Tang Rui, graduated in electronic engineering from Tsinghua University in 1999. The founder of Rejoin, Li Xiang, has an electronic engineering doctorate in integrated circuitry from Zhejiang University. Although Cao Yueqiong worked in China for a local company before establishing her firm, Wu Yuchun spend four years in the United States working for the electronics distributor ADI, and Tang Rui worked over ten years in various oversea companies before he established his new venture, Zongmu. Li Xiang, on the other hand, never worked in any company and established his company before finishing his doctorate. Li Xiang always dreamed of becoming an entrepreneur. As an undergraduate student, he was a member and later chairperson of the Future Entrepreneurs Club of Zhejiang University and developed an independent vision. In 2006, as an undergraduate, he founded Rejoin Technology with two friends. Huang Dinglong, the cofounder of Malong Technologies in Shenzhen, received his doctoral degree in human machine interaction from Tsinghua University. He worked at Microsoft, Tencent, and TripAdvisor before founding his company in 2014 with an American cofounder Matthew Scott, a graduate of Boston University and a top scientist with over sixty patents in computer science. Malong Tech has developed a breakthrough deep learning and computer vision technology platform for business applications. Finally, the founder of Juzix, Shun Lilin, is a graduate of Beijing University of Aeronautics and Astronautics and has a doctorate from Wuhan University in electronic engineering and remote sensing. Before founding Juzix, he worked for Union Pay, China's Visa. Juzix is an infrastructure provider for distributed data exchange using distributed ledger technology and multiparty computation.

Unlike copycats and businessmen, these new elite entrepreneurs distinguish themselves by bringing science and technology to the market. Although not all of them have been educated abroad, all have received elite education before starting their technology ventures.

Early International Exposure

Often the "China goes global" trend is linked to large, even state-owned enterprises from China. Especially in the last decade, the Chinese government strengthened its "going abroad" policy, which aimed to help Chinese companies acquire strategic assets, further develop internationally competitive "global champion" enterprises, secure resources abroad, overcome intensified competition and overcapacity in the domestic economy, acquire advanced technology to address competitive disadvantages, and acquire brands and managerial know-how.[4] Our research, however, shows that the underdogs are often already at an early phase of being present in international markets. In this section, we discuss various ways that they are participating in international markets—through collaboration, original equipment manufacturing (OEM), the overseas markets, international promotion, and pilot projects.

In 2010, Weihua Solar was established in Xiamen with support from the local government. Its founder, Fan Bin, was recognized as part of the Thousand Talent Program and an internationally renowned scientist, so it is not surprising that Weihua has an international outlook. In its early years, the team focused on research and development and patented several inventions. By 2013 (before Weihua had a commercial product), Merck, a German chemical giant, contacted Weihua, and in October, the two companies reached an agreement to be strategic partners, where Merck would offer advanced materials and authorize Weihua to use Merck's relevant patents.

Unlike Weihua, Zongmu focused in the beginning on developing and commercializing high-quality advanced driver assistance system (ADAS) products for their domestic clients. After undergoing several rounds of fund raising and successfully being listed on the over-the-counter market in China, Zongmu developed an international partnership with Qualcomm. At the 2017 CES conference in Las Vegas, the two companies launched the latest ADAS prototype, which is based on the Qualcomm Snapdragon 820A processor and deep learning technology, while Zongmu began steering the company's vision from ADAS to self-driving technology.

Rejoin followed a different route. At a 2007 international trade fair, Li Xiang met a Canadian client. Earlier that year, Rejoin had already acquired two technologies—optical character recognition (OCR) and text-to-speech (TTS) technologies. Based on these new technologies, the company's ten employees launched eight products in 2007. At the end of 2007, they signed a partnership agreement with the Canadian client to develop and produce visual aid devices. Until 2011, most of their sales were overseas, but in 2011, the collaboration ended when Rejoin decided to sell its own branded products abroad. Globally, only two companies have developed low-vision, high-definition (HD) lens technology—Sony and Sentech, which are both Japanese companies. In 2014, Rejoin acquired a British company called Zoomax, which became its overseas brand.

Similar to Rejoin, Shining 3D started early to export its products to Europe, America, and other regions. Clients include global companies such as Adidas, Bosch, Cherry, Haier, Hikvision, Huawei, Intel, Midea, and Wahaha. Universities such as Tsinghua University and Zhejiang University also are buying the company's 3D scanners and printers. Shining 3D is active in twenty foreign markets, opened branches in the United

States and Germany in 2017, and aims to earn 50 percent of its revenues overseas by 2022.

In the artificial intelligence (AI) technology field, Malong started to expand overseas in 2017, only three years after its founding. In that year, the company received a large investment of 200 million renminbi (RMB) from Softbank. It intends to increase its exposure outside of China by attending AI contests like Google's first WebVision (which it won in 2017) and by having a presence in North America, Western Europe, and Japan.

Some underdogs already have an overseas presence. For instance, in 2012, Royole started operations in Hong Kong, Shenzhen, and Silicon Valley. In 2014, it claimed to have developed the world's thinnest flexible full-color display. Since 2015, the founder has received increased media attention, and in September 2015, he topped the list of *Forbes*'s most innovative U.S.-China entrepreneurs. One month later, the Chinese premier, Li Keqiang, visited Royole. At CES 2015 in Las Vegas, Royole launched new flexible electronics–enabled smart home products and a curved vehicle dashboard, which Reuters named the best of CES 2015. Royole is not likely to stay hidden for much longer, especially after hiring R&B pop star Akon as its chief creative officer in 2016.

Some underdog companies are still in the early phase of commercialization but are keeping an eye on foreign markets. Gago, for instance, has launched several pilot projects in Australia, Bangladesh, and Mongolia. Gago was established in the Silicon Valley in 2014, and it moved back to Beijing later while keeping an office in the United States in order to mobilize all the resources the founding team has there. It also is active in different kinds of oversea engagements. For instance, cofounder Wang Yungang gave a speech at the University of California, aiming to recruit international interns who can be "stored" in the company's international talent pool for further development of the international markets such as Canada, Mexico, and the United States.

Considering the international backgrounds of these entrepreneurs, it is perhaps not surprising that their ventures are active internationally. Nevertheless, despite their small size and early introduction of product commercialization, it appears they are at the brink of a new trend. Unlike the previous generation of entrepreneurs, new technology ventures are increasingly looking beyond the Chinese market. Some of them are perhaps "born global" in the sense of being familiar with the foreign environment and having an international mindset and ambitions.

Under the Radar

Underdogs normally share two important features—a disadvantaged position and a passion and determination to triumph against the odds.[5] In our research, we find that underdogs tend to operate under the radar: they have limited media exposure or visibility in the market. We analyzed the media exposure of our case studies in comparison to the book's other innovators—pioneers, hidden champions, and changemakers. In figure 4.1 we show the media exposure for the underdogs.

The underdogs have the least number of employees (on average 250 people) and most limited domestic and international exposure. The underdogs do not show up in international specialized media and show up very limitedly on Google, the world's largest search engine. There were fewer than two thousand hits for all underdogs combined (to compare, the first author of this book has 36,000 hits and second author 500,000 hits). Most striking is that these underdogs have very limited exposure, even in domestic specialized media, and that 60 percent are not visible at all.

The least visible of our cases is Ease Power. This partly is due to their young age but also probably due to the company's niche industry

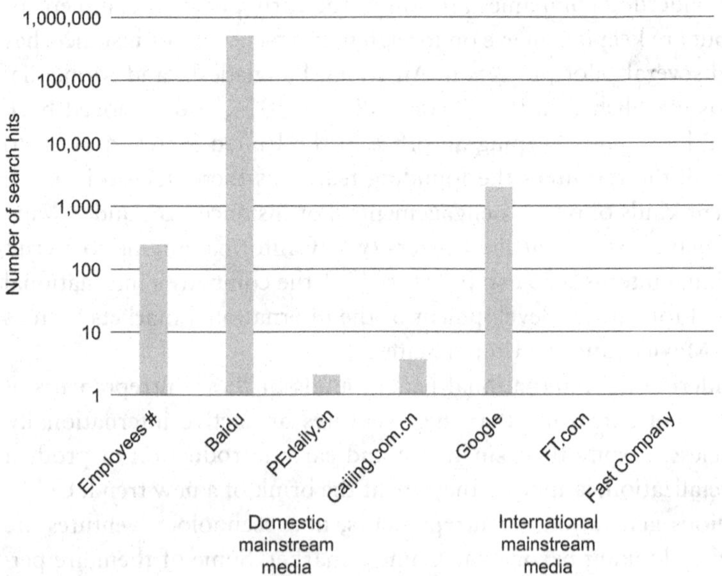

Figure 4.1
Media exposure for underdogs
Source: Authors' database, search date May 10, 2017.

(industrial design for power electronics) and low-profile founder. The most visible is GeneChem, the oldest in our sample, and it already has raised venture capital investments. Among the older underdogs, Shining 3D has some visibility in specialized media mostly because the company is on the OTC market, is raising capital, and expects to be an IPO in the near future. Royole has raised several rounds of venture capital and therefore has appeared in domestic investment media like *PEdaily* and *Caijing*. According to some valuations, Royole already has reached "unicorn" valuation of over $3 billion.

Although the age of a company matters in amount of media exposure, the more important factor is the founder's personality. Companies like Royole and Gago are both very young but more visible than other underdogs. Royole is not happy with its under-the-radar status and actively is looking for media attention by appointing an American rap star as a brand ambassador and arranging a site visit by Premier Li Keqiang. Nevertheless, according to our data, the company's plan has not yet worked well internationally. It does not yet have extensive exposure. For startups and small companies that seek to take on big competitors, underdog status can be an asset. With an element of surprise, these underdogs may become competitors in incumbent markets.

Because this is a large group of technology ventures, the competitive threat for domestic and foreign champions is significant. First of all, since 2016, fifteen thousand new companies register every day according to Chinese national statistics, up three thousand per day compared to 2015.[6] In 2016, over 5.4 million new companies registered. Second, China's government runs one of the world's largest nationwide competitions for technology ventures—the China Innovation and Entrepreneurship Competition—with thirty-three regional competitions across almost every province in 2016.[7] This competition focuses on six fields—advanced manufacturing, mobile Internet, electronic information, new energy and environmental protection, new materials, and biopharmaceuticals. This competition alone attracted over an estimated 50,000 new ventures in 2016, up from 27,000 in 2015. Third, China's private sector is now the world's largest creator of inventions, as measured by patents registered: it registers over 65 percent of all inventions. Fourth, Chinese companies have become the world's largest spender on R&D, with over $160 billion (nominal) in 2015 or over 75 percent of the total R&D expenditures in China.[8] The underdog group is not only large and growing but also increasingly technology driven.

Cutting-Edge Technology

Not often are Chinese companies, especially small Chinese companies, characterized as cutting-edge technology leaders. Nevertheless, the underdogs are not only technology driven, but they are emerging as global technology leaders. In the past decade, China's output in measures such as patent applications and input in terms of R&D expenditures have increased significantly. Figure 4.2 illustrates the trend of China's patent applications in the United States as compared to India, Japan, Mexico, South Korea, and the United States. Figure 4.3 illustrates the R&D expenditures of China compared to the same countries.

In fact, the patent and R&D expenditure boom is due to not only the pioneers and large innovators but also the underdogs. Key sectors in technology development include telecom, information technology, electronics, chemicals, automobiles, Internet and digital sectors, and new energy. In 2015, over fifteen hundred new companies ventured in new energy, including solar, wind, biopower, and water. Of these, 90 percent are in the seed or growing phase. Although they may not have as many patents as the pioneers have, the collective efforts and output of the many underdog entrepreneurs cannot be ignored. In what follows, we discuss six technologies in which China is advancing quickly and illustrate each technology with an underdog technology venture—solar technology, genetics, display technology, new materials, artificial intelligence, and agritechnology.

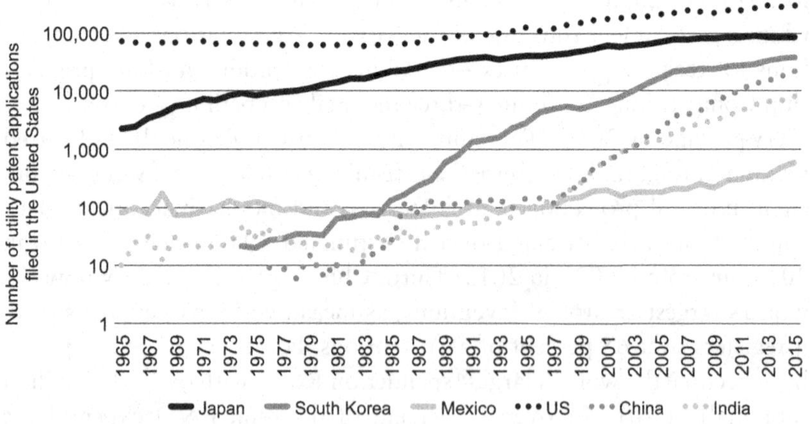

Figure 4.2
Number of utility patent applications filed in the United States
Source: U.S. Patents and Trademark Office, accessed February 1, 2018, https://www.uspto.gov/patent.

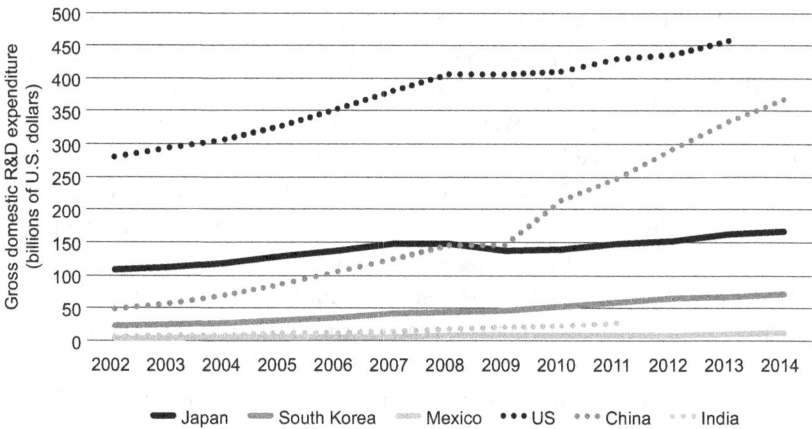

Figure 4.3
Gross domestic R&D expenditures of selected countries (billions of U.S. dollars)
Source: "Gross Domestic Expenditure on R&D by Sector of Performance and Source of Funds," Organisation for Economic Co-operation and Development, accessed February 1, 2018, http://stats.oecd.org/Index.aspx?DataSetCode=GERD_FUNDS.

Solar's Third Generation: Weihua Solar

Although Chinese companies did not play a role in researching and developing the first- and second-generation solar technologies, they are at the forefront of third-generation technologies. The first-generation photovoltaic cells were based on crystalline silicon and almost exclusively developed by Germany, Japan, and the United States. By 2016, Trinasolar, a Chinese giant in the solar industry, was still crystalline silicon–driven but as one of the largest players in the world. The second-generation photovoltaic cells are based on thin-film technology developed primarily in the same group of countries (Germany, Japan, and the United States)—such as copper indium gallium selenide (CIGS), cadmium telluride (CdTe), and gallium arsenide (GaAs). The second-generation cell is much easier than crystalline silicon to produce but is less efficient. Chinese companies have adopted this technology and are able to produce various types of thin-film solar cells. The third-generation photovoltaic cells are often organometallic but also inorganic compounds and substances that are mostly in the experimental stage of development and not yet commercialized on a large scale. Weihua is developing a type of third-generation photovoltaic cell that is based on perovskite structured compounds, commonly a hybrid organic-inorganic lead or tin halide-based material.

Fan Bin established Weihua in Xiamen in 2010 with a 3 million RMB starting fund from the local government and a free factory of 500 square meters. In the company's early years, Fan, a scientist who has published many academic papers, had his team focus on research and development, and the firm patented several inventions. In 2013, Merck, the German chemical giant, contacted Weihua and reached an agreement to be strategic partners, offer Weihua the most advanced materials, and authorize the Chinese firm to use Merck's relevant patents. By January 2015, Fan and his team produced the first batch of perovskite solar modules in the laboratory. In May 2015, the company built the world's first pilot production line to move toward a production capability of perovskite solar cells, starting with large-scale plate spread testing and by August reaching a high cell efficiency. By the end of the year, the first outdoor power station was operational, and in 2016, worldwide module efficiency was attained. Weihua has only fifty employees, is based out of the relatively unknown city of Xiamen, and has limited visibility in the market, but regardless of this underdog status, the company is developing breakthrough technology that may change the solar industry.

Weihua is not the only company that is changing the new energy market. In our own studies, we identified over 150 Chinese companies with significant intellectual property in photovoltaic cell technology and found that the current global top ten solar companies are predominantly Chinese. Moreover, a large group of newcomers, such as Xiamen's Weihua, is changing the market outlook. An interesting company is Advanced Solar Power from Hangzhou, established in 2008, which develops and produces CdTe-based thin-film modules and is one of the few companies worldwide that have CdTe thin-film mass production facilities. The founder, Wu Xuanzhi, is a leading scientist in CdTe thin-film cells and claimed an early world record in 2001.[9]

Genetics Frontier: GeneChem

Genetics research in China is at the forefront worldwide. The Beijing Genomics Institute (BGI), founded in 1999, was one of the key sequencing facilities for the Human Genome Project. BGI has continued to make headlines, sequencing other flora and fauna, such as pandas, rice, and silkworms. Recent reports in *Nature* summarize the research on genetic engineering being done by Chinese teams of scientists in Guangzhou, including claims to have edited genes in human embryos.[10] This introduces ethical concerns, but the knowledge of technologies such as CRISPR (clustered regularly interspaced short palindromic repeats) is available in China, which does not have strong regulations. In fact, overall relaxed laws have created a gray area in which many startups and companies have sprung up. Genetic testing is another hotly debated field in China, and startups such as 360 Gene and WeGene are offering consumer-focused services. Setting aside genetic engineering and testing, China has been steadily developing large research databases of genes and the advances of functional genomics (such as discovering the genetic basis for diseases). Companies such as GeneChem are leaders in utilizing such data and capabilities to become R&D powerhouses for hospitals.

GeneChem has established the largest lentivirus library with nearly 150,000 independent clones that cover almost all human genes. The company's research has identified hundreds of tumor-specific candidate genes. It collaborates with over three hundred hospitals and two thousand clinical doctors and scientists in the field of cancer research. For instance, in 2016, an ongoing collaboration between GeneChem and the Shanghai Changhai Hospital began to do clinical research on anti-CD19-CAR-T cells transduced with lentivirus, aiming to develop an immunotherapy for leukemia.[11] Although GeneChem originally offered R&D services to hospitals and doctors, it has transformed itself into a company that engages in the field of translational medicine and quickly transfers research results into products and services to benefit patients. The company is often used for research and has over sixty invention patents and over 2,500 academic papers cited by the Science Citation Index (SCI) in journals such as *Nature* and *Cell*. Over half of the company's 350 employees are from Fudan University, the alma mater of the founder, and 40 percent have a master degree or above. The low-profile founder Cao Yueqiong has built up world-class technology and a reputation in the genetics field, while maintaining an underdog status with limited visibility in the business and financial markets. Science is at the core of this company, not business.

Artificial Intelligence: Malong Tech Is One in a Million

Artificial intelligence (AI) became known to the business community in China probably in 2014, when Baidu hired Andrew Ng from Google to work on the Baidu Brain. As a search term in the Baidu search engine, AI took off in early 2016. Since then, China has seen a spike in academic publications by Chinese scientists on deep learning, one of the key technologies in AI. In 2015, China surpassed the United States in terms of journal articles that were cited at least once and mentioned the term *deep learning*. Moreover, the number of patent applications in the period 2010 to 2014 increased by over 180 percent to 8,410, as compared to the United States' 15,317. China has become the second-largest nation for AI within the last decade, leaving Europe, India, Japan, and South Korea far behind. China's State Council issued the Next Generation Artificial Intelligence Plan with the goal of becoming the top global AI innovation center.[12]

The dominant players in AI in China are without doubt Baidu, Alibaba, and Tencent (BAT). Driven by big data, infrastructure, capital, and AI talent, these three companies are well positioned to develop an all-in AI—Baidu with a variety of applications, including human resources, autonomous cars, and search; Alibaba with Apsara, an independently developed supercomputation system for AliCloud; and Tencent with an AI laboratory with over seventy top-tier AI scientists. In the slipstream of BAT, other data-rich ventures (such as Didi Chuxing and Meituan Dianping) and a host of new technology ventures (such as Malong Tech in the field of voice recognition and computer vision) have had successes.

Malong's cofounders met while they both were working for Microsoft. In 2014, they saw a megatrend in technology happening, and when they registered in Shenzhen, they were officially the millionth company in the city. Their original focus was on flexible material image recognition, a complex version of image recognition compared to static object recognition. The first prototype was developed in 2014 and called StyleAI. The founders and a small team entered global AI competitions and joined the Microsoft Accelerator program in Beijing. The company graduated with honors from the Microsoft Ventures Startup Accelerator in 2015, won the first AI Pioneer award from Microsoft in 2016, and received other awards for its AI technology from Amazon and NVIDIA. Although the company's first product (StyleAI) was consumer focused, it changed focus to business products in 2016. The key product currently is ProductAI, which offers visual product recognition at humanlike performance to any customer via a public cloud platform, private cloud, or embedded module hardware for Internet of things scenarios. By early 2018, the platform had over three hundred business customers. Malong Tech was recognized by *Fast Company* as China's most innovative company.

Many AI tech ventures are starting to emerge in China. For instance, there are over eighty AI-driven health tech ventures. The leading face-recognition venture, Face++, which supplies Uber, is from Beijing and defeated fifteen AI firms, including Facebook, Google, and Microsoft. Another fast-moving venture is SenseTime, a deep-learning developer that raised $600 million in financing led by Alibaba. Westwell Lab presented the Westwell Brain in 2016, a brain simulation said to have 10 billion neurons with hardware running on the company's own DeepSouth neural processor. AI in China is benefitting from the sheer amount of data, AI talent, capital, and government support and a market looking for new products and services.

Superthin Screen: Royole

Display technology and the superthin-film industry is highly concentrated in the hands of a few global players. Most current displays are TFT-LCD (thin-film transistor, liquid crystal display) screens. OLED (organic light-emitting diode) screens—whether AMOLED (active-matrix organic light-emitting diode) or PMOLED (passive-matrix organic light-emitting diode)—are still expensive and not commonly seen in households or electronics products. Globally, only a handful of companies are developing and producing such displays, including Everdisplay Optronics (Chinese), Japan Display, LG, Samsung, and Visionox (Chinese). The capital investments in these companies are significant and often include local governments, as in the case of Everdisplay (Shanghai) and Visionox (Jiangsu province). The technology barriers are high, and mass-scale production is complex. Royole appears to be a new kid on the block of middle-stream display technology development and production. Their upstream suppliers (none Chinese) are basically companies such as LG and Samsung, a handful of suppliers with bargaining power. So far, Chinese companies that have announced they are building an AMOLED production line have strong government backgrounds, support, or ownership. Royole is highly ambitious about developing flexible AMOLED displays, something that has not yet been done in China or in successful mass production globally.

Royole is an innovator of flexible displays, flexible sensors, and smart device technologies and offers display solutions and IP licensing. Its star technology is the world's thinnest full-color flexible display (0.01 millimeter). In August 2013, the company demonstrated the first thinnest flexible backplane, and in 2014, it claimed to have developed the world's first thinnest flexible full-color display. In 2015, the company started mass production of flexible sensors and display modules with series-C funding of $172 million raised, becoming a global unicorn startup. In 2016, Royole built a variety of partnerships with domestic incumbents like China Mobile, iQIYI, and Li Ning. Although Royole has not yet succeeded in mass producing the new superthin displays, the company is among the global leaders in technology.

Although mass-produced flexible displays have not yet been seen, many ventures are developing display technologies. Everdisplay, for example, was established in 2012 with the support of the Shanghai government. The company develops only flexible AMOLED displays and has an actual production line. Newvision Opto-electronic Technology is a company from Guangzhou established in 2010 with the support of Huanan Polytechnic University. The company develops OLED display technology and in 2013 claimed to have developed the first flexible AMOLED display, although by 2016, it had produced only small-batch and customized products.

High-Performing Nanotechnology: Uninano

In 2014, the Ministry of Industry and Information Technology (MIIT) announced in the Twelfth Five-Year Plan that the size of the new materials industry in China has reached over $200 billion, less than 4 percent of the materials industry but with an annual average growth rate of 25 percent.[13] China's new materials industry is still at the tracking and imitation stages, and the recent fusion of traditional materials with nanotechnology poses opportunities for breakthrough innovations. Companies like Uninano may play a crucial role in China's industrial transformation. Various factors—such as rising labor costs, an oversupply of low-end manufacturing, limited R&D, and an ongoing transformation from a production- to a consumption-driven economy—require China's manufacturers to upgrade. Large utility and resource providers in areas such as petroleum, electricity, and chemicals, for example, are searching for new technologies to support their existing businesses. Thermal insulation solutions for pipelines and plants have developed considerably in China in response to the large market demand: roughly 13 billion square meters were manufactured in 2014.[14] For the past twenty years, the industry has developed to a point where it now includes a wide variety of products such as cotton insulation, expanded perlite, foam, fireproofing fiber, silicate, rock wool, and polyurethane. Uninano's nanoporous materials are higher performing than traditional insultation materials and are considered part of a new generation of technology.

After establishing the company in 2008 in Shenzhen, the founder and his team have focused on R&D and product development. Their first experimental production line was built in Shenzhen in 2010. In 2011, after Uninano had been three years in R&D, Softbank China did a seed investment and followed it with an A round in the same year. In 2012, pursuing its long-term strategy, the company moved the sales and R&D groups to Shanghai, where they shared a coworking space with iStart. In 2013, the company established a production base in Suzhou, and in 2014, it received a B round investment to fuel further development. By 2015, Uninano released its fourth generation of nano porous thermal insulation products, called ThermalSaver. The next step for the company is to enter the construction market, where there is a lot of potential with industry trends such as green buildings, low-energy buildings, and urban sustainability. Uninano is the least visible of the underdogs, with only fifty employees, and although it is at a disadvantage compared to the large players in chemicals, insulation materials, and construction, the company is making serious strides and gaining traction in these markets.

Agritechnology Revolution: Gago

In the United States and Europe, many companies operate data-driven platforms and solutions for agriculture, including with drones, geographic information systems (GIS), and various other climate and satellite data. U.S. companies such as the Climate Corporation (a company acquired by Monsanto for $930 million in 2013), Descartes Labs, FarmLogs, and Mavrix are all mature leaders in the industry. However, most of the solutions used by these existing players are not directly applicable in China. The largest difference between China and the United States and large parts of Europe is that the arable land plots in China are dispersed and scattered. Moreover, China has many independently operated farms instead of large farm companies (as in the United States) or cooperatives (as in Western Europe). Zhang Gong and his three cofounders acknowledged and embraced this difference in developing a China-specific solution, Gago. There are large market opportunities because the farming population is shrinking and the total land for each farmer to manage is expanding. Currently half of the 2 billion *mu* of arable land in China are classified as the latter.[15]

Gago's key advantage is its access to original satellite data from China and the world, including thirty years of world vegetation data of the world, fifty years of meteorological data, machine learning algorithms that process the data, and big data integration and analysis. Gago's particular advantage lies in processing, interpreting, and visualizing large amounts of data in a meaningful way. Currently, Gago provides farming management solutions for five crop types—corn, hay, pitaya, potato, and rice. The company aims to expand its solutions to other crop types, such as sugar cane. Clients currently are farmers with plots of around 1,000 *mu*, and according to Gago, they have reported a 15 percent increase in productivity.

Although Gago's focus is China, it has been reported to have launched pilot projects in several other countries (such as Bangladesh, Pakistan, and Thailand), with plans for further internationalization.[16] Zhang also is trying to connect agriculture to finance and develop a risk evaluation tool that would be useful for investors, insurance companies, and banks and would transform Gago from an agritechnology company to an environment technology company. Although few people have heard of this young company, it may become a changemaker in China's agricultural landscape.

Gago is not the only player in the agritechnology field in China. This industry has two types of players—the ones focusing on data from the sky and the ones focusing on data from the soil. The latter companies are in the field of the Internet of things and include sensors inserted into farmland. For instance, a company called Insentek from Beijing was established in 1999 and originally focused on watering equipment. It incubated a project on farmland sensors and big data in 2011 and eventually launched a land probe. Compared with Gago, Insentek's business model has higher costs but may work out for niche crops and specialty use. Besides these high-technology solutions, many other ventures are operating in the field of farmland management and optimization systems. For example, GeoHey is an interesting venture that focuses on developing an online cloud-mapping environment based on open-source data and development. Another company called ControlEasy Automation Software is focusing on smart farmland water management. As a promising market, many more solutions are to come.

Niche Innovators

The underdogs focus on new product development for niche markets. In China, we see increasingly more product innovations, but many remain incremental rather than radical. According to a survey conducted by China's National Bureau of Statistics, 19 percent of large Chinese manufacturing companies reported that they invested in significantly improving existing products or developing new products—that is, product innovation.[17] Strong economic growth and the rise of the middle-class consumer in the past decade have pushed many companies to come up with improved products or new products. The more radical product innovations are more often reported to come from the pioneers (such as Huawei) or large hidden champions (such as Hikvision and Positec). Our research, however, shows that the underdogs develop new products with disruptive features. Although the focus is on new product development, the underdogs often innovate their production processes and business models as well. The resulting innovations are often more systematic and more difficult to imitate than purely new products. Two types of niche innovations stand out—product and process innovations and product and business model innovations.

Product and Process Innovation: Uninano, Gago, and Zongmu

Uninano, Gago, and Zongmu are examples of technology ventures that combined a new product with a process innovation. Uninano's product innovations are based on the founding team's research and experience with nanoporous materials. The products are considered to be a new generation of thermal insulation with better performance. The advantages of this material lay in its extremely low thermal conductivity, nonflammable and low volatile organic compounds, and nontoxic safety properties. The company has a handful of patents registered in China for this material. Although the current product offering is limited, the potential applications are wide. If the company succeeds in entering the construction market with high-performing but cost-effective solutions, it may be disruptive. In the words of the founder:[18] "The largest boundary to enter the construction industry is cost. Therefore, our company innovates the recipe, raw materials, production process, and equipment to save about 10–30% of the cost. Our product is not only innovative, but we also innovate our cost and business process."

Along the same lines, Gago's innovation combines product innovation (cloud-based farming platform) with process innovation (big data–driven and machine learning processes). The announced moves into financial solutions—risk evaluation of agriculture loans and agriculture insurance assessments based on big data analytics—suggest that the company is also rethinking its business model to include financial services. The key drivers of Gago's innovations are the market and its customers. In Zhang's words in 2016:[19] " the key is not technology but closely connecting with the market and deeply understand the customer. ... A lack of technology can be solved, but with a changing market only when technology keeps up with the market, the technology can be used powerfully." Gago's competitive strategy has been disruptive from the start, and time will have to tell which markets it will disrupt.

Like the above two fellow companies, Zongmu has innovated in both products and process, with a focus on cutting costs. For instance, by using virtual vehicle technology, the navigation vehicle can be integrated with the panoramic system, thus significantly saving hardware costs. The high-quality price-to-performance ratio of the products of Zongmu and other Chinese underdogs in this field forced the dominant player in the

Chinese advanced driver assistance system (ADAS) market—Mobileye, an Israel-based company listed on the New York Stock Exchange—to decrease its product price by about 50 percent in the past few years. The disruptive price also allows middle-end Chinese car brands (with a sales price at around $30,000) to afford an ADAS system now.

Product and Business Model Innovation: Magnity, Ease Power, and Shining 3D

Magnity, Ease Power, and Shining 3D illustrate how technology ventures combine product and business model innovations. Magnity's innovations are all technology-driven product innovations. The product innovations satisfy a wide variety of industrial use needs, and the company offers customized services. According to the founder, Shen Chongfei, the company seeks to satisfy the current industrial clients' needs but also pioneer in developing a good enough product for the commercial civilian market at a reasonable cost. It aims to get nonconsuming customers to become users. This is illustrated by his announcement to move into more consumer products, such as security solutions for houses and outdoor applications.[20] Magnity also was the earliest in the infrared industry to adopt a "fabless" model for production by outsourcing the fabrication of its devices instead of building a heavy-asset business model. These innovations—large product variety, diversification using economies of scope, a fabless model, and good enough cost innovations—have given the company a competitive advantage in the market. If the company succeeds in offering low-cost, medium-quality products to new commercial users, Magnity may disrupt this currently small commercial market without entering the military market.

Ease Power's innovation early on included expansions of the business model. In 2012, the company received a technology innovation project fund from the Kunshan government, which was a necessary input of capital and support. In 2013, it developed nonisolated direct current to direct current (DC to DC) converter chips. By 2014, just three years after establishment, the company had developed a wide range of chips, built up significant knowledge and expertise, and reached sales of over 30 million RMB. In 2015, the venture capital market began to pay more attention to its industry. The company received an A round investment of 10 million RMB from a local venture capital firm followed by a much larger B round in 2016. Since 2015, the applications of their chips have expanded into many other downstream industries, and they introduced a new product for wireless charge solution providers.

Beyond product innovations, the company has introduced process innovations, such as customization of integrated circuits (IC) at low cost and high speed, using small sizes, reducing required components compared to analogue power, controlling software, creating flexible parameters, and producing stability. In 2015, Ease Power introduced its own design concept—the restructurable power integrated circuit (RPIC). This design concept allows the company to produce ICs quickly according to the requirements of both consumer- and business-focused clients. The customization service is an interesting business model innovation in the IC design industry while at the same time is based on a core technological advantage (RPIC). Although a whole IC development cycle takes two years, the company has redesigned and modularized its chip structure to allow flexible customization in the field of digital power IC design in a few days.[21] Although Ease Power's core innovations are not disruptive, as evidenced by their mostly utility model patents, its new design methodology makes it possible to break through the design cycle, serve the many specialized needs of clients in a short time frame, and offer a low-cost way to customize a digital power chip quickly.

Shining 3D's first product was deep-surface laser-engraved crystals, whose most common applications are engravings of photos and pictures. In 2005, the company launched the laser-engraving control software 3D-Engraving and 3D-Camera. Since 2007, Shining has been doing R&D in 3D scanner technology, which turned out to be its core advantage and was launched in 2008. This was also the year when the company entered the industrial manufacturing field. In 2010, it expanded into healthcare 3D printing and opened a 3D printing service center. In 2011, the Ministry of Science and Technology appointed the company as a National Core High Technology Enterprise in its famous Torch program. In 2012, the company received a national innovation fund, and in 2013, it launched its first 3D printing machine. Also in 2013, in collaboration with local university professor Xu Mingen, Shining 3D incubated a new company—Regenovo Biotechnology—that focuses on 3D printing for biomedical technology, software, and new product development.[22] Clients include global companies such as Adidas, Bosch, Haier, Hikvision, Huawei, and Intel and also universities such as Tsinghua University and Zhejiang University.

The company's core technology is 3D scanning, and it has developed a whole ecosystem around 3D printing, including services, cloud, software, and hardware products. The innovations are technology driven. In 2004, Shining 3D was a first mover driven by insights from the university.

It developed a range of products around its core advantage, 3D scanning, making incremental improvements with some products (such as 3D printing machines) and making radical innovations with other products (such as its 2013 newly established biomedical 3D printing business). Li Chen is not a scientist or technology entrepreneur but a typical Wenzhou businessman with vision. With only five hundred employees (50 percent who work in R&D), Shining 3D has developed a business ecosystem around 3D printing and several niche sectors.

Insights into the Underdogs

The technology-driven underdogs are elite entrepreneurs who have cutting-edge technologies and operate mostly under the radar. This group of innovators is extremely large and includes a wide variety of technology sectors. Five insights stand out from our empirical research:

- *Elite entrepreneurs:* Underdogs are often ventures established by overseas returnee entrepreneurs who have top educational backgrounds in science and technology. Since the early 2000s, a new type of technology enterprises has emerged in China built around elite entrepreneurs who returned from overseas studies to become entrepreneurs and seize opportunities in China's emerging economy and booming middle class. Although their international education experiences are similar, their roads to entrepreneurship vary from beginning with student entrepreneurship to starting a venture after an international corporate career.
- *Early international exposure:* Underdogs often internationalize early with export and technology partners abroad, international markets, and overseas facilities. The underdogs are often already present in international markets while still in the early phases of their development. These small technology ventures operate internationally through collaboration, original equipment manufacturing, overseas markets, international promotions, and pilot projects.
- *Under the radar:* The market visibility of the underdogs is limited, and most of these companies are young and small. Underdogs share three important features—a disadvantaged position, a passion and determination to triumph against the odds, and a tendency to operate under the radar. Although the age of the company surely matters in the amount of media exposure it receives, the founder's personality is a more important factor. These underdogs may prove to become

competitors in incumbent markets by leveraging the element of surprise.

- *Cutting-edge technology:* Underdogs compete on cutting-edge technology, often driven by technological and scientific advances rather than advances that address customers and engineering solutions. The underdogs are emerging as global technology leaders. The collective efforts and output of the many underdog entrepreneurs cannot be ignored. We found cutting-edge technology development by technology ventures in six advanced technologies—solar technology, genetics, artificial intelligence, display technology, new materials, and agritechnology.
- *Niche innovators:* The innovations of underdogs are often in niches (although niches of global market size) in business-to-business markets and combine new products with new processes and business models. The underdogs focus on new product development for niche markets. Underdogs develop new products with disruptive features. Although the focus is on new product development, the underdogs often innovate their production processes and business models as well. The resulting innovations are often more systematic and more difficult to imitate than purely new products. Two types of niche innovations stand out—product and process innovations and product and business model innovations.

5
Changemakers: NextGen Entrepreneurs

Who Are the Changemakers?

The changemakers are unicorns—startups valued at more than $1 billion (USD)—that are driven by digital disruptive innovations, have significant venture capital support, and are less than ten years old. The previous chapters have discussed three types of technology ventures—pioneers, hidden champions, and underdogs. This chapter focuses on a fourth type—the changemakers who are the future generation of entrepreneurs. Previous Chinese innovators often came from manufacturing and technology backgrounds. Our empirical research on Chinese innovators distinguishes a group of entrepreneurs who are different in that they are digital natives and have no clear industry boundaries for their operations and markets. These next-generation entrepreneurs are not difficult to spot because they are highly visible and seek attention. Their ventures have grown quickly into several hundred renminbi (RMB) unicorns and over eighty USD unicorns. This group of several hundred high-impact changemakers is growing. Our empirical research reveals five distinguishing features of the changemakers:

- *Next-generation entrepreneurs:* This group of young changemakers disrupts traditional ways of thinking about business.
- *Digital disruption:* Digital technology disrupts the dominant business models of traditional industries.
- *Innovation fueled by venture capital:* Professional and corporate venture capital play an important role both domestically and internationally in the rapid growth of the changemakers.
- *High visibility:* The changemakers are extremely adept at promoting their new products and services. They are born marketers and create high visibility for their ventures from the beginning.

- *Need for speed:* These ventures have grown quickly and focus on expanding their user base and market share rather than profits.

China's next-generation entrepreneurs are true changemakers. First, they embrace and exploit digital technologies to rethink product offerings in traditional industries. Unafraid and perhaps unaware of the complexities and legacies of traditional industries, these young changemakers innovate across industry boundaries. Armed with novel business models, they disrupt traditional industries such as catering, finance, healthcare, media, and transport. Second, these entrepreneurs change the rules of the competitive game and displace incumbents. Their services reach previously unreached markets at a low cost to users. Third, this new generation of entrepreneurs is digital savvy, showcases strong public identities, and have excellent marketing capabilities. Unlike entrepreneurs such as Huawei's Ren Zhengfei and Wahaha's Zong Qinghou, who are known for their modesty and low public profiles, they are not afraid of the spotlight. Finally, they display a supergrowth mindset where users always come first and profits later. Driven by venture capital investments, their business models focus on growth and the expansion of China's booming consumer market.

In this chapter, we examine eight illustrative cases of changemakers (table 5.1). These changemakers are active in catering, ecommerce, fintech, healthcare, location-based services, media, and transportation. Some of the changemakers are USD superunicorns like Didi Chuxing, Meituan, and Toutiao. The changemakers are coming from Beijing, Shanghai, Shenzhen, and Zhejiang, which is also reflected in our empirical research and the eight illustrative cases. Although these changemakers are promising, their youth and limited experience mean that history will decide whether the markets will be truly disrupted and these ventures can be transformed into sustainable innovators. Some of these interesting ventures and companies have been some more successful than others. The key message is that Chinese changemakers are plentiful and are not to be underestimated on the global stage.

Next-Generation Entrepreneurs: The Fifth Generation

The changemakers are a new generation of entrepreneurs. In table 5.2, we compare the five generations of entrepreneurs and highlight their differences. The changemakers stand out with their market disruption and wide variety of industry activities.

Table 5.1
Eight changemakers: Next-generation entrepreneurs

Case	Location	Year	Valuation (U.S. dollars)[a]	Field
Didi Chuxing	Beijing, Hangzhou	2012	$55 billion	Transportation
Ele.me	Shanghai	2009	$9.5 billion[b]	Catering
51 Credit Card	Zhejiang	2012	$1 billion	Fintech
Meituan	Beijing	2010	$30 billion	Location-based service
Mobike	Beijing	2015	$2.7 billion[c]	Transportation
Pinduoduo	Shanghai	2015	$15 billion	Ecommerce
Toutiao	Beijing	2012	$30 billion	Media
We Doctor	Zhejiang	2010	$1.5 billion	Healthcare

Notes: a. Valuation as of April 2018. b. Acquired in April 2018 by Alibaba. c. Acquired in April 2018 by Meituan.
Source: Authors' research.

The first generation of entrepreneurs, starting as original equipment manufacturers, can be illustrated by people like Lu Guanqiu, the founder of Wanxiang Group, a Chinese multinational manufacturer of automotive components. Wanxiang was built from Lu Guanqiu's agricultural machines factory, its stock is now listed domestically, and it acquired the leading transportation battery manufacturer A123 Systems from the United States in 2013. Similarly entrepreneurial during a time of high political risk was Zong Qinghou, the founder of Wahaha, China's largest beverage manufacturer, which employs thirty thousand people and internationalizes its brands across the world. These first-generation pioneers were true grassroots entrepreneurs.

The "92 *pai*" (a term invented by Taikang Life's founder Chen Dongsheng) is considered the second generation of entrepreneurs. After Deng Xiaoping's public endorsement in Shenzhen, private companies obtained clear legal status, and many former government officials jumped into the private sector. In 1996, Feng Lun founded the Vantone Group, a company operating in real estate and asset management with total assets over 14 billion RMB (2 billion euros). Feng Lun had been a teacher at the Party School of the Central Committee of the Communist Party of China,

Table 5.2
Five generations of Chinese entrepreneurs

Generation	Representative	Birth period	Type	Industries	Education
1. Pioneers	Lu Guanqiu	1940s–1950s	Grassroots	Manufacturing	Limited
2. 92 *pai*	Feng Lun	1960s	Political	Manufacturing, real estate, finance	Limited, political
3. Internet	Ma Yun	1970s	Market makers	Consumer	University
4. Technology	Fan Bin	1970s–1980s	Science engineers	Manufacturing niche	Elite overseas
5. Digital	Cheng Wei	1980s–1990s	Disruptors	Diverse	University

Source: Authors' research.

the breeding ground for top cadres, and was a senior adviser for the State Commission for Restructuring the Economic Systems, the think tank for China's economic reform. An outspoken person whose opinions are influential in China, he has become a critic of China's government policy in the property sectors and a proponent of "retreating the state and advancing the private sector." The second generation of Chinese entrepreneurs transferred political power into economic gains.

The third generation of entrepreneurs was driven by the information technology revolution and is exemplified by the entrepreneurs who founded Alibaba, Baidu, and Tencent (the BAT companies). Ma Yun founded Alibaba's ecommerce platform in 1999 and now operates the world's largest online business-to-business platform and largest online consumer marketplace. Recently, it broke records with the biggest IPO in U.S. history. The BAT companies are among the largest investors in China's booming high-technology sector, fueling a new generation of entrepreneurs. The third generation of Internet entrepreneurs are true market makers.

The fourth generation of entrepreneurs, the underdogs, is driven by science and technology. Companies such as Weihua and Gago (chapter 4) were founded by this fourth generation of entrepreneurs, who received strong educations internationally in the sciences and engineering. These companies are technology focused and tend to leverage their international experiences early on. This fourth generation of entrepreneurs is debunking the myth that Chinese ventures are copying rather than innovating technologies. They are the scientists and engineers, and although less impactful in the market, they bring cutting-edge technology to global markets.

A possible fifth generation, sometimes referred to as mobile digital or the "after 1980s," includes entrepreneurs like Cheng Wei, the founder of Didi Taxi, and Chen Ou, the founder of Jumei.com cosmetics. They utilize an emerging mobile Internet society and display radical business mindsets. In 2012, Cheng Wei started a revolution in the taxi world, and in 2010, Chen Ou transformed the Chinese cosmetics industry. The Didi Taxi app received large investments from the Tencent Group. In 2012, Chen Ou became a *Forbes* top entrepreneur, and in 2014, his company Jumei.com was listed on the New York Stock Exchange. These radical entrepreneurs are often still in their early twenties and getting more and more attention. IDG, a global venture capital group, even has a special fund for "after 1990s" entrepreneurs. One such entrepreneur is Zhang Xuhao, the founder of Ele.me.

In 2008, Ele.me was established by a group of students from Shanghai Jiaotong University, and by 2015, it had grown to unicorn status with a valuation over $1 billion (USD). Zhang Xuhao (born in 1985) comes from a Shanghai family of successful businessmen. The family culture encouraged him to take risks and achieve financial independence at an early age, and he had competitive hobbies like boxing and car racing. When he was studying architectural engineering at Shanghai Jiaotong University, he met his cofounder, Kang Jia. Both grew hungry during overnight gaming sessions, so they often ordered takeout food and had unsatisfactory experiences with paper menus, limited choices, and phone ordering. In 2009, when Zhang was only twenty-two years old, they decided to improve the situation and established Ele.me. By 2015, Zhang Xuhao had overshadowed his family's success and was one of *Harper's Bazaar*'s breakthrough entrepreneurs. The current company still has a very young average age of twenty-five years.

Pinduoduo was established by Huang Zheng, who is a graduate from Zhejiang University and studied computer science at the University of Wisconsin at Madison. He joined Google in the United States and reunited with Li Kaifu to start Google China in 2006. A year later, he left Google China and started an ecommerce platform for multinational corporations and an independent gaming company. In 2015, he started Pinduoduo, his current venture in social ecommerce, with the endorsements of Netease founder Ding Lei, SF founder Wang Wei, Oppo/Vivo's largest shareholder Duan Yongping, and Taobao's cofounder Shun Tongyu. In a market where Taobao, Tmall, and JD.com had by far the largest market share and dominated the ecommerce market in China, Huang started a new ecommerce platform. We call this next generation of disruptive entrepreneurs the changemakers.

The most recent generation of entrepreneurs fits the trend of consumer boom in China. Chinese consumers have become a driving force for global innovation. In China, people born in the 1950s, 1960s, and 1970s are known as the "last generation," and people born in the 1980s, 1990s, and 2000s are known as the "young generation." Those who were born after the 1980s and 1990s are the "spenders." The success of transitioning China's economy away from investment and more to consumption will be spearheaded by China's 1980s generation.[1] Unlike the generation of people who were born between the 1950s and 1970s and grew up in a tough economic environment, those born after 1980 are much more active shoppers and demand quality products and services as they pursue diverse lifestyles. This new generation of consumers, who will make up 46 percent of the population between the ages of fifteen and seventy in the next five years, will help services gain a greater share in total consumption. One of the implications for a market dominated by a new generation of consumers and an upper middle class is that domestic brands now have the opportunity to grow.[2] Changemaker entrepreneurs are tapping into this opportunity.

Digital Disruption

The changemakers employ digital business models to disrupt established industries. By the end of 2017, China had over 750 million Internet users, up from just 22 million in 2000. One fifth of the total world population online is now Chinese. Although this growth and these numbers are remarkable, China has reached a penetration rate of only just over 55 percent of the population, just about the global average, but less than the United States' 88 percent (or 287 million users), according to Internet Live Stats.[3] The most recent trend is full connectivity, where mobile Internet, manufacturing, marketing data, and sales channels are increasingly being integrated. According to recent statistics from the China Internet Network Information Center, the number of mobile Internet users is over 680 million (93 percent of Internet users), compared to 225 million mobile Internet users in the United States (78 percent).[4] Although China is far behind the United States in terms of Internet penetration, mobile Internet usage is ubiquitous and higher than in the United States.

The high proportion of mobile Internet usage has interesting consequences. For instance, mobile payments in China are far more accepted by Chinese consumers than American consumers, an advantage that perhaps was gained by leapfrogging over personal computer payments and going directly to mobile digital payments.[5] In fact, the percentage of users frequently using online payment and mobile payment is similar, around 60 percent. It is therefore not surprising that China is leading global developments in fintech, especially mobile digital solutions. For instance, in 2012, 51 Credit Card was established in Zhejiang, starting out as a management tool for managing consumers' credit cards. By 2012, the majority of Chinese people who had credit cards had multiple credit cards. The service reminds users of their payment due dates and analyzes spending patterns across credit cards from different banks. This company later transformed itself into a platform for peer-to-peer lending services. Leveraging its large user base and associated user data, the company is well positioned to offer individual lending services. By April 2018, the company had a pre-IPO valuation of over $1 billion and was planning to go public on the Hong Kong Stock Exchange in 2018.

The changemakers are disrupting not just the financial industry but also many different traditional or established industries and is going so in short time frames. For instance, Toutiao, established in 2012, uses artificial intelligence to provide mobile customized news recommendations. By analyzing online social behavior and profiling each individual user, founder Zhang Yiming's service develops news interest maps. His biggest competitor is Tencent News, an incumbent Internet giant and China's highest-valued company. Toutiao's success comes not from early adopters in first-tier cities but from users in other cities, especially users who are under thirty years old: 90 percent of its users come from outside the first-tier cities. By 2018, the company was valued at over $30 billion. With over 700 million registered users, it has over 140 million daily active users who spend on average over one hour a day in the Toutiao app.

In the catering industry, Zhang Xuhao and his classmates created a true disruption. Ele.me is a logistics service provider and an eBay-style catering company in one. The cofounders started out by collecting menus of small restaurants on or near the university campus for their classmates. In just over five years, they developed a large delivery fleet and had a presence in over seven hundred cities reaching 300,000 restaurants. They guarantee that you can find any type of food near your location, even $2 dumplings, and have it delivered to your home. Small restaurants suddenly had access to a sales channel and a wide reach in their nearby markets, and larger restaurants and chain stores followed suit as soon as they became aware of the advantages of Ele.me's localized search, logistics fleet, and large user base.

In an overcrowded ecommerce market, Pinduoduo focused on social ecommerce with group buying features for third- and fourth-tier cities. Pinduoduo found a quickly expanding niche as connectivity increased in the less developed parts of China and millennials boomed in those areas. By 2018, the platform was second only to Taobao in China. Within one year, Pinduoduo had over 1 million users, 1 million daily orders, and a gross merchandise volume (GMV) of 1 billion RMB per month. By early 2018, the GMV reached 40 billion RMB per month, one third of JD.com's size. Moreover, the company was planning to go public on NASDAQ in the second half of 2018. Neither Alibaba nor JD.com had expected a new player to become that large in such a short period of time.

Another case is We Doctor, which was established in 2010. The venture started as an online hospital registration application for Chinese hospitals. Within five years, it connected over 1,600 Chinese hospitals, 190,000 doctors, and 100 million patients. These patients register their hospital visits, do online consultations, and make online payments. We Doctor also offers complete family healthcare management services, including insurance and family doctors, aiming to become an accountable care organization. This changemaker is playing an increasingly large role in the healthcare system in China and fills in many voids, especially in terms of service provision and customer experience.

In most cases, changemakers do not start their ventures within the industry they have worked in. For instance, Toutiao's founder Zhang Yiming (born in 1983) comes from an ordinary Fujian family and has an interest in coding, computers, and reading. After receiving a software engineering degree from Nankai University, he started working for Kuxun, a leading online travel agent, and later Microsoft in China. Realizing that a corporate career was not for creative types, he decided to try venturing. By 2012, he successfully founded Toutiao, currently China's leading online mobile news portal. Also from the south, Mobike's founder Hu Weiwei graduated from Zhejiang University City College as a journalist. She gained experience in the media field and worked for several local news media outlets. After ten years working as a journalist, she founded Mobike in 2014. By 2017, Mobike was one of China's hottest startups, was its most popular bike-sharing company, and had started to branch out overseas. Didi Chuxing's founder Cheng Wei also had a corporate career before founding Didi Taxi. Born in a small city in Jiangxi, he studied administration management at the Beijing University of Chemical Technology. His only corporate job was at Alibaba, where he spent eight years before founding his venture Didi Taxi. Inspired by Alibaba's success in the Internet industry, Cheng Wei looks for opportunities in digital enterprises. Not unlike Travis Kalanick at Uber, the story goes that Cheng Wei waited in the cold Beijing rain one time too many, which led to the idea of a mobile taxi hailing application. Changemakers disrupt traditional industries, often those that they are not even familiar with.

Innovation Fueled by Global Venture Capital

In 2015, Didi Chuxing raised more venture capital than the combined VC industries of Israel, Japan, and Singapore—$3 billion. And Didi Chuxing is not an exception. In the same year, Ele.me had its fifth fund raising round, collecting over $350 million from CITIC, Dianpin, JD.com, Sequoia, and Tencent. Round six was even bigger—$630 million. In 2016, Toutiao's

D round of financing collected over $1 billion from CCB International, Sequoia, and other institutions. In 2018, Ele.me was acquired by Alibaba. Table 5.3 summarizes global venture capital for our eight selected cases.

Against the backdrop of the venture capital boom in China (chapter 1), it is not surprising that there was a large amount of VC available for changemakers. Several things stand out. First, changemakers raise large sums of capital early in their existence, up to billions of U.S. dollars in financing rounds pre-IPO. Second, changemakers raise multiple rounds in a short timeframe. This is especially striking with Mobike, which was established in 2015 and by 2017 had raised five rounds. Third, investors include a wide variety of stakeholders—domestic and international funds, domestic tech giants, and also a few domestic state funds, such as China Development Bank Capital. An exception is perhaps 51 Credit Card, which attracted mostly local venture capital. Meituan is the only changemaker that also raised capital from a traditional institutional investor (Canadian Pension Plan Investment Board). Fourth, the role played by domestic tech companies is significant. In some outlets and investor circles, changemakers that get funding from the dominant BAT companies start to belong to distinct groups—the Baidu club, the Alibaba club, and the Tencent club. China's three Internet giants are heavy investors in startups, including changemakers, whose total investment amount in 2015 reached $30 billion and in 2016 surpassed $80 billion.

The three BAT companies invested in Internet-related business such as online takeout ordering and mobile taxi booking. They also paid close attention to the health, financial, and culture and entertainment sectors. The majority of their investments were made during a startup's nascent stage—VC series A or VC series B. By comparison, Tencent invested heavily in games (such as Riot Game and ZAM), social networking services (SNS), mobile phone apps (such as Kakao, Snapchat, and Zhihu), and other Internet-related businesses, and such investments aimed at consolidating its strength in mobile-related business.

The Internet pioneers have also jointly created new ventures to disrupt traditional markets. For instance, the current Didi Chuxing is an amalgamation of three companies. In 2013, young entrepreneur Chen Weixing founded Kuaidi Taxi in Hangzhou, and from 2013 to 2015, Alibaba was a significant supporter of Kuaidi with three rounds of investment. Also in 2013, another young entrepreneur, Cheng Wei, founded Didi Taxi in Beijing, and from 2013 to 2014, Tencent was a strong supporter of Didi with three rounds of investment. In 2015, both companies merged into Didi Chuxing, and both Alibaba and Tencent invested a combined two rounds

Table 5.3
Global venture capital for eight changemakers (as per April 2018)

Company	Year of entry	Valuation (U.S. dollars)	Latest round (U.S. dollars)	Number of rounds	Examples of venture capital or corporate venture capital
Didi Chuxing	2012	$55 billion	$4.5 billion	F+	Alibaba, Apple, BAIC, CDH Investments, China Investment Corporation, CITIC PE, DCT, GSR Venture, Sina Weibo, Softbank, Temasek, Tencent
Ele.me	2009	$9.5 billion	$630 million	Acquired	Alibaba, Citic PE, Didi Chuxing, Dianping, GSR Venture, JD, Matrix Partners, Sequoia Capita, Tencent
51 Credit Card	2012	$1 billion	$310 million	C	A+ Fund, Guosen Investment, Tiantu Capital, Xinhu Zhongbao
Meituan	2010	$30 billion	$4 billion	F	Alibaba, Canadian Pension Plan Investment Board, China Development Bank Capital, DST, General Atlantic Investment, Sequoia Capital, Temasek, Tencent, Today Capital, Trust Bridge Partners
Mobike	2015	$2.7 billion	$600 million	Acquired	Bertelsman Asian Investment, Hillhouse Capital, Joy Capital, Qiming VC, Sequoia Capital, Sinnovation Ventures, Tencent, Warburg Pincus
Pinduoduo	2015	$15 billion	$300 million	C	IDG Capital, Sequoia Capital China, Tencent Industry Win-Win Fund
Toutiao	2012	$30 billion	$1 billion	D	China Construction Bank International, Sequoia Capital, Sina Weibo
We Doctor	2010	$1.5 billion	$394 million	E	China Development Bank Capital, Fosun, Goldman Sachs, Hillhouse Capital, Tencent

Notes: Valuation as of April 2018; investment up to date until April 2018. In 2015, Meituan merged with Dianping as China Internet Plus, and Meituan took the lead. We followed the investment trail from Meituan before the merger. Didi Taxi and Kuaidi Taxi merged in 2015, and Didi took the lead. We followed the investment trail from Didi Taxi before the merger. Both Ele.me and Mobike were acquired in April 2018.
Source: Authors' research.

of investments in the newly merged company. Moreover, in September 2015, Didi Chuxing invested $100 million in Lyft, the main competitor of Uber in the United States, and Tencent and Alibaba also invested in Lyft. The close connection generates several avenues of cooperation, such as allowing users to summon rides through both networks. Didi Chuxing is also expanding in Southeast Asia with investments in local taxi-hailing companies like Ola and Grab. The taxi-hailing business was not safe from disruption, however, and Didi Chuxing acquired Uber China in August 2016. This pulled Baidu into the game because Baidu had invested two rounds of investments in Uber China. Within three years, the BAT companies (and other external investors, such as Apple) have created a superunicorn that has disrupted the Chinese taxi-hailing market.

Another example is Meituan Dianping (also referred to as China Internet Plus or XinMeiDa in Chinese), a location-based service (LBS) platform that focuses on catering and is valued at $30 billion. Meituan, established in 2010, received two rounds of investment from Alibaba, and Dianping, China's earliest consumer review platform (established in 2003), was supported by Tencent with two rounds of investment. In 2015, the two companies merged into Meituan Dianping. By 2016, DST, Tencent, and others had invested $3.3 billion in the company, which is another example of how Tencent and Alibaba have supported the rise of another changemaker. Meituan Dianping has started to become a national champion itself. In February 2018, the company added a taxi-hailing service, directly competing with Didi Chuxing, and in April 2018, it acquired Mobike, thereby becoming a major player in the mobility sector in China. Its latest valuation of over $30 billion makes Meituan a contender with the BAT companies for top player.

High Visibility

Although the changemakers are young ventures, less than ten years old, they are far more visible than the underdogs, which are often older. In fact, they are more visible than the large and experienced hidden champions (chapter 3). Their early and wide visibility can perhaps be explained by the qualities of their entrepreneurs and their extreme focus on marketing and public relations. These companies also have focused on raising capital well before they were making any profits, so visibility was not only the result of their business approach but also a necessity. Attracting capital also increased the visibility of the changemakers. They are the "salesmen entrepreneurs" of the Chinese innovators who are looked at in this book.

This new generation of entrepreneurs is certainly different from the previous generations. These changemakers born in the 1980s and 1990s want to make an impact. For instance, Zhang Yiming, founder of Toutiao, is a serial entrepreneur, is one of *Fortune* magazine's 2016 business pioneers, and has shaken up the traditional media landscape in China. He is also on two of *Forbes*'s lists—China 30 under 30 and China 40 business elites under 40. By 2015, Zhang Xuhao had surpassed his entrepreneurial family's early successes and was named *Harper's Bazaar*'s breakthrough entrepreneur. Didi Chuxing's Cheng Wei was named *Fortune*'s businessperson of the year in 2016 and was on *Wired*'s top hundred list as well. These entrepreneurs are by no means hidden. They are in the spotlight.

Another reason for their high visibility is that many changemakers received early support from big names in the Internet business in China. For instance, Toutiao received an angel investment from Zhou Hongyi, who is the founder of Qihoo 360, one of China's top five Internet groups. 51 Credit Card received an angel investment from the young Chen Weixing, who had just founded Kuaidi Taxi and now has merged into Didi Chuxing. Hu Weiwei received angel investments from Wang Xing, the founder of Meituan and another changemaker. It is clear that the changemakers are good at networking with influential investors and Chinese entrepreneurs.

We also have looked at the overall media appearance of the changemakers in Chinese and international leading media—general, financial, and technology news portals (chapter 4). Figure 5.1 summarizes the main findings. First, changemakers are highly visible in domestic and international media, almost as visible as their "big brother" pioneers. Second, the average size of the changemakers is still small—about 6,300 employees, mostly due to one large outlier, Meituan, that has over 35,000 employees. Third, the changemakers are highly visible in general media. Baidu and Google have had 45 million and 22 million total hits, respectively. Didi Chuxing and Meituan are the most visible in domestic media. Toutiao and Meituan are the most visible in international media. Fourth, considering their strong venture capital support, they are also visible in financial media such as *PEdaily*, *Caijing*, and even the *Financial Times*. 51 Credit Card, which received mostly local venture capital support, is the most visible in *PEdaily*, with over 1,400 articles. Didi Chuxing received the most attention in international specialized media such as

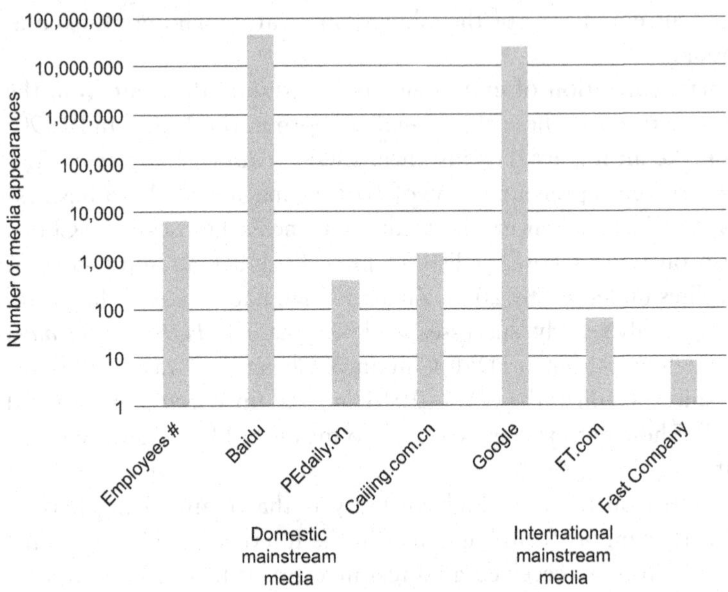

Figure 5.1
Media appearances of changemakers
Source: Authors' database, search date May 10, 2017.

Fast Company and the *Financial Times*, with over 170 articles on the company appearing in the *Financial Times*.

Need for Speed

Probably one of the most important features of the changemakers is their need for speed. As is seen in many industries in China, large numbers of new competitors have appeared in newly emerging sectors. For instance, after Didi Taxi was launched, dozens of other taxi apps entered the market, such as Dahuangfeng, Diandian Taxi, Kuaidi Taxi, and Taxi Secretary. Second, these markets are all winner-take-all markets, where the competitors are narrowly focused on getting market share rather than making profits. Many of these changemakers burned up large sums of venture capital before making any profit. In a way, the investments from venture capital mostly bought time rather than strategic resources or other advantages. Third, these newly emerging markets have increasing returns to adoption for users, especially because these markets did not exist a few years ago. Therefore, it makes sense to focus first on attracting more users, usually for free or even with subsidies, before earning money from the users. Finally, the products that these changemakers launch are at first often just good enough with simple features. However, all of them quickly upgrade their products, not in years but with iterations in weeks and days. This approach guarantees speed and user engagement, all in order to keep users as close as possible. As is illustrated below with the cases of Didi Chuxing and Mobike, these business battles are fought out over several years before a dominant player emerges.

Didi Chuxing

Didi Chuxing is a location-based car service matching platform that originally was designed for taxis but later expanded to include private car services as well. The company has grown at breakneck speed, and today receives 20 million orders per day, processes 2,000 terabytes of user data per day, employs 15 million drivers in 400 cities, and has close to 7,000 employees. After merging with its largest competitor (Kuaidi Taxi) in 2015 and acquiring Uber China in 2016, Didi Chuxing's market share reached 90 percent and a superunicorn valuation of $50 billion, second only to Uber globally. Uber was established in 2009, and only in its fourth year did it receive its first $100 million investment, whereas Didi is three years younger and has grown more quickly than Uber—not bad for a Chinese venture founded just five years ago.

Didi Chuxing was established in 2012 and in September of that year launched its first version of a taxi-hailing app. The first app was actually not developed by the founding team but outsourced to external engineers for 80,000 RMB. The product had a lot of problems, such as consuming too much energy and data. However, three months later, after receiving feedback from the first users, the company iterated the product and added new functions. By May 2013, dozens of competitors had emerged in China, but first-mover Didi's app was the top download. By November 2013, Didi had spread to thirty-two cities and claimed 10 million users. In January 2014, the company shifted gears and started its famous "red envelope" subsidy strategy via WeChat. In this way, they attracted many new taxi drivers and new users, who basically received 10 RMB's worth of free travel. After this round of promotion, spending 1.4 billion RMB in four months, Didi's daily orders reached 5 million per day.

In 2015, Didi introduced several new products and functions—in May, Didi Kuaiche (a private car service that is lower priced than Didi Zhuanche); in June, Didi Shunfeng Che (a car pool service); in July, Daijia (a designated-driver service) and a new bus-hailing function; in August,

Didi Zhuanche (a private taxi service); and in October, Shijia (a test drive app that allows you to try out a car). In between (February 2015), Didi merged with its largest competitor, Kuaidi Taxi, and in 2016, it launched more services like Didi Zuche (a car rental service). Beginning in December 2015, Didi started to collaborate and invest in overseas car services like Grabtaxi, Lyft, and Ola. In 2016, the company integrated Alipay and Wechat Pay for cross-border payments for their overseas business, and by the end of the year, the company collaborated with Avis and Budget car rental companies to offer Chinese users car renting services in 175 countries.

Although the collaborations were adding new functions for existing users, investors sought to have Didi become a real global player. Didi raised nine rounds of capital, totaling $16 billion with a latest valuation of $55 billion. Such numbers come with high expectations. In early 2017, Didi founded its international business department and made its first real market entry with investment in the Brazilian taxi hailing service 99Taxi. It next plans to enter markets in Japan, South Korea, and then Europe. Although Didi is going to step into the saturated markets of Uber, which basically controls the main five hundred cities globally for such services and has five years of international experience, its approach will differentiate itself by making strategic investments in combination with technology support.

However promising Didi Chuxing's sharing economy business model may be, at least two challenges await to be tackled. First, although ride hailing was not officially regulated in China until November 1, 2016, new regulations on drivers and cars in cities like Beijing, Shanghai, and Shenzhen will force Didi Chuxing to standardize and operate more like a traditional taxi company. Second, exciting profits have yet to turn up. In its search for more revenue, the company has added private taxis, high-end drivers, and other functions to its platform. Since the Uber China acquisition, the company has launched three new initiatives—"drive to own," which seems similar to the traditional taxi business that it set out to disrupt; "car rental," which would be a new revenue stream; and "bike sharing," which is in collaboration with the dockless bike-sharing service Ofo (which is also the largest competitor of Mobike). In April 2018, Meituan, a fellow changemaker, became a competitor in Didi Chuxing's space by adding taxi-hailing and bike-sharing services with the acquisition of Mobike. Even with a dominant market position and large amount of investor cash, speed and innovation are necessities for Didi Chuxing and many other Chinese changemakers.

Mobike

One of the newest changemakers is Mobike, the world's largest bicycle operator (with 6 million bikes) and arguably one of the most interesting startups from China. Mobike is a dockless bike-sharing service that allows users to ride and leave the bikes whenever and wherever, using smart locks with GPS and other innovative features. The platform claims that it has 25 million orders per day, creating large amounts of user and location data.[6] Although Didi Chuxing has at least one strong global competitor in Uber, Mobike has only domestic competitors, particularly Ofo. With less than two years' experience, today it claims 100 million registered users across more than a hundred cities in China and recently in Fukuoka, Manchester, and Singapore and launching in Milan and Florence. Speed is everything for Mobike's expansion.

As cofounder Hu Weiwei, a Chinese female entrepreneur in her early thirties, said at the 2017 Summer Davos Forum in Dalian, making profits is not a priority, but market expansion is. Mobike's expansion is venture capital driven. By August 2017, it had raised $1 billion, and this was its fifth round in just one year. Its real operations started in April 2016 in Shanghai, after a successful development of the first version of its new bicycle. The first launch was only a business prototype in Shanghai to test the model, improve the user interface, and develop the first group of seed users. After only three months, it added Beijing as a second city. In its second step, Mobike focused on upgrading the hardware of the bike. It innovated the bikes significantly by developing solid tires in collaboration with Dow Chemicals; a shaft drive transmission instead of a traditional chain transmission; a smart lock with telecommunication, GPS, and an embedded alarm module; and self-power generation by bicycling. In just six weeks, the app downloads increased four times, and within nineteen days, the company put ten thousand new bikes in Beijing (it took four months to reach the same amount in Shanghai).

By November 2017, Mobike was operating 500,000 bikes. Optimizing the bike supply chain and cutting down the hardware cost became urgent because the bikes were expensive to produce due to their advanced features and other special design features. The company also continued to innovate its business processes. It introduced a feature that provides credit or cash rewards for users who find and ride bikes left in remote areas. They even have designated some vehicles as "bonus bikes" (they are labeled with a red envelope) to encourage users to move bikes from low-traffic areas to high-traffic spots, thereby helping reduce the operational costs of the company.

New technologies were increasingly explored. In May and June 2017, Mobike start using its big data on locations and user behavior by introducing the AI Magic Cube, features on Baidu Maps, and its Internet of things platform in collaboration with China Mobile and Ericsson.[7] The Magic Cube forecasts supply and demand for its bike rentals and provides guidance for bike dispatching, scheduling, and operation. Mobike is moving rapidly, and Ofo, its main competitor, is hurrying to follow. In fact, Ofo, which announced a partnership with China Telecom and Huawei in March 2017, is playing catch-up because it originally did not plan to leverage Internet of things technology on its bikes. Another new technology was integrated in May 2017, when Mobike announced a partnership with China's leading thin-film solar cell manufacturer Hanergy to integrate solar cells into the smart locks for energy efficiency.

The first half of 2017 saw other important developments, such as the TUV quality certificate, ISO standards, and collaborations with Axa Insurance, Microsoft, Stripe Payment, and Vodafone. In a race between Mobike and Ofo (arguably more aggressive than the race between Didi and Kuaidi), Mobike started to internationalize less than two years after its founding, first to Singapore and then to the Italy, Japan, and the United Kingdom. In August 2017, the company was active in a hundred cities and had a goal to reach two hundred cities worldwide in 2018. In order to build lighter, more environmentally friendly, and more comfortable bikes, Mobike signed a strategic partnership with DuPont, a global chemicals company from the United States, to develop new materials. The need for speed (in terms of expansion over profits) and continuous innovation of technology and new product launches is remarkable. In April 2018, Mobike was acquired by Meituan.

Insights into the Changemakers

The changemakers are potentially the disruptors of the near future. Although many entrepreneurs who started disruptive ventures are still young and relatively inexperienced, we are witnessing the rise of a whole new generation of entrepreneurs who are native to digital technology, are driven by venture capital, and have a strong sense of growing fast before turning a profit. The following five insights stand out:

- *Next-generation entrepreneurs:* The changemakers are a group of next-generation entrepreneurs that disrupt traditional ways of thinking in business. The changemakers utilize an emerging mobile Internet society and showcase radical business mindsets. However, they are emerging hand in hand with a new generation of consumers. Unlike the previous generation of Chinese, who were born between the 1950s and 1970s and grew up in a tough economic environment, those born after 1980 are much more active shoppers and demand quality products and services as they pursue diverse lifestyles.

- *Digital disruption:* The changemakers employ digital business models to disrupt established industries. The shocking fact is that although China is far behind the United States in terms of Internet penetration, Chinese mobile Internet usage is ubiquitous and much higher than in the United States. This leads to a very different mobile digital business scope. Mobile payments, for instance, are far more accepted by Chinese consumers than American consumers. The changemakers are leveraging this to disrupt many different traditional or established industries with digital business models.
- *Innovations fueled by global venture capital:* The changemakers raise large sums of capital early in their existence, up until multiple billion-dollar financing rounds pre-IPO. The investors include a wide variety of stakeholders, including domestic private funds, a few large Chinese state funds, and dozens of international funds. The Internet pioneers (chapter 2) are supporting the next generation of digital disruptors and want a piece of the cake.
- *High visibility:* The changemakers are extremely adept at promoting their new products and services. They are born marketers and create high visibility for their ventures from the start. Although the changemakers are young companies that are less than ten years old and receive less media attention than the pioneers, they are far more visible that the underdogs and hidden champions. The changemakers are the "salesmen entrepreneurs" who excel at delivering business pitches and convincing investors as well as the public. They are often the opposite of the rather media-shy underdogs or purposely hiding hidden champions.
- *Need for speed:* As is seen in many industries in China, the number of new competitors in newly emerging sectors is large. These markets are all winner-take-all markets, where the competitors are obsessively focused on getting market share rather than making profits. The increasing returns for users who adopt are significant. For the sake of speed and instant user feedback, many changemakers launch inferior products but then quickly iterate and upgrade. Upgrading refers to improving the product, the business model, the technology behind the product, and the marketing approach as well.

6

The Chinese Innovators' Way

What Is the Chinese Innovators' Way?

In examining the four types of Chinese innovators and analyzing their innovations—from novel technologies to disruptive business models—certain features of their innovation approaches emerge. Whether the approach is to put the customer at the center of innovation or to follow the herd rather than look for unique opportunities, our research reveals at least six distinct ways of innovating that characterize the Chinese innovators' way:

- *Swarm innovation:* Collectively pursuing opportunities
- *Tinkering:* Fast trials and fast learning
- *A strong customer focus:* Local needs and product variety
- *Quick technology upgrades:* The red queen race and staying ahead of copycats
- *Rapid centralized decision making:* A sense of urgency
- *A network mindset:* Recognizing opportunities and accessing resources

Although critics may claim that any one of these six approaches is not unique to China, together they have fostered a distinctive style of Chinese innovation. We consistently find these ways of innovation regardless of firm size, experience, or sector. These findings at least question the assumption that companies from developing economies can catch up only slowly. China's large entrepreneurial class and the rapid expansion of its middle class have accelerated innovation in unexpected ways.

Swarm Innovation: Collectively Pursuing Opportunities

According to Chinese national statistics, on every day in 2016, fifteen thousand new companies were registered, an additional three thousand more per day than in 2015, totaling 5.4 million newly registered companies in 2016 in China.[1] Not so long ago, private entrepreneurs were symbols of unwanted capitalism, but now the country is flooded with startups. More often than any time before, young people are choosing to start their own businesses. The total early-age entrepreneurial activity in China is higher than in India, the United Kingdom, and the United States, according to the Global Entrepreneurship Monitor.[2] Although government promotion of the private sector and student entrepreneurship is certainly a driving force, many societal reasons are contributing to the expansion, such as a tight labor market, peer pressure on earning more money, success examples, and an overall culture of entrepreneurship in many parts of China. For whatever reasons, China has one of the most active entrepreneurial ecosystems in the world.

Startups in China are booming, especially in the high-tech sector due to many government initiatives. Besides the newly promoted university entrepreneurship courses, rise of incubators, and science parks, a multitude of competitions have emerged. One of the world's largest nationwide competitions for ventures is based in China (chapter 1) and held thirty-three regional competitions across almost every province in 2016. This competition focuses on six fields—advanced manufacturing, mobile Internet, electronic information, new energy and environmental protection, new materials, and biopharmaceuticals.[3] Nationally, this competition attracted over 50,000 new ventures in 2016, up from 27,000 in 2015. A true population of entrepreneurs has emerged and has become a force that cannot be ignored.

The drivers of China's innovations—the size of China's market, its booming middle class, intense competition, a large population of entrepreneurs, diverse domestic business systems, and continuous changes in the market, regulations, and competition—all contribute to a unique phenomenon we call swarm innovation. Numerous, nimble, often short-lived Chinese companies quickly copy existing products, make minor upgrades, and become superseded by the next wave of small companies. Literally millions of entrepreneurs collectively innovate and push technology and market boundaries. Although many of these ventures fail, some emerge as strong competitors and even market leaders. Considering the overall size of the startup pool, this number in absolute terms may not be small and run into the thousands. Collectively and over time, the market evolves, while multinationals that encounter such competitors find the swarm difficult to outmaneuver. According to the founding partner of a Chinese venture capital, ten thousand people in China see an opportunity, a hundred of them start a business, ten keep tinkering, and one wins the market in the end.

Swarm innovation—or the collective pursuit of similar opportunities in the market—contrasts sharply with the way that innovators compete in most other global entrepreneurship ecosystems, such as Amsterdam, Berlin, Boston, London, and Silicon Valley (table 6.1). Where for most foreign entrepreneurs the game is to identify unique opportunities and develop competences and business models that are distinct from their competitors, Chinese entrepreneurs are doing almost the opposite. Although there are exceptions, one feature of these innovators is that they are less concerned with being different and more concerned with grabbing a piece of a growing market, which leads to intense competition between innovators for similar opportunities. Innovators in developed markets are more concerned with fighting old-model incumbents or proving that the opportunity actually exists—that is, they are competing with nonconsumption. Swarm innovation is often a winner-take-all market, where a few dominant market leaders emerge over time and most competitors do not survive. Finally, not only is there a swarm of innovators, but in many sectors, these innovators and new ventures pursue similar

Table 6.1
Swarm innovation versus developed market innovation

Swarm innovation	Developed market innovation
Go for proven opportunities	Go for unique opportunities
Many selling points	Unique selling points
Market driven	Technology driven
Intense competition among a large number of peers	Competition with incumbents and nonconsumption
Winner-takes-all markets	Diversified markets[a]
Strong geographic market clustering	Technology clustering

Note: a. Exceptions are platform technology companies such as Amazon, Apple, Facebook, and Google.
Source: Authors' research.

opportunities in the same geographic locations—that is, there is strong geographic concentration. In contrast, developed market innovators tend to cluster around technology and not around specific geographic markets.

These phenomena of swarm innovation and geographic clustering have their origin in the way that Chinese entrepreneurs have been doing business for a long time. The legacy of state socialism and the early steps taken in market development have part of their origin in specialized market exchanges where entrepreneurs and businesspeople came together to sell the same products in a physical marketplace.[4] Even today, in many Chinese shopping streets and local markets, there are clusters of the same type of products together in one place. Zhejiang province is the home ground for such developments, not surprising given its strong entrepreneurial culture.

The earliest modern markets in Zhejiang were observed in August 1979 in Wenzhou.[5] The Qiaotou ("next to the bridge") town button market started when two brothers traveled to search for business opportunities and brought back to their hometown a bag of buttons that they started to sell on the roadside. Seeing that the business was doing well, neighbors also started to source and sell buttons, and a market was formed spontaneously. By 2008, Zhejiang, one of China's smallest provinces, had over four thousand such markets with over 950 billion renminbi (RMB) in transaction volume.[6] Other examples of specialized markets that evolved into industrial clusters that showcase innovative learning and cross-cluster exchanges include the Yongkang hardware cluster, the Yueqing low-voltage apparatus cluster, and the Haining leather cluster.[7] Swarming of entrepreneurs and innovation is part of how business is done in China's emerging market economy. The sectors discussed in this book are full of examples of swarm innovation. In what follows, we illustrate the swarm innovation competitive pattern for four types of innovators.

Underdogs Swarming in Competition

The underdogs are technology-driven ventures in niche business-to-business markets. In the solar industry in China, where Weihua competes, the market is large and competitive. In our own studies in 2016, we discovered that over 150 Chinese companies had significant intellectual property in photovoltaic technology and that the current global top ten solar companies are predominantly Chinese. A large group of newcomers, such as Weihua, is changing the market outlook. In the broader new energy industry, over fifteen hundred new companies were started in 2015, with at least 50 percent of the ventures in solar technology. A striking two hundred of the startup projects that made it to the finals of the China Innovation and Entrepreneurship Competition were in the solar technology field.[8]

In the case of big data technologies, a field where Gago competes, there has been an explosion of big data industry parks in China, the largest being in Guiyang with over seventeen thousand registered big data companies. Although Guiyang is in the southwest hinterland of China, it has specific advantages: it is less affected by solar storm and sunspot activity; it is so remote that crimes are rare; and its mild average temperature yields lower energy consumption, which is ideal for big data centers. In addition, big data technology has found applications in a wide variety of industries—including agriculture, ecommerce, education, electricity, finance, marketing, recruitment, and retailing—and Chinese innovators are particularly strong in developing such applications. In addition to Gago, many companies are competing in the narrow field of big data agriculture, including ControlEasy, GeoHey, and Insentek (chapter 4), which are innovating, competing, and swarming the market.

A Boom in Changemakers and Accelerated Consolidation

The pattern of swarm innovation is visible in the way that changemakers compete. The market opportunities and disruptions that new digital technologies bring attract many young people who start digitally driven businesses that are fueled by global venture capital. For instance, the food delivery sector started in 2008 with the founding of Ele.me, but it has boomed since 2013. Over a hundred new ventures have entered the market, but most did not survive until 2017. A handful of large companies remain, including Baidu Takeaway, Ele.me, and Meituan Dianping. There has been strong consolidation in the industry. For instance, Meituan Dianping, a $30 billion (USD) market valuation company, is the result of a large merger between Meituan (a company established in 2010) and Dianping (China's earliest consumer review platform, which was established in 2003). This superunicorn was backed by Alibaba and Tencent as the main investors. Another example is the merger between Baidu Takeaway and Meituan Takeaway and the acquisition of Ele.me by Alibaba.

Driven by a strong need for speed (chapter 5), the changemakers are competing almost exclusively in winner-takes-all markets. For instance, similar to the food-delivery sector, in the last five years, the taxi-hailing markets and bike-sharing markets have exploded and then consolidated but at an accelerating speed of consolidation. Although the consolidation in the food-delivery market took close to eight years, the taxi-hailing war took only around four years, and the bike-sharing competition was more or less settled after only about a year. The first players in the taxi-hailing apps were Didi and Kuaidi, which were set up around 2012. At the height of the market, there were around a hundred taxi-hailing apps in China, and by 2013, only fifty had survived. One year later, basically only Didi and Kuaidi were left and had the majority of the market. After merging with its largest competitor Kuaidi Taxi in 2015 and acquiring Uber China in 2016, Didi Chuxing's market share reached 90 percent and a superunicorn valuation of $50 billion.[9] In the case of bike sharing, the winner-takes-all competition was mostly settled by 2017. After the entry of around seventy bike-sharing companies since the middle of 2016, by the end of 2017, the main competitors were Ofo and Mobike. The acceleration of consolidation in the changemaker markets is unheard of in other countries or, for that matter, in most other industries in China.

Swarming Is Not Only for New Ventures

Swarm innovation is relevant not only for the new ventures of the last decade but also for the older generation of pioneers and hidden champions. According to our interview with a Haier Group vice president, there are over 25,000 domestic players in small household appliances in China, and more than 5,000 of these players export products, directly competing with Haier. The construction industry also has been extremely attractive since the 1990s with a booming real estate and infrastructure market. Even companies such as Geely, a car manufacturer, and Wuliangye, a Chinese liquor company, started to make excavators. By about 2000, over a hundred Chinese companies were producing excavators, but by 2011, the top fifty accounted for 90 percent of the total market.[10] Fierce competition followed, and by 2016, only twenty competitors were left, and fourteen of these were publicly listed companies.

The hidden champions are also subject to swarming. A good example is the solar industry and the hidden champion Trinasolar. The solar industry started to boom in about 2000, and by 2013, Jiangsu province alone had over a thousand companies. One year later, only roughly 50 percent survived.[11] Currently, China has only 149 registered members in the China Photovoltaic Industry Association, the industry's largest association. Another example is the medical equipment industry. Driven by China's aging population, booming middle class, and increased demand for quality healthcare, there are abundant opportunities in medical equipment for years to come. This sector used to be dominated by foreign companies such as GE, Philips, and Siemens, but China's healthcare companies have been upgrading significantly. Moreover, because the foreign companies are not strong in the lower and middle segments of the medical equipment industry, a huge market void has emerged in China. The number of new entrants is significant. In 2014, there were twelve thousand registered companies in this sector, and by 2016, there were sixteen thousand companies—a 30 percent increase (four thousand companies) in just two years. Clearly, swarming is not only for new ventures but also a competitive pattern for pioneers and hidden champions.

Tinkering: Fast Trials and Fast Learning

Chinese innovators use fast trial and error to test the market, adjust, and learn. Testing the market, developing the product, and designing the business model often are done at the same time. Chinese companies—not only the startups but also giants such as Alibaba and Haier—tend to be good at early market validation and iterated development. Rather than just experimenting, which assumes a large failure rate, Chinese innovators tend to tinker—or in Karl Weick's term, use bricolage—in their organizations.[12] Tinkering refers to constructing something based on whatever things happen to be available. Rather than planning for a specific objective that requires a prearranged set of resources, tinkerers do not assume that the objectives can be reached only by using a fixed set of resources. Rather, the processes of tinkering is a continuous iteration of building, searching resources, testing, and rebuilding. Rather than a process of planning, it is a process of learning by combining existing resources and knowledge and recombining previously unrelated knowledge. In the tinkering approach, mistakes are small and easily overcome, in contrast to the large and potentially disruptive mistakes in planning that can be made under conditions of uncertainty and limited information.

The tinkering process has several preconditions for being successful in organizations, as outlined by Weick's bricolage concept—an intimate knowledge of available resources, careful listening to and observation of the customer, confidence in one's ideas, and self-correcting feedback. Intimate knowledge of available resources is not the same as having access to abundant resources, but Chinese innovators have both. In fact, as is shown later in this chapter's discussion of a network mindset, Chinese innovators are continuously searching for resources and are highly aware of what resources are readily available. In many ways, Chinese innovators are better at searching for than developing resources. Careful listening to the customer is also a precondition for the next feature—a strong customer focus. Many observers have applauded Chinese companies' ability to listen to the market. Confidence in one's ideas is one of the features of a decisive boss. Chinese leaders are known to be confident and decisive, as is illustrated below. Iteration and feedback are related to the habit of many companies that develop good enough products rather than perfect products, in response to changing customer needs. Our research reveals that Chinese companies meet most of these preconditions for successful tinkering.

Tinkering fits well with Chinese pragmatism and the transitional nature of a market where there is much uncertainty. Moreover, Chinese entrepreneurs are known to be comfortable in turbulent waters. Almost by nature, younger ventures, such as the changemakers and underdogs, tinker continuously. However, the large incumbent's embrace of this approach stands out. For instance, Alibaba is good at trying out new initiatives, such as Internet finance and digital healthcare, and connecting to new innovation opportunities. At the same time, it also allows failure, such as with the instant messenger Laiwang (which was supposed to compete with WeChat) and the collaboration with Wasu TV to create digital content in the joint venture with Taobao.[13] None of these failures was fatal. Nobody talks anymore about the Laiwang failure, but Alibaba's experience with Laiwang did help the company develop better social tools that later became crucial in other products. Another example in the digital sphere is Xiaomi, which started as a software company because it was most familiar with software development. Its first product was a new smartphone operating system. The development of this operating system was based completely on the tinkering process—launching a product early in the market, carefully listening to users, updating on a weekly basis, and iterating the cycle between user and product development. The confidence of the founding team was obvious, and many of its members were successful entrepreneurs and business leaders before starting Xiaomi.

More striking examples are TCL and Geely. TCL is now a leading consumer electronics manufacturer, but it started by developing recording tape before switching to the telecom business and becoming the leading provider for phone terminals in the 1980s. Then in the 1990s, founder Li Dongsheng realized that color TV had a great potential and, starting from nothing, built up what is now one of the largest TV businesses worldwide. Every transformation was highly risky, and TCL did not have any relevant technology at the time, but trying and learning brought Li great success. Similarly, Li Shufu, the founder of Geely, started by making motorbikes but, in 1997, saw that cars had great potential. Without any of the assets, knowledge, or experience needed to make cars, he was not taken seriously. Li famously said that "cars are just motorbikes with two extra wheels." In 1998, his first car rolled off the production line, with a car manufacturing license that he acquired from a prison and that, in fact, allowed only the production of trucks. In 2001, the government gave Geely an official license for producing cars. In 2010, Geely acquired Volvo, and, similar to TCL, it has been a tinkerer and risk taker from the start.

Another example from the hidden champion group is Lens Technology. Originally, the company produced watch glass, similar to the company that the founder, Zhou Qunfei, used to work for. This traditional industry was characterized by fierce competition. The turning point was in 2001, when one of Zhou's friends got a deal from TCL to develop flip cell phone panels. Based on Zhou's experience in making products for watches, Lens Technology suggested to TCL that it should use glass instead of acrylic plastic. After this experiment, which TCL accepted, Lens Technology sensed an opportunity and decided to focus on mobile phone screen products. Observing the potential and the start of a trend, the tinkering of a confident founder led her to a new opportunity in an unfamiliar industry. In a different but more traditional industry, changemaker Three Squirrels, an innovative online business selling edible nuts, has showcased tinkering as well. After it was established in 2012, the company reached a turnover of 4.5 billion RMB by 2016 by sourcing, packaging, branding, and selling nuts online. Its initial success came from trying to promote and sell a new type of pecan nut that was not yet popular with Chinese consumers. After its success, the company kept trying out new things, including an innovative marketing approach and new product design, thereby distinguishing itself. A process of tinkering allowed the company to find new opportunities and quickly learn from the market.

A Strong Customer Focus: Local Needs and Product Variety

Beside the enormous size, a key feature of China's market is continuous development and change. The country's wide diversity of geographic markets makes it a highly segmented business system (chapter 1), so customer development and the ability to understand and meet changing customer requirements are crucial conditions for the success of Chinese innovators. Although critics explain the obsession that Chinese companies have for listening to the customer as being triggered by a lack of technological capability, these companies are stars at customer-driven innovation, and multinationals often comment their own lack of local market understanding. Our studies confirm that Chinese companies not only respond more quickly than multinationals do to the needs of local customers but also cater to a larger variety of needs. The latter is not done by building more sophisticated products but by bringing more versions of the product to market.

China's rapid and lower-cost execution capability and well-developed manufacturing capability and infrastructure actually allow its companies to pay attention to special needs. One example is Haier's Crystal washing machine series, which is the outcome of several series of user surveys and innovations in terms of spin speed and operating noise. TCL's innovative TV products have a large variety of features, such as karaoke, smart touch pens, and dual display. Most of these are not radical innovations but combinations of existing technologies that create something that the customer values highly. Another example of a changemaker that pays special attention to the customer is Three Squirrels, which rethought the consumer experience of buying and eating nuts. Considering specific customer requirements, it invented a new product that is complementary to the actual nuts: it sells nuts in bags that include a wet tissue, a rubbish bag, and a nut opener. None of its competitors had packaged these items together, and by 2016, the company was the largest nut brand in China. To give a sense of this market size, during the Alibaba Shopping Festival in 2016, Three Squirrels sold 500 million RMB worth of nuts in one day.

The many reasons behind this strong customer focus vary according to type of innovator. For the hidden champions and underdogs, it is not surprising that they have a strong customer focus. Their business positioning is niche and most often business clients, so they have a strict customer focus as their competitive advantage. For the pioneers, there is an historical reason because originally they did not have a strong technological basis. They had to be close to the customer while launching good enough products. Good enough innovation results in a low-cost, fit-for-purpose product that has a great appeal for customers who are buying for the first time. In the beginning, Huawei's products were not of good quality, and after installing the product, company staff members usually had to stay nearby for several months to provide maintenance and repair. Huawei has said that in the past decades this customer proximity helped it to develop thousands of micro-innovations. It should be noted that "good enough" does not necessarily refer to poor quality or low safety standards. The aim is to develop exactly the product that the market can accept—nothing more but also nothing less. Like Chery's QQ subcompact car or Haier's middle-market version of the wine cooler refrigerator, the products are positioned between the high-end premium segment and the low-cost mass segment, a niche that has been growing significantly in China.[14] Practically speaking, good enough innovation requires a highly localized, customer-focused innovation approach, in contrast to the technology-driven innovation approach that multinationals often follow.

Another case in point is Sany, a heavy construction equipment manufacturer that probably is one of the most international Chinese companies. It is far from a traditional low-cost manufacturer. One of Sany's innovations is the development of more robust, easy to maintain and repair construction equipment that operates under the harsh conditions in many developing countries, where the lack of engineering skills and limited availability of components otherwise would severely limit operations. Sany listened to its foreign and local customers. Within China, for instance, acknowledging a large variety of ground and soil conditions, it has developed many models for each application. While focusing on market reach, it also is expanding its capabilities.

The changemakers are another group of innovators. Three features make deep customer focus a competitive advantage for changemakers. First, the changemakers are young companies with limited legitimacy and brand reputation. The more they focus on the market and gain traction with large groups of customers, the better. Second, because they are digitally driven and have a variety of tools at hand, including social media and creative marketing approaches, they have many possibilities for reaching their customers quickly and all at once. Third, the market positioning of the changemakers is focused on mass markets, usually of consumers. For example, Yunmai's smart scale has many locally relevant functions, such as weights in the Chinese traditional weight unit *jin* rather than kilos, mandatory reminders for everyday weighing, and rechargeable rather than disposable batteries. These functions were identified by its first group of users, a group of loyal fans organized in communities, not unlike Xiaomi's fan culture. After success in China and South Korea, the company entered the United States with the same approach. Within nine months after entering the U.S. market, it had already surpassed the market share of the local competitor, Fitbit.

A special group of Chinese companies, perhaps not really innovators but surely innovative in their approach, are the *shanzhai* companies.

Although they do not develop much in terms of technological innovation and often copy existing design and technology, they are an example of how Chinese companies are obsessed with the market and customer needs. For instance, G'Five caters to specialized requirements, such as preinstalled religious software for Middle East markets or extraloud loudspeakers because Indian families like to dance together. Such special needs are not considered by technology-driven incumbents such as Apple. The obsession of Chinese innovators with the customer and their needs is striking.

Quick Technology Upgrades: The Red Queen Race and Staying Ahead of Copycats

In China, being a copycat is no longer enough to become a top cat. Although companies used to be able to get away with simple technologies and attractive business models, quick technology upgrades have become a necessity for most technology industries in China. There are several reasons for this. First, customers increasingly demand better and more advanced products. In many cases, this means that the companies need to increase their technological capabilities. Second, market competition has intensified to the extent that it has become more and more necessary to have intellectual property (IP) and strong technology as competitive advantages. For many industries, upgrading technology is much like a running the red queen race in Lewis Carroll's *Through the Looking-Glass*, where upgrading very fast allows you just to stay in the game. Third, copycat behavior is still widespread in China, and companies need to stay ahead of copycats. On the one hand, copycats can preempt the market that a company tried to capture. On the other hand, patent trolls and copycats can patent a company's own technology and then pursue the original company in court. Finally, and connected to copycat behavior, IP protections are improving but with significant limitations. Formally, IP has been acknowledged and protected in China since 1979. But there are many deficiencies in the protection of intellectual property rights (IPR). Some multinationals hesitate to enter China because of valid concerns about loss of IP.[15] This concern applies even more when it comes to innovation or conducting R&D in China. However, in 2016, there were more IPR lawsuits filed by Chinese companies against other Chinese than were filed by foreign companies.

Although many Chinese companies did not have a strong starting point in terms of technology, knowledge, and experience, our studies find that they are eager to upgrade quickly. Many interviewees view the competition as a red queen race where constant upgrading is necessary to compete in a market with multinationals' technology advantages and state-owned firms' resource advantages. Companies such as Positec, the power tools giant, and Ecovacs, the successful sweeper robot company, have been upgrading their technological capability from original equipment manufacturing to their own technology within a decade. Goldwind, a wind turbine manufacturer, gained its competitive advantage by continuously upgrading its technology until it reached a breakthrough with direct current drive permanent magnet engine technology. Damon Group has been steadily upgrading its technology and transformed from producing components for conveyers to full-scale conveying and sorting solutions.

Hikvision is also a good illustration of how quickly technology can be upgraded. In 2002, Hikvison launched MPEG4-based products such as a video compressor card for computers. In 2003, the company launched a new product series called DS-4000H that was based on an H.264 technology standard. The latter is an advanced video coding standard for video compression and is one of the video encoding standards for Blu-ray Discs. Hikvision kept upgrading this product series until the ninth-generation DS-9000H. In 2014, the company launched H.265-based products. This high-efficiency video coding is one of the potential successor technologies. Hikvision was globally among the first to adopt this standard, and it also quickly developed new technologies such as cloud computing and 4K resolution technology.

These companies see quick technology upgrades as a way to stay ahead of both competitors and copycats. After facing copycats in their early days, innovative companies such as Hikvision realized that their advantages could quickly erode and have focused on upgrading technology ever since.

Rapid Centralized Decision Making: A Sense of Urgency

China is not a market for slow starters. Our interviews and observations reveal three reasons for this (table 6.2). First, intense competition among the many companies and startups in China's economy creates a need to make rapid decisions. Many of our interviewees said that they often traded speed of decision making for product quality or formalized organizational processes. They claimed that if they do not make a decision quickly, their competitors will do so. It is not just one nearby competitor

Table 6.2
Rapid centralized decision making

Internal drivers	**External drivers**
Decisive leadership	Intense competition
Flat and flexible organizational structure	Changing market behavior
Cultural acceptance	Regulatory void
Sense of urgency	

Source: Authors' research.

but a whole swarm of entrepreneurs who are eager to exploit a similar opportunity.

Second, the changing nature of the market is a strong incentive for making decisions quickly. Customers are still developing their behavioral profiles and have fewer fixed preferences, leaving companies vulnerable to disloyal customers. Market research shows a trend of a booming middle class that will have money for new, better, and more diverse products. Innovators need to innovate new products, services, and business models quickly to avoid missing the boat. At a more fundamental level, switching costs for customers are still relatively low, which on the one hand, increases the chance of walkaways but on the other hand, makes the market fluid. In other words, today's champion and market leader may not be tomorrow's.

Third, regulatory changes and regulatory voids are more of an opportunity than a problem—as long as they are captured quickly. For instance, Alipay, Alibaba's online third-party payment service, was launched in 2004 when there was no regulation on third-party payments. It took years for the government to catch up with regulatory requirements, but by then, Alipay had already gathered a critical mass of hundreds of millions of users. Alipay also launched Yu'ebao, an online monetary fund investment product that can be used at any time, before regulations were available for this new financial product. By the time that regulations caught up, plenty of competitors were flooding the market. Another more recent example is the taxi-hailing app business. When the product was launched in 2012, Didi and Kuaidi were basically not subject to any particular regulation regarding their drivers. The answers to questions about who owns the car, who drives the car, and who is liable for problems were all unclear at the start. Nevertheless, Didi and Kuaidi quickly gained users. It used venture capital cash to attract as many users as possible within a couple of months, knowing that eventually regulators would catch up and competitors would do the same.

Besides the external drivers for making quick decisions, there are internal drivers as well. The way that Chinese innovators are organized facilitates rapid decision making. First, decision making in most Chinese companies is centralized with strong leaders. Chinese companies innovate faster than multinationals do. Geely's transformation from motorbikes to cars took only one year. Haier's new product development cycles are shorter than those of most competitors. Lenovo's new global customer buyer system allows processes to run in parallel, thereby speeding up the entire buying process. Because many Chinese companies are young and lack bureaucratic management structures, they tend to be less formal and listen more to decisive bosses.

BYD's high-speed but risky step into electric vehicles has been driven by founder Wang Chuanfu's decisiveness. Although BYD performed well below expectations, 2015 became its most profitable year ever. Ren Zhengfei's leadership style is often called military style. He has a large personality and influence on the company. In 2002, when Huawei had its historical negative growth, Ren's decision to commit to international market expansion and make Huawei a global technology leader was met with skepticism and criticism. It was a turning point in Huawei's history. Even today, Ren Zhengfei's influence on the multibillion USD company is significant. Although he implemented a rotating CEO system, he holds the final veto right on any executive decision. Other examples of strong leaders include Ma Yun, who is still the brain behind Alibaba even though he retreated from the CEO position many years ago. In the smaller and lesser-known ventures, the founder is often said to be like the father of the company and the one who makes all decisions. This pattern actually starts at the founding of new ventures. Whereas Western ventures often have founding teams, Chinese ventures tend to be almost exclusively founded and run by one or two founders. Xiaomi is an exception and has seven cofounders.

Second, the organizational structures of Chinese innovators tend to be either flat or flexible. Underdogs and changemakers have relatively flat structures because they are young and small. The question is how the larger and more mature Chinese innovators organize themselves for rapid decision making. We distinguish two types of large innovators.

One type of large innovator is a company like Haier or Xiaomi that has reorganized its organizational structure to be as flat as possible. Haier's motto is zero distance to the customers, and its organizational innovation of work units—that is, micro-enterprises or ZZJYT (in Chinese, *zi zhu jing ying ti*)—is its organizational answer. A crucial difference is that all decision-making power lies within the twenty-person work unit, not unlike any other startup company. Xiaomi is another example where a company with eight thousand employees has only three organizational layers. According to traditional management theory, it is not possible to manage in such a flat but large organization, but Xiaomi succeeded. The seven cofounders direct one layer of directors, who in turn manage the engineers and salesforce directly. The cofounders also are required to communicate directly with the engineers. A crucially different way of thinking is in the role played by key performance indicators (KPIs). Xiaomi has significantly reduced the number of KPIs, instilled a culture of fans (chapter 2), and provided generous bonus options, which all have given employees a large degree of autonomy.

Another type of large innovator does not necessarily have different organizational structures but has complemented its hierarchies with specific practices. For instance, Huawei's matrix organization has a flexible approach with a forward-moving team structure—iron triangle teams. Huawei's small teams have three crucial roles—improving customer relations, providing solutions and delivery, and increasing the speed of decision making. Another example is the business ecosystem structure of Baidu, Alibaba, and Tencent (the BAT companies). Although each of the companies in the Baidu, Alibaba, and Tencent groups are organized according to traditional structures, the individual unit companies never become too large. The ecosystems consist of dozens, if not hundreds, of small companies that are held together by shared users and services. Decision-making power lies at the company level more than at the group level.

Third, the leadership style of Chinese leaders is traditionally mostly patriarchic and top down and would not be easily accepted by American or European employees. Chinese employees have less difficulty with accepting a strong leader. Sometimes referred to as the traditional culture of Confucius and later the philosophy of Communism, Chinese culture is more accepting of top-down leaders and has less need for consensus building. Concepts such as loyalty, filial piety, and face are still widespread in the Chinese business world. Moreover, the upside is that employees have stronger expectations of their leaders in terms of giving direction, showing vision, and speaking for their employees. One consequence is that values are important in employee assessment and decision making. In a way, values function as heuristic decision-making logics. For instance, Alibaba is famous for its organizational values—such as customer first, embrace change, and dedication—that guide decision making and employee performance appraisals. Chinese employees have a widespread acceptance of being guided by relatively abstract values and tend to follow leaders by default. In contrast, most Western employees are guided by relatively specific and concrete operating principles that vary somewhat by company.

Fourth, and perhaps most noteworthy, is the sense of urgency of Chinese innovators. Although intense competition, changing market behaviors, and increasing regulations create a strong sense of urgency for Chinese innovators, they also have created clever incentives to keep a sense of urgency, even when the company has grown up. The underdogs naturally have a sense of urgency because they are startups that are short of resources. Changemakers have an even stronger sense of urgency due to the need for speed and user acquisition (chapter 5). But it is the large innovators' sense of urgency that is remarkable. For instance, Huawei's Ren Zhengfei is famous for his belief that Huawei should remain in a continuous state of growth rather than become an established organization. Moreover, the company is employee owned, and Ren Zhengfei wants everyone to act like the boss, so the sense of urgency and pressure on performance is high. Finally, by asking senior employees to resign and reapply in 2007. he shook up the organization and showed that apparently nobody was safe from the pressure to perform. In a similar fashion, Zhang Ruimin of Haier strongly feels that there is no such thing as a mature company, only a changing company. Since the late 1990s, he has continually reorganized the company, most recently in reforming toward a platform organization of micro-enterprises. Basically, most employees work for micro-enterprises, as startups, on a larger Haier platform. Haier also has instilled a catfish effect by putting a strong competitor next to the current unit leader, which creates a sense of urgency.

A Network Mindset: Recognizing Opportunity and Accessing Resources

Chinese entrepreneurs traditionally have been characterized as being strong networkers who are oriented toward personal relations. Innovation in China often is explained by the tendency of Chinese companies to connect extensively to external partners.[16] Because the government plays a more significant role in the market in China than in other countries and China's institutional landscape is still changing and forming, the ability to connect externally and build alliances is a crucial source of competitive advantage.[17] In our research studies, we find that a network mindset is one of the typical features of Chinese innovators. Such a mindset allows the early identification of opportunities in an emerging market, not unlike open innovation initiatives, and it also is a way to overcome resource limitations.

Although China's resource environment for talent, capital, and knowledge is good, accessing those resources is not always easy. According to the China Innovation Survey 2014, talent access and talent retention are among the largest challenges.[18] Our studies of over two hundred local Chinese companies also have confirmed the difficulty of finding and keeping the right employees. Although China has an absolute advantage in terms of the number of graduates, engineers, and scientists, the labor market mismatch should not be underestimated. Rising labor costs are another challenge for many Chinese innovators that started out with cost innovations, which they need to upgrade quickly to product, process, and business model innovations.

The Chinese innovators described in this book have a network mindset. For instance, Xiaomi started out its MIUI operating system development in direct collaboration with its user community and now is building its own network of a hundred hardware companies. Huawei has set up twenty-eight joint innovation centers with fourteen leading telecom operators worldwide. Haier employs the HOPE (Haier Open Partnership Ecosystem) initiative to tap into thousands of external experts in an online community. Haier also has a big data-based platform called 360 Global Talent Engine that allows anyone in Huawei to search for relevant talent inside and outside the Haier Group. Damon Group has built extensive partnerships to upgrade its technology and develop new product systems. Alibaba's smart logistics initiative, Cainiao, is a large-scale supply-chain innovation that collaborates with a range of external partners in trying to overcome the logistics limitations in China. To establish the National Wind Power Engineering Technology Research Center in 2008, Goldwind benefited from strong government relations, (former) cross-positions of executives in government, subsidies, and R&D collaboration with seventeen higher-education institutions. Another organizational example is the business ecosystem structure of the BAT companies (Baidu, Alibaba, and Tencent) that is basically a large and interdependent network of companies that develop customer-centric offerings across industries. Although networks are always important for innovators, Chinese companies utilize networks to innovate products, business models, and supply chains.

Overall, Chinese innovators have a mindset to look across their corporate boundaries for resources and opportunities.

We also can find this mindset with Pingan, one of the largest Chinese financial groups. Pingan is a holding company whose subsidiaries deal mainly with insurance, banking, and other financial services. The company was founded in 1988 with its headquarters in Shenzhen. The company is not only the world's most valuable insurance brand (worth $16 billion) but also a well-known innovator. Its innovations come primarily from its network mindset and especially its habit of making unusual partnerships. For instance, Pingan incubated two companies that became small ecosystems themselves. Pingan Good Doctor has, in turn, developed many partnerships with care providers and also with real estate developers to find entries into communities. Pingan Lufax, a unicorn-valued fintech startup, recently signed agreements with Ele.me and Durex.

Pingan also is active in the fintech industry in collaboration with the leading digital giants of the BAT companies. In November 2013, Pingan partnered with Alibaba and Tencent to establish China's first online insurance company, Zhongan Insurance, which has already launched over three hundred insurance products, some of which are widely considered to be star products and quite innovative. For instance, Bububao is a health insurance which connects consumers' smart wearable step counters to its insurance premium so that the more they walk, the less they need to pay. Pingan also collaborates with Baidu on big data analytics. The two jointly conduct fundamental research to see where and how big data analytics can help any of Pingan's services, such as consumer behavior profiling. Pingan also entered into a strategic collaboration with JD.com, one of China's largest ecommerce platforms, to connect the ecommerce and Internet financial businesses of the two companies.

Insights into the Chinese Innovators' Way

Chinese innovators have developed distinct ways of innovating. In this chapter, we analyze and illustrate six ways that set apart Chinese innovators:

- *Swarm innovation:* Swarm innovation can be summarized as the collective pursuing of innovation opportunities by large groups of enterprises. This approach is different from innovation in most developed markets because swarm innovators go for proven opportunities, are market driven, face intense competition between innovators, cluster geographically, and compete in rapidly consolidating markets. Although the underdogs swarm in competition, changemakers grow and see accelerated consolidation. Swarming is not only about startups, however, and we see the same competitive pattern for pioneers and hidden champions.

- *Tinkering:* Tinkering refers to constructing something based on the diverse range of things that happen to be available. It requires fast trials and fast learning. Rather than planning for a specific objective that requires a prearranged set of resources, tinkering does not assume full information and thrives on uncertainty. Chinese innovators showcase most of the preconditions for successful tinkering in organizations—an intimate knowledge of available resources, careful listening to and observations of the customer, confidence in one's ideas, and iterated, self-correcting feedback.
- *A strong customer focus:* The hidden champions and underdogs focus on market niche business clients, which requires a highly customer-centric approach that looks for local needs and provides product variety. The pioneers historically did not have a strong technological basis and developed only good enough innovations. Later, this became a competitive advantage because the pioneers were close to customers for long periods of time, and their organizations have grown into a customer-centric logic as well. The changemakers benefit from being highly customer focused because they start with limited legitimacy, can use their competitive digital capabilities, and can focus on mass market positioning. Our research reveals that Chinese innovators are not only highly customer focused, in the sense of being market driven, but also cater to local, special needs and develop a wide variety of products.
- *Quick technology upgrades:* Although companies could get away with simple technologies and attractive business models, quickly upgrading technology has become a necessity for most technology industries in China. This requires running the red queen race and staying ahead of copycats. Many Chinese companies did not have a strong starting point in terms of technology, knowledge, and experience, but our studies find that they are eager to upgrade quickly. Quickly upgrading technology is seen as a way of staying ahead of competition and also copycats.
- *Rapid centralized decision making:* China is not a market for slow starters. Chinese innovators have a sense of urgency and

excel in rapid centralized decision making. On the one hand, the innovators are characterized by decisive leadership, flat and flexible organizational structures, cultural acceptance of strong leaders, and a sense of urgency. On the other hand, intense competition, the changing market behavior of customers and consumers, and regulatory opportunities are another set of drivers for rapid decision making.

- *A network mindset:* Chinese innovators have a mindset to look across their corporate boundaries to recognize opportunities and access resources. In our studies, we find that a network mindset is one of the typical features of Chinese innovators. Such a mindset allows the early identification of opportunities in an emerging market, not unlike open innovation initiatives, and it is often a way to overcome resource limitations. Chinese companies are not afraid to enter into unusual partnerships to create innovation across industry boundaries.

7

China's Innovators Going Global

China's Innovators Emerging as Global Players

While China is playing a large role as a host location for foreign R&D centers, Chinese companies are developing strong technological competences and increasingly embed themselves in global R&D networks. Chinese outbound investments are reaching all corners of both the developing and developed world. In 2000, China's outward foreign direct investment (OFDI) was only 0.1 percent of total global foreign direct investment (FDI), but by 2015, it was already 8.7 percent. In 2016, there was a 44 percent year-on-year increase with a total of $170 billion (USD) invested in around eight thousand overseas projects. The China Innovation Survey indicates that over 80 percent of responding Chinese firms intend to expand abroad in the next ten years.[1] In terms of geographic locations for OFDI to date, the majority is in Asia (74 percent), Latin America (8.6 percent), the United States (7.4 percent), and Europe (4.9 percent). Leasing, finance, and business services take up most of the investments, with mining and retail a distant second and manufacturing only 7 percent. Our research shows that up to 70 percent of Chinese OFDI goes via four offshore centers—Bermuda, British Virgin Islands, Cayman Islands, and Hong Kong.[2]

Generally, Chinese companies invest in developed countries to obtain technologies, R&D capabilities, sales networks, and brands. According to a report by Alberto Di Minin, Jieyin Zhang, and Peter Gammeltoft, for example, Chinese R&D internationalization in Europe is mostly motivated by learning rather than technological innovation.[3] Nevertheless, intentions aside, a European Commission report found that fifty-six Chinese companies invested significantly (over $35 million) in R&D in Europe, with one of the fastest growers, Huawei, leading the way.[4] Nevertheless, Chinese R&D investment in Europe as a percentage of total

R&D investment by the top fifteen hundred companies in the European Union was only 2.7 percent in 2015 (Taiwan, 1.4 percent; South Korea, 2.9 percent; Japan, 21.9 percent; the United States, 34.9 percent). The top destination in terms of value is France, followed by the United Kingdom and Germany. However, France owes its first place to a single transaction, China Investment Corporation's $3.2 billion investment in Gas de France in 2011. Were it not for this transaction, France would be in the fourth place, just after Sweden. Except for the extractive and natural resources sectors, Chinese companies invest in a broad range of industries and assets in both manufacturing and services spread widely across Europe. In terms of value, the biggest deals have been in utilities, chemicals, and automotive.

Going beyond macroeconomic statistics, we focus on actual behavior and strategy at the company level, which may not show up in the numbers. Drawing on our extensive database and empirical research, we can draw a more comprehensive picture. Our empirical research reveals three distinguishing themes of the Chinese innovators that are going global:

- The BAT companies (Baidu, Alibaba, and Tencent) are internationalizing rapidly and building up the infrastructure for a comprehensive global digital ecosystem.
- Technology-driven innovators are building up global innovation networks, innovation bases, and technology outposts.
- Next-generation enterprises are exporting their disruptive business models.

Our study shows that all four types of innovators, particularly the younger generation, are actively going abroad. As a result, the number of innovative Chinese companies abroad will significantly increase in the years to come. They will include several dozens of competitors that are similar to the pioneers, large numbers of small and medium-sized enterprises, and new ventures in traditional and newly emerging industries. These Chinese innovators are not just selling products abroad but are developing global R&D capabilities and innovating products, process, and business models for overseas local markets. Our research reveals five different ways that the Chinese innovators go global:

- Building global digital ecosystems,
- Building global innovation networks,
- Establishing overseas innovation bases,
- Establishing technology outposts, and
- Exporting disruptive business models.

Global Digital Ecosystems: BAT

In recent years, Alibaba and its peers Baidu and Tencent (the BAT companies) strategically shifted focus to explore foreign markets. They gained hundreds of millions of users in international markets; established footholds in America, Europe, and Asia; made over 150 direct overseas investments and acquisitions; and rapidly spread pioneering payment, cloud, and communication technology services. Although BAT's internationalization is still in its early phase and data and performance are relatively limited, our research indicates that the BAT companies are adopting hybrid internationalization strategies. According to our research, Alibaba's internationalization consists of at least six components:[5]

- Internationalizing shared services such as Alipay, Alibaba Cloud, and Alibaba Cainiao Smart Logistics Network;
- Setting up overseas subsidiaries such as greenfield initiatives in Dubai, France, India, Japan, the Netherlands, and the United States;
- Expanding cross-border ecommerce by Alibaba.com, AliExpress, and Tmall Global;
- Creating an international reputation by listing on the New York Stock Exchange;
- Investing overseas with a diversified approach initially targeting the United States and nearby Southeast Asian markets; and
- Developing a global leadership academy to train the future ambassadors and overseas managers of Alibaba.

In terms of cross-border ecommerce, Alibaba's Tmall Global is highly successful as the dominant platform for shopping for overseas products with close to fifteen thousand brands from over sixty countries, 34 million sellers, and about 100 million buyers in over two hundred countries. Moreover, Alibaba's payment service Alipay succeeded in becoming a major payment alternative for Chinese consumers abroad and domestic consumers shopping overseas. Finally, Alibaba has invested in about forty overseas entities in ten countries and thirteen sectors, thereby significantly extending Alibaba's ecosystem footstep abroad and allowing the company to be close to overseas digital and related technology developments. By 2015, close to 10 percent of Alibaba's ecosystem revenues came from abroad.

In general, the BAT companies favor direct approaches, such as establishing subsidiaries, directly launching international products, and using investment and acquisition approaches to expand overseas, and they encounter strong competitive peer pressure (table 7.1). In terms of the

Table 7.1
The internationalization of the BAT companies

	Baidu	Alibaba	Tencent
Year of establishment	2000	1999	1998
Foreign market entry	2006 as Baidu Japan	1999 as Alibaba.com	2005 in South Korea
Number of offices	7 offices	5 offices	Not available
International users or shipments as of 2016	300 million monthly active users of mobile products by 2015	Tmall Global: 14,500 foreign brands and 3,700 product categories in over 60 countries AliExpress: 34 million sellers and 100 million buyers	270 million monthly active overseas users of WeChat by 2013[a]
Revenues overseas as of 2015	\$109 million (1.1%)	\$1.1 billion (9%)	\$1.3 billion (8%)
Cumulative overseas investments	15 deals	44 deals	79 deals
Focus countries and regions	Brazil, Egypt, India, Southeast Asia, United States	India, Southeast Asia, United States	India, Southeast Asia, United States
Investment focus	Acquisition	Mixed	Early phase

Note: a. This is the latest available information on international WeChat users. In later annual reports, Tencent provides only combined user numbers, suggesting that the growth of international users has stalled.
Source: Adapted and updated from Mark J. Greeven and Wei Wei, *Business Ecosystems in China: Alibaba and Competing Baidu, Tencent, Xiaomi, and LeEco* (Abingdon, UK: Routledge, 2018).

direct entry approach, Baidu was the first to start internationalization by initiating Baidu Japan in 2006. Instead of marketing its domestic core business search engine abroad, Baidu currently focuses on developing and promoting mobile software tools in overseas markets, avoiding competition with Google Search in other countries. By 2015, Baidu's mobile products had over 300 million monthly active users overseas. Tencent started by internationalizing the game business but also its new core WeChat. Competing with other successful instant messengers such as WhatsApp and Line, it has achieved over 350 million monthly active users in Europe, Southeast Asia, and the United States. Tencent's overseas revenue is also close to 10 percent of its total revenues.

In terms of investment approach, Tencent was the earliest overseas investor among the three BAT companies. It made its first overseas deal in 2005, whereas Alibaba's first was in 2010, and Baidu's first was in 2013. Tencent also was the most active BAT, with about eighty deals by 2016, particularly after 2013. Baidu was the least active BAT. Tencent is strategically focusing on early-phase investments. Pre A or A round investments account for over 40 percent of its overseas investments. Baidu and Alibaba have far fewer early-phase investments. Baidu is clearly not focusing on early-stage ventures abroad, and Alibaba is following a more hybrid strategy, with 16 percent in early-phase investments, similar to its domestic approach. Tencent appears more interested in pioneering technologies and new gaming ventures overseas. Baidu's investments have no specific sector focus, and Alibaba and Tencent have preferred sectors, such as ecommerce and the associated logistics for the former and games for the latter. Tencent also is an active overseas investor in social network services (SNS) and digital healthcare.

Fueled by abundant cash, investments, retained profits, a larger user base at home, a comprehensive digital architecture, and pioneering mobile technology, the BAT companies are not just exporting products and services or setting up subsidiaries but expanding their digital ecosystem globally. The BAT companies both expand organically (with subsidiaries and new products) and inorganically (with investments and acquisitions) to speed up the process of capturing international markets and technologies.

Global Innovation Networks

Chinese innovators, especially technology-driven enterprises, are building global innovation networks. These innovators first built a strong home base before internationalizing. Because these pioneers are established and often led by early generations of entrepreneurs, they are less familiar with foreign markets and have less experience abroad. In addition, because their businesses are more traditional and their channels are initially offline, these innovators have more operational boundaries to internationalize. Nevertheless, Chinese pioneering innovators are building up global innovation networks to support and boost their international business. In what follows, we describe this pattern with two illustrative cases—Huawei and Haier.

Huawei

Huawei's internationalization started in 1997, when it entered the largest emerging markets, Russia and Brazil. The move mostly failed, and by 2002, Huawei had its first historical negative growth in domestic markets. Facing a need to grow in the domestic market, it decided that it had to become a real international company to be able to survive. With the lessons learned from its first international trial, Huawei's strategy changed, and it entered markets in Africa and the Middle East. These regions did not yet include any emerging markets and were growing more slowly than Brazil, Russia, India, and China (the BRIC economies). Huawei succeeded in these markets by building on three success factors—overseas market analysis capability, a localized market approach, and an "iron triangle" sales team that includes a customer manager, a delivery manager, and a solution manager.[6] By 2005, its overseas revenues surpassed domestic revenues. A new internationalization phase had begun.

Since 2006, Huawei has explored European and American markets and acquired global clients, such as NTT and BT, and by doing so, it started to build a global network for operations, resources, and R&D. By 2017, Huawei had set up R&D centers in eight countries, all with a specific technology focus. For instance, in the United States, Huawei runs a New Technology Innovation Center and an Integrated Circuit Research Center; in India, the focus is on software research in its local Software R&D Center; a 5G Innovation Center in the United Kingdom focuses on next-generation telecommunication technology and standards; in Japan, Huawei leverages that nation's tradition of and widespread expertise in industrial engineering in its Industrial Engineering Research Center.

Besides R&D centers, Huawei also has initiated various research collaborations. It has set up twenty-eight overseas joint innovation centers since the start of this initiative in 2006.[7] These innovation centers are primarily with telecommunication operators (its main clients) but also with universities and foreign governments. By 2017, a hundred successful projects were completed through such innovation centers. For instance, Vodafone and Huawei started six joint innovation centers together. In fact, SingleRAN, one of the leading technology breakthroughs, originates from one of these joint innovation centers with Vodafone. The collaboration with Vodafone is continuous, and every few years since 2006, a new innovation center has been started. Besides direct collaborations, Huawei also established a joint innovation center for enterprise cloud technology in Canada with Carleton University and Telus, a provider of wireless and Internet services throughout Canada. A third leg in the joint innovation centers is foreign governments. In 2016, Huawei initiated a new innovation center with the Polish state-owned institute Poznan Supernetwork Computing Center. In Indonesia, Huawei started to collaborate with the Indonesian government's Ministry of Telecommunications to build an innovation and communication technology (ICT) center.

Huawei develops collaborations in telecommunication technology but also in several other promising fields, such as new energy, digital healthcare, and smart transportation. Huawei is developing a global R&D network in emerging and developed economies all over the world. It is leveraging the specializations of each region and country by focusing on specific fields in single locations. The deep immersion in local markets and wide network of R&D and innovation centers allow Huawei to develop locally relevant products while exploring global technology standards.

Haier

Haier's internationalization took off after it opened production facilities in Indonesia in 1996; the Philippines, Malaysia, and Yugoslavia in 1997; and Iran in 1998. A major step was the opening of a factory in the United States in 1999. This move was considered rather bold and brought Haier into direct competition with GE, Maytag, and Whirlpool. A domestic magazine even wrote an article to "remind Zhang Ruimin" about this seemingly reckless move, especially because of high labor costs and fierce competition. Normally, Chinese competitors would rather leverage their cheap labor advantage in China than establish factories in developed economies. Nevertheless, Zhang Ruimin saw the trend of globalization and the advantages of being close to the customer and having access to more advanced technologies and talent. Initially, Haier did not explicitly identify itself in the United States as a Chinese company, and the fact that Haier's products sold in the United States were truly "made in the U.S."

significantly increased acceptance by local customers. To fight off competition, Haier initially focused on only two niche markets—compact refrigerators and electric wine cellars. Zhang Ruimin's reputation almost immediately went international, and in 1999, the *Financial Times* named him one of the world's top thirty most reputable entrepreneurs. Eventually, Haier's bold move proved itself to be smart. From 1998 to 2001, Haier overseas' revenues increased from $60 million to $420 million. By 2016, overseas revenues were 56 percent of total revenues. Every minute, Haier sells 125 units overseas. It is one of the few Chinese companies that have fully localized operations outside of China.

In the following years, Haier built up production facilities in Algeria, Egypt, Jordan, Nigeria, Pakistan, South Africa, and Tunisia; acquired a Meneghetti factory in Italy; and began placing its products in European retail chains. By 2003, Haier was already the largest refrigerator producer worldwide, although at the lower end of the market. In a search to upgrade its brand and after the failed acquisition of Maytag, Haier launched its own high-end brand in 2006, Casarte. This new brand was independent from the original Haier brand, just as Lexus was separated from Toyota. The new brand received several design awards from *Business Week* and *Red Dot*. At the same time, Haier followed a strategy of acquiring technologies and brands and over the years acquired Fisher & Paykel, GE Appliances, and Sanyo (chapter 2). By 2017, Haier had three brands in Europe, three brands in the United States, and two brands in Japan, all focusing on different segments.

In order to support the multibrand approach worldwide, Haier built a global innovation capability with two components—R&D labs and the Haier Open Partnership Ecosystem (HOPE). First, Haier has five R&D labs in Australia, China, Europe, Japan, and the United States. After acquiring GE Appliances, Haier added another five R&D labs, totaling ten R&D labs worldwide. Since 2015, Haier's Asian R&D headquarters has been based in Japan, where it has invested over 400 million renminbi (RMB). In the past two years, it has applied technology and design patents such as a tandem shaft drive for washing machines, ultrasound local washing, and the technology that can keep frozen products fresh. Haier's R&D centers are platform-based and form an open system. Each Haier R&D center can operate independently but also can coordinate when needed. Not unlike Huawei, Haier's R&D centers have different technological specializations according to local technical advantages. For example, the U.S. scientific and technological innovation advantages are prominent, so Haier put its forward-looking R&D and creative platform in North America. Europe has advantages in technology transfer, incubation of products, and industrial design, so Haier put its core technology research and technical feasibility analysis in Europe. The Japanese center focuses on fine management and control advantages, and the office in China focuses on the industrialization of products.[8]

Second, Haier employs the HOPE initiative to tap into thousands of external experts in an online community (chapter 2) and aims to develop over half of its innovations by open innovation. Research and development personnel can interact with 2 million users through the Internet, acquiring a large amount of data on user needs. One interesting product that came out of the HOPE initiative is the Air Cube, which launched in 2014. It is a smart air quality control device with humidification and purification functions built into four modules that can be assembled by the user into eight different combinations. Users have a large degree of freedom to customize its air quality control within one device. Air Cube was developed by Haier and involved a team of 128 internal and external experts and researchers from eight countries, via the HOPE platform. After consulting with more than 9.8 million users from across the globe over a six-month period, the team eliminated 122 product sore points and developed a solution that met consumer needs.[9]

Haier did not only develop a full localized operation in overseas markets but also has a unique innovation approach overseas. In fact, Haier developed a platform through its ten R&D centers in combination with its open innovation platform, HOPE. As a truly global innovation network, Haier leverages talents and technologies to develop customer-driven innovations all over the world.

Emerging Overseas Innovation Bases

Another approach that emerges from our empirical research is that hidden champions appear to set up overseas innovation bases. Hidden champions often are already true market leaders with much or even most of their revenues coming from international markets. They have not set up comprehensive innovation networks worldwide and often are not looking (yet) for specific localization of their products. They are niche innovators, and their products often do not need to be locally customized. Therefore, their emerging overseas innovation bases focus more on being close to certain technology developments, building up an international intellectual property (IP) pool, and leveraging their presence outside of China to build their reputations.

Hikvision, for instance, is much younger than Huawei and Haier, but as a hidden champion, it has built up a global footprint, with roughly 30 percent of its revenues coming from overseas. Hikvision's internationalization predominantly consists of a global sales network and subsidiaries, collaborations with leading industry partners, and two recently established R&D centers in North America.[10] Hikvision also has established research partnerships, including joint labs, product development, and IP licensing. It has a joint lab with Texas Instruments in Hangzhou, does product development with Intel in China, and has an IP sharing agreement with ObjectVideo, a leading video analysis company in the United States. The newly established Montreal R&D Center focuses on engineering development for applications, and the second overseas facility in the United States, the Silicon Valley Research Institute, focuses on broader technology research. All in all, Hikvision has an overseas innovation base.

Another example in the new energy industry is the hidden champion Envision. Envision, founded in 2007, is a global top ten wind turbine manufacturer and the second largest in China. Besides wind turbine technology, Envision innovated Internet of things solutions that allow smart energy asset management—Wind OS for wind power, Apollo Platform for solar power, and total management of 50 gigawatts of new energy capacity globally.[11] The company is active in both domestic and overseas markets. Its wind power business has been successfully internationalized and developed in Europe and America, and its energy asset management system won large international clients such as Atlantic Power, Brookfield, and Patter, the largest independent new energy operator in the United States. Based on our 2016 interview with Envision's global R&D director, we conclude that Envision is a highly innovative new energy company that leverages its manufacturing experience in wind energy, solar energy, and smart energy asset management. Its overseas innovation capability is significant, especially considering the young age of the company. For instance, Envision's Global Innovation Centre in Denmark is staffed by forty engineers who focus on advanced turbine technology and are mostly locally hired from the Danish wind industry. It also has a battery storage R&D center in Osaka, Japan. To develop its energy Internet platform, it also founded a Global Digital Energy Innovation Lab and Center in Silicon Valley and Houston and a Digital Energy Software R&D Center in Nanjing. Recently, it received a European Union fund's Horizon 2020 citation for its technological research on a superconductive wind turbine project called EcoSwing. The fund is valued at around 100 million RMB and is used by a consortium including a German engineering institute called Eco5, the Dutch Twente University of Technology, and several other industry partners. A superconductive wind turbine prototype is planned to be launched in two years, and Envision claims that this revolutionary technology can lower the levelized cost of energy (LCOE) by 30 percent.[12] All in all, Envision has built up overseas research bases to develop specific technologies and be at the front end of new developments.

In a different industry, Yili Group is another good example of a hidden champion that has built an overseas innovation base. Yili is a privately owned company in the dairy industry that was established in 1993 and currently is number one in China with a 20 percent market share in 2016.[13] Besides a baby formula factory in New Zealand, Yili has no production facilities outside China, and it is currently focused on the domestic market. In 2014, the Yili R&D Center Netherlands was opened in Wageningen after setting up collaborations in Denmark, Germany, and Italy. These are collaborations with local institutions but not Yili's own R&D centers. The Wageningen R&D Center is the first such Center for Yili outside of China. Based on our interviews with the R&D director of the Yili R&D Center Netherlands, it becomes clear that the motivation for establishing an R&D center there is that Wageningen is world famous in the food business. It is in the center of the "Food Valley NL," which combines many institutions, R&D expertise, and technologies.[14] Yili's main goal is to obtain knowledge that can be used in the home market and help solve specific problems. The company wants to focus on five identified projects for which it has allocated a budget of 1 million euros—projects such as doing big data collection for food safety, establishing a mother milk bank, and creating dung treatment technology for large cow farms. Local partners include DSM, Friesland Campina, Nizo Food Research Institute, TNO, and Wageningen University. The focus is on R&D, with the center looking to serve headquarters with useful technologies and solutions. There are no plans to enter the Dutch market or start local production in Holland, though. The same applies to collaboration in other European countries such as Denmark, France, Germany, and the United Kingdom. The purpose is primarily to serve research and product development for China.

Technology Outposts

In addition to the above three innovation globalization approaches, our research reveals that small and medium-sized technology-driven ventures have implemented another interesting approach called *technology outposts*. Such technology ventures or underdogs (chapter 4) start internationalizing early, their employees often have elite international experience and education, and they do not hesitate to mobilize foreign resources. Considering the size of the ventures, their market focus, and their experience, the purpose of technology outposts is mostly to learn and monitor. In a way, the technology outposts are the first step in building up innovation networks worldwide. Pioneers like Huawei and Haier also started with single-technology outposts in the 1990s and since then have built up truly global innovation networks.

Weihua is a pioneering third-generation photovoltaic (PV) technology venture from Xiamen (chapter 4). Since its start, it has focused on developing a core technology (perovskite-based solar cells), and the founder has a strong science background as researcher for the Swiss Federal Laboratories for Materials Science and Technology (Eidgenössische Materialprüfungs- und Forschungsanstalt) (Empa).[15] Although the majority of its R&D efforts are in its Xiamen facilities, Weihua has started to reach out internationally and create technology outposts. In 2013, the company's first international technology collaboration with Merck, a leading German chemical and pharmaceutical company, allowed them to use state-of-the-art intellectual property from Merck in order to develop further. Weihua also collaborated with top universities and institutes in its technology field, including Empa, the École Polytechnique Fédérale de Lausanne (EPFL), and the Hong Kong Nano and Advanced Materials Institute (NAMI). These are the early beginnings of an innovation network that can leverage the international outlook of the venture.

Another example comes from industrial automation. Established by Zhuo Xu in 1997, Damon is a domestic private enterprise that started in Zhejiang province and now locates its headquarters, marketing department, and R&D center in Shanghai. In 2016, its revenues exceeded 400 million RMB. As one of the largest logistics component suppliers in China, the company offers integrated service for logistics automatic conveying and sorting systems for ecommerce, express delivery, pharmaceuticals, and apparel. In the Chinese market, Damon is twice the size of Interroll, the global market leader. The company has 150 patents, thirty global sales centers since 2011, four domestic manufacturing bases, and one overseas assembly factory. Success in today's China has been far from easy, however, and Damon has been a technology underdog for a while.

Damon's challenge was to compete with dominant foreign companies that had superior technology and with domestic companies that often were either state owned or publicly listed companies with abundant resources. A clear positioning in a growing niche is what often characterizes technology underdogs, and Damon is not an exception. But the thirst for learning at Damon sets it apart. The company learns by interacting with customers and has established partnerships for developing technology with international industry partners and institutions such as Ancra, CSi Industries, Egemin, EuroSort, Fraunhofer Institute, and Hokusho. These technology partnerships include technology transfer and licensing, but the collaboration with Fraunhofer Institute is R&D driven. Although Damon is far from having an established global R&D capability and its market is so far mostly domestic, Damon has created overseas technology listening posts to learn about and develop new technologies. Damon is not yet an international player and still resides under the radar, but it has the potential to grow into a global champion.

Chinese private small and middle-sized enterprises are not the only Chinese companies that have set up overseas technology outposts. In a study of Chinese R&D in the Netherlands, we observed at least eight Chinese state-owned firms that were establishing overseas technology outposts.[16] Companies such as XCMG (machinery and construction equipment), CIMC (transportation equipment), and XEMC (wind power equipment) have acquired (near) bankrupt Dutch technology companies in order to have access to new technologies and monitor new developments. Others, such as Jiangling Motors and Hisense (now divested), have established subsidiaries to focus on R&D in the Netherlands. Their key motives include access to technology and market access, but they focused mainly on exploring technology with limited transfer back to China. Chinese parent companies do not seek to transfer a specific technology and wrap up the subsidiary but instead wish to maintain the acquired companies as they are and tap into their capabilities to innovate, which include the harder technology development aspects but also the softer innovation management capabilities.

Born Global: Exporting Disruptive Business Models

A fifth approach we observe in our research is specific to next-generation enterprises. The changemakers and young ventures founded in the last few years are different from the technology-driven pioneers, hidden champions, and underdogs. The new generation has produced entrepreneurs who are younger, are digital natives, and often have overseas experience. The ventures that were founded by or focus on the 1990s generation are less cautious and more willing to take risks. Second, because most of the new ventures founded by this next generation of entrepreneurs are digital and online from the start, there are lower barriers to export their business models abroad. Operations and facilities are generally simple and small and can avoid many of the traditional offline challenges abroad. For instance, ventures such as Mobike and Didi Chuxing are exporting their disruptive business models (chapter 5). One major reason for this is the need to scale up as quickly as possible, especially considering the huge valuation of these ventures. We also see a lot of other next-generation ventures that perhaps have lower market valuations but export their disruptive business models from day one—the Chinese "born global" ventures (table 7.2).

Cheetah Mobile was established in 2010 as a merger of Kingsoft Security and Conew Image. The venture develops tools for mobile phone use, like browsers and tools for system cleaning, photo retouching, and battery management. In the category of nongames, Cheetah Mobile's apps are in the global top three of the Google Play android app market. Its product Clean Master reached number one in the mobile tool list in sixty-three countries in 2014, with a user score of 4.7, which is even higher rated than Google Maps and Facebook. Another app, Battery Doctor (which is a free tool), is in the top five on the app list in over fifty countries. The photo app Photo Grid is highly popular in the United States. In 2016, it launched its first social media product, a live streaming app called Live.me, and by January 2017, it was the top social app in the United States.[17] Cheetah was from day one a listed company due to the listing of Kingsoft Security on the New York Stock Exchange. It reported 4.6 billion RMB revenue in 2016, with over 65 percent coming from overseas. With a $1.6 billion valuation, it is in the same size category as our changemakers.

Another young but global venture is Yunmai, which was founded by a young entrepreneur, Wang Yang, in 2014. Wang Yang, born in 1990, is a serial entrepreneur and started his first company while still in high school. Before starting Yunmai, Wang founded two different ventures, one of which has been acquired by Cheetah Mobile. Moreover, the connection to Cheetah Mobile is significant because the founder of Cheetah Fu Sheng is also the angel investor of Yunmai. Yunmai produces a smart body fat scale, including affiliated app and health data cloud. Its first hardware prototype was launched within two months after founding and sold a thousand products within one month. In the first year, during the JD.com sales festival, Yunmai sold five thousand units in a single day, which was the best result in its product category. The product includes

Table 7.2
Chinese "born globals"

	Year of entry	Sector	Countries	Overseas market (percentage)	Size	Venture capital
Cheetah	2010	Mobile internet	Europe, North America	67% (2017)	5 billion RMB (2017)	Listed on NYSE
DJI	2006	UAV	Africa, Europe, Southeast Asia, North America	80%	18 billion RMB (2017)	C round
Musical.ly	2014	Social media	North America	100%	200 million users	Acquired by Toutiao in November 2017
NIO	2014	Automotive	Germany, United Kingdom, United States	Not available	Not available	Pre-IPO
Papaya	2008	Digital marketing	Europe, North America	100%	460 million RMB (2016)	Listed on the new OTC market
Yunmai	2014	Smart Home	Japan, North America, South Korea	30% (2016)	100 million RMB (2016)	B round

Source: Authors' research

several customer-centric innovations, such as usability on a carpet, customization according to Asia's physical features, and a mandatory daily alarm for reminding users to measure. Sold at a disruptive price setting, 99 RMB, it can undercut most competitors. Its overseas development was as quick as its domestic one. In 2015, it entered South Korea with smart social media marketing and was endorsed by Korean stars, leading to a top market position and the sale of 600,000 units in one year. Following the initial success, it entered markets in Canada, Japan, the United Kingdom, and the United States in 2016 and sold 30 million units outside China. In May 2017, Yunmai raised roughly $10 million in series B funding led by a Korean investor.[18]

In 2016, *Forbes* called musical.ly "America's hottest new app." In 2014, cofounders Zhu Jun (formerly of eBaoTech) and Yang Luyu launched musical.ly after their first venture in Shanghai—an Internet education video app—failed. The idea for musical.ly came from the founders' trip to Silicon Valley, where they observed a group of youngsters making short videos on the road.[19] Zhu Jun thought that they could do something similar but with music clips. In July 2014, after just one month of development time, the company launched the product simultaneously in the United States and China. The product is basically a database of songs, and users can video record themselves for 15 seconds to match the music. The resulting creation is then shared on all available platforms and can be forwarded, commented on, and liked. Every day since the launch, there have been five hundred to a thousand new downloads in the United States. Originally, the company expected that university students would be the first to adopt this product, but high school students have been the largest group of adopters. In April 2015, the first round of investment came from Cheetah Mobile with 5 million RMB. In July 2015, musical.ly became the top app in the United States, and it stabilized in 2016 at around an impressive 55 million monthly active users.

Papaya Mobile is a mobile social gaming platform that was established in 2008 by female entrepreneur Shen Si, who worked as a product manager at Google after receiving her degrees from Tsinghua University and Stanford University. In 2008, the smartphone market in China had not yet taken off, so it was too early to launch this social gaming platform in China. Shen Si decided to start in the U.S. and European markets. Papaya's main product was a mobile community that integrated hundreds of social games. By 2011, Papaya had over 23 million registered users, 80 percent from Europe and the United States. Because its community is mostly international, Papaya began to attract Chinese users, who used the platform to connect to new foreign friends. In order to monetize users, the company built an ad platform that was later spun out as a new advertising technology (ad tech) company. Chinese Internet companies that are expanding into global markets are seeing growing demand, and Papaya has gained many notable clients, including Alibaba, Baidu, Qihoo 360, and VIP.com. With a valuation of 2.2 billion RMB, Papaya Mobile is projecting a revenue of 1 billion RMB with 100 million RMB in net profit for 2016.[20] Despite its promising performance, Papaya is facing fierce competition in the Internet advertising field from companies like Xiaomi, which launched an ad platform called Xiaomi Marketing to make advertising a main source of revenue; Cheetah Mobile, which launched its global ad platform in June 2015; as well as the international incumbents, such as Facebook.

NIO is a truly global startup. Li Bin founded his company in November 2014 with the support of high-profile investors such as Baidu, Hillhouse Capital, JD, Lenovo, Sequoia Capital, Shunwei Capital, Temasek, and Tencent. By April 2018, the company employed four thousand employees, mostly engineers, from forty countries in four locations—London, Munich, Shanghai, and Silicon Valley. The company is headquartered in Shanghai, its product designs come from Munich, and its autonomous driving research and development team is based in San Jose in the United States. In 2016, the company's first global launch was the electric racing car NIO EP9 in 2016, and in December 2017, it launched the NIO SUV ES8. The first batch of licenses that Shanghai issued for road tests of driverless vehicles went to NIO. NIO is one of many electric vehicle (EV) startups in China but one of the few born globals.

DJI is a Chinese company that manufactures commercial and recreational unmanned aerial vehicles (UAV), accounting for 70 percent of the global consumer drone market. DJI was founded in 2006 by Wang Tao in his dormitory at the Hong Kong University of Science and Technology, where he was studying engineering. DJI did not sell any products during the first year of its existence and spent nearly all of its money on research and development and nothing on advertising. Two of the company's biggest shareholders are a family friend, Lu Di, and his former robotics professor, Li Zexiang. The contributions of these two individuals allowed him to survive during the lean beginning years. From 2010 to 2013, the number of employees grew from fifty to fifteen hundred, and the release of its first model, the Phantom, in 2013 quickly proved to be a success.

DJI now has offices in the Beijing, Germany, Hong Kong, Japan, the Netherlands, and the United States that provide customers with the necessary services. It has business partners for distribution all over the world and is selling drones on its own webpage. The main focus is on R&D, which takes 10 percent of revenues. In 2015, DJI received more than $100 million from well-known investors such as Accel Partners, Maison Capital, and Sequoia Capital, with a valuation of about $8 billion. DJI has built up many international partnerships—such as with Leica Geosystems, a global leader of measurement and reality capture technology—to develop the best camera incorporated in a drone, which helped DJI ride the drone wave easily in 2016. To stay ahead of its competitors, DJI is also trying to enter lucrative markets such as agriculture, science, search and rescue, and surveillance by investing in its software development kit, a platform that allows individuals and companies to program DJI drones to suit its needs. All in all, DJI has been exporting its UAVs with a disruptive business model from the start, and its achievement so far is impressive.

Challenges for China's Global Innovators

Despite the advantages held by Chinese innovators, we cannot ignore the many challenges that they face when globalizing their innovations. These challenges include licensing, technology transfer, joint innovation centers, and overseas research projects. We can distinguish three types of innovation globalization practiced by Chinese innovators according to the targeted countries:

- *Innovating in other emerging economies such as Brazil, India, and Russia:* Because there is significant institutional similarity between China and the other emerging countries, there are probably limited challenges for Chinese innovators who choose to innovate in these markets.
- *Innovating in developing economies in Africa, Eastern Europe, South America, and Southeast Asia (including Bangladesh, Nigeria and Vietnam):* Considering the limited economic prosperity and relevant resources such as talent in these regions, it is not really an option now for Chinese companies to innovate in these markets. The companies featured in this book have, indeed, not chosen to innovate in such economies. However, developing countries are good choices for production considering local cost advantages. Currently, under the pressure of the rapid growth of manufacturing costs in China, many Chinese companies are moving their factories from China to these countries. In the longer term, R&D capability might

be developed connected to local production capability, similar to how multinationals transformed their capability in China from only production in the beginning to innovating locally later and even innovating locally for global.

- *Innovating in developed countries such as North America and Western Europe:* Developed countries are the most interesting because they offer most possible gain as well as the most challenges for Chinese companies. With the most sophisticated markets, richest talent pools, finest scientific research, and most creative technology invention, developed economies are fertile soil for innovation. In our research, we found that Chinese innovators currently are mostly globalizing their innovation into developed countries.

Here we summarize the key challenges for Chinese innovators that are globalizing innovation in developed countries:

- *Global talent development:* In order to globalize their innovation activities, Chinese innovators need to develop a global talent pool. They can either develop talent by themselves, such as by recruiting local fresh graduates, or lure experienced talent away from competitors. Either way, there are many challenges in competing with established local firms and other Western multinationals to hire top talent.
- *Limited intellectual property (IP) management experience:* The IP strategies of Chinese innovators are probably not sufficient to deal with patent management and engage in patent wars with overseas incumbents.
- *Negative reputation of Chinese companies:* Despite the successes of Chinese innovators such as Haier and Huawei, the overall negative impression of Chinese products and companies abroad cannot be underestimated. The stereotypes that the Chinese lack creativity and original ideas will be barriers for gaining relevant resources for innovation.
- *Locally embedded business models:* Many of the business models of Chinese changemakers are built around locally embedded ecosystems of companies, products, services, and technologies. Building up such locally embedded systems overseas, even if possible, will take at least as long as it did in China and probably longer.
- *Building up a fundamental technology capability:* Although the strong customer focus innovation approach in China works well because Chinese companies understand Chinese customers very well,

abroad this will not work as easily. In fact, a highly customer-driven R&D culture may become a barrier for building up a fundamental technology capability abroad.

- *Unfamiliar institutional environment:* Chinese companies have little overseas market experience in general, despite the latest generation of entrepreneurs who mostly have international experience. Thus, they may not be familiar with the institutional environment and industry regulations, such as in information and communication technology, the Internet, and new energy, which are crucial for conducting successful innovation activities.
- *Separation of production and R&D for hardware companies:* Most Chinese innovators do not have production facilities in foreign countries. Doing R&D without a manufacturing function nearby will prove to be a big challenge for Chinese hardware innovators.
- *Language and cultural distance:* It may sound trivial, but language is actually the greatest barrier for Chinese companies that are seeking to internationalize. The cultural distance between China and the West may also cause problems. Without developing a real cross-cultural capability, Chinese innovators will face significant drawbacks with their overseas innovation practices.

Concluding Remarks

Although foreign companies have been discovering that China has great potential as an innovation economy, Chinese companies have been exploring international markets for innovation opportunities as well. In particular, three insights stand out:

- Chinese innovators—not only the pioneers and hidden champions but also the young underdogs and changemakers—are going global.
- Chinese innovators follow five different routes when globalizing their innovation capabilities—global digital ecosystems, global innovation networks, overseas innovation bases, technology outposts, and the exporting of disruptive business models.
- Chinese innovators face significant challenges in globalizing their innovations. So a sudden boost of new innovative competitors from China is not expected, but an increasingly deeper involvement of Chinese innovators in global innovation is a foreseeable trend.

8

China's Emerging Innovators: Lessons from Alibaba to Zongmu

China's innovators have emerged as significant competitors in a variety of business sectors inside and outside China. In the last decade, many incumbents and multinationals have been taken by surprise, and newcomers have eagerly joined the game. China's innovators include not only pioneers but also hidden champions, underdogs, and changemakers. In this concluding chapter, we discuss insights into and lessons learned from China's innovators based on a set of managerial questions. These questions were generated from our interactions with business leaders and experts, when we asked them, "What would you want to know about China's innovators?"

- Who are China's innovators?
- What is unique about China's innovators?
- Can China's innovators replicate their successes outside China?
- What are the challenges for China's innovators?
- What should multinationals do to deal with China's innovators?
- Are China's innovations sustainable?
- How is China changing the global innovation arena?

Who Are China's Innovators?

Our research identified four types of innovators in China. Table 8.1 summarizes key features of these four types of China's innovators.

The *pioneers* are companies that began from zero and became large, successful, innovative national or international enterprises. Their revenues are at least $10 billion (USD) in revenues and in the national top three in terms of market share. Most of these enterprises were established by grassroots, first-generation of entrepreneurs (chapter 1) who

Table 8.1
Four types of innovators in China

	Market	Experience	Size	Visibility
Pioneer	Mass	Incumbent	>$10 billion in revenue	High
Hidden champion	Niche	Incumbent	<$5 billion in revenue	Low
Underdog	Niche	Newcomer	<$60 million in revenue	Low
Changemaker	Mass	Newcomer	>$1 billion in valuation	High

Source: Authors' research.

built their companies over three or four decades. A special subgroup of the pioneer innovator group is the Internet entrepreneurs. They were pioneers in industries that began to emerge at the end of the 1990s and have been transformed into digital giants in China and the rest of the world.

The *hidden champions* are midsized niche market leaders. Their revenues do not exceed $5 billion, and they are in national and often the global top three in terms of market share. The founders of these companies are almost invisible and maintain low public profiles, and the companies have low levels of overall public awareness, although the recent successes of, for instance, Goldwind, Hikvision, and Mindray have gradually increased their media attention.

The *underdogs* are small and medium-sized enterprises (smaller than $60 million in revenue or a thousand employees, according to the standard set by China's Ministry of Industry and Information Technology) that were established after 2000, are driven by innovative technology, and own significant intellectual property. The founders are often low-profile scientists and engineers with overseas educations and work experiences. Their companies are the smallest of our set of innovators, but they are, by far, the largest group in quantity. Their specific niche focus, low-profile founders, and small size make them almost invisible in national and international public media. Figure 8.1 compares the media appearances of the four types of innovators.

The *changemakers* are unicorns (larger than $1 billion market valuation) that are driven by digital innovations, have significant venture capital support, and were recently established (established after 2007). These companies are the youngest of our set of innovators, but their visibility is almost equal to that of the experienced incumbent pioneers.

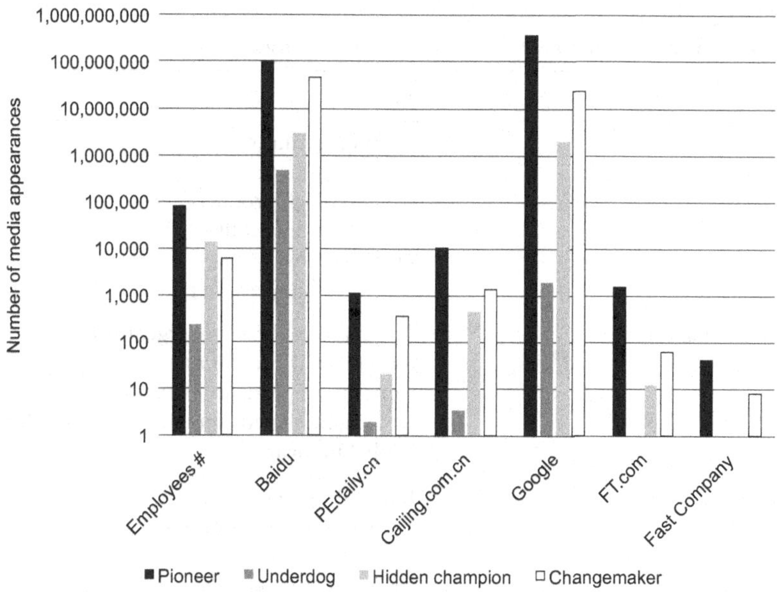

Figure 8.1
The media exposure of four types of Chinese innovators
Source: Authors' database, search date May 10, 2017.

These companies focus on creating digital products and disrupting existing markets rather than opening up new technological fields or sectors.

The Key Themes of China's Innovators

The four types of innovators in China are not only different in characteristics such as age, size, market focus, and visibility. Our research has identified key themes for each, as summarized in table 8.2. First of all, these themes help us better understand what and how these companies innovate. For instance, the hidden champions excel at product innovation, and the pioneers are strong in organizational innovation. Second, comparing these themes helps us understand that there is no such thing as *the* Chinese innovator. The differences between these four types of innovators are striking and warrant different competitive approaches. For instance, the changemakers move quickly because speed is more important than profitability to them, and the underdogs focus on technological breakthroughs to outcompete other players in the market. Third, the themes help us understand the competitive advantages held by these companies and the ways that international companies can either leverage

Table 8.2
The key themes of the four types of Chinese innovators

	Themes
Pioneer	Technology innovation Agile organizing Good enough product innovation Innovation by acquisition Business ecosystems Social media marketing
Hidden champion	Rapid growth from divergent roots Strong R&D capability Continuous product innovation Leveraging the advantage of being hidden Global innovators
Underdog	Elite entrepreneurs Early international exposure Under the radar Cutting-edge technology Niche innovation
Changemaker	New-generation entrepreneur Digital disruption Fueled by global venture capital High visibility Need for speed

Source: Authors' research.

those advantages in collaborations, invest in the advantages, or compete with these advantages in domestic or international markets. For instance, the hidden champions accumulated technological advantages as well as a strong position in their niche, and the changemakers have high visibility and capital support.

An Iceberg of China's Innovators

When we look at the numbers of innovators, a striking pattern emerges. There are about thirty to forty pioneers with global impact and around 200 to 250 hidden champions. These innovators have been around for many years and have built up experience and reputation. However, this is just the top of the iceberg. In 2016, there were an estimated eighty unicorns in China, of which the majority were digital changemakers. Therefore, we estimate that there are around fifty changemakers—that is, innovators with the potential to become global champions in a relatively short time frame. There also are tens of thousands of underdogs. A careful estimation would include only those that participate in technology-focused startup competitions, which already number over fifty thousand. If we look at specific sectors, such as the solar industry, fifteen hundred new technology ventures were established in 2015 alone. In the case of big data, the national industry base in Guiyang province has over seventeen hundred registered technology ventures. Therefore, over a hundred thousand technology ventures of various sizes are competing in China's market under the radar. They are a true iceberg of innovators in China.

What Is Unique about China's Innovators?

We acknowledge the unique features of China's innovation ecosystem (chapter 1). First of all, the continuous changes in the market combined with regional diversity have created a strong sense of urgency for Chinese companies to innovate. Without continuously developing new products, services, processes, business models, and technologies, Chinese companies could easily lose the competitive game or miss emerging opportunities. This need to innovate did not arise from international pressure or foreign firms in China. It is a grassroots driver that should not be ignored. Second, the conditions for innovation in China are good and improving (chapter 1). Even the often-quoted disadvantage of weakly protected intellectual property rights is no longer a critical limitation to China's companies. Access to critical resources such as capital, talent, and knowledge is good, although geographically concentrated. It is against this unique background that we assess Chinese innovators and their approaches to innovation.

Thriving on Uncertainty: Six Actions

Chinese innovators have developed a specific way of innovating. Chapter 6 outlines six approaches that characterize the Chinese ways of innovation. Here we summarize the key features with examples:

- *Swarm innovation:* The term *swarm innovation* refers to the collective pursuit of opportunities by entrepreneurs rather than an individualized focus on differentiation and unique advantages. Large numbers of Chinese innovators, particularly underdogs, swarm around specific emerging opportunities. For instance, after Alipay's launch and success, other online and offline players jumped into this opportunity, and by late 2016, over 250 licenses for third-party payment services had been issued by the Chinese government. In a similar way, dozens of new bike-sharing companies, many extremely local, popped up around the country after the initial successes of Ofo and Mobike.

- *Tinkering:* Fast trials and fast learning have led entrepreneurs to put good enough products and services on the market rather than develop close to perfect products. With continuously shifting demands and the rising sophistication of customers, it is close to impossible for innovators to follow the traditional logic of market research that calls for focus groups, stage gating, and linear planning of new product development in broad portfolios of strategic emerging business opportunities. Rather, Chinese innovators tend to tinker (or in Karl Weick's term, use bricolage) in their organizations by having an intimate knowledge of available resources, doing careful listening to and observing of the customer, having confidence in their ideas, and seeking iterated and self-correcting feedback. For instance, Xiaomi launched its MIUI operating system well before it was ready and after the launch had weekly iterations to upgrade it. Similarly, Mobike initially put inferior bikes on the street to share, learned what consumers wanted, and then quickly upgraded the bikes with technological innovations such as solid tires, shaft drive transmission instead of traditional chain transmission, smart locks with telecommunication, and embedded GPS and alarm modules with self-power generation by bicycling.
- *A strong customer focus:* Focusing on customers led to a deep market understanding and a focus on local and special needs rather than standardization and mass manufacturing. Chinese innovators are highly aware of specific and sometimes special customer needs. Partly due to the large market size, niche markets have a different scale in China, but Chinese innovators have been willing to customize and take an extra step for customers. For instance, Hikvision has the world's largest variety of smart security cameras for any type of application, from small street shops and baby rooms to Amazon-sized warehouses and airport security. Similarly, the famous Goodbaby baby strollers have such a wide assortment that even foreign parents have been convinced about their customer-focused development.

- *Quick technology upgrades:* Chinese innovators are often in a "red queen race" as they try to stay ahead of competitors.[1] The struggle for survival in a highly competitive environment often encourages innovators to recombine existing technologies just enough to adapt to the changing business environment. Many innovators innovate to keep their current competitive position rather than to stay ahead of the crowd. Although Chinese innovators, especially pioneers and hidden champions, operate at a lower-end technological base, they continuously push for incremental and basic R&D to upgrade their technology quickly. For instance, hidden champions like Mindray continuously upgrade their products to keep their leading niche position. This does not usually give them a new advantage, but it does allow them to stay competitive enough to survive. Moreover, the ability to upgrade technology quickly suggests that even though the majority of Chinese innovators are not radical technology innovators, they are quickly learning and catching up. The underdogs are the significant exception to this rule because they aim for developing cutting-edge technology from the very beginning.
- *Rapid centralized decision making:* More intervention by the founder and boss ensures a less formal and faster process for making decisions and results in flexibility and willingness to resolve problems quickly. Chinese innovators are highly decisive and sometimes even ignore potentially relevant information just for the purpose of making quicker decisions. Although consensus building may have certain social benefits, Chinese innovators are more focused on speed. For instance, Geely's transformation from motorbikes to cars took only one year. BYD's high-speed but risky move into electric vehicles was driven by Wang Chuanfu's decisiveness. Lenovo's new global customer buyer system allows processes to run in parallel, thereby speeding up the whole purchasing process. Haier's new product development cycles are shorter than most competitors' cycles. For instance, the smart cool cooker hood took only four months from the initial market need to the product launch.
- *A network mindset:* A mindset that quickly connects and disconnects with external partners for opportunities and resource mobilization is widespread among Chinese innovators. Whereas casual observers might find these innovators sometimes random, naive, and uninformed, they are always on the lookout for relevant resources

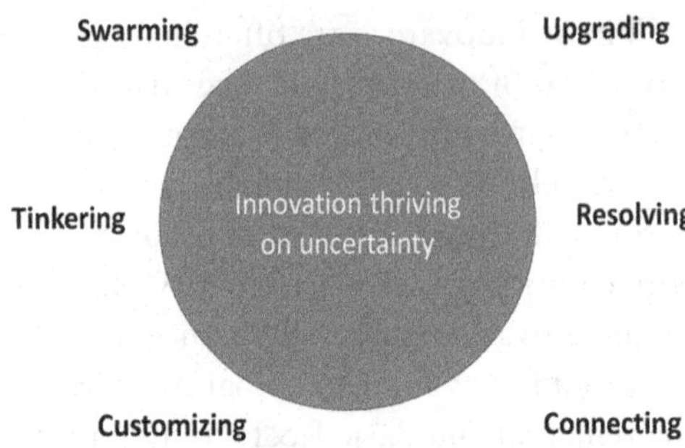

Figure 8.2
Innovation thriving on uncertainty: Six actions
Source: Authors' research.

to integrate or recombine. A network mindset allows them to adapt more quickly to changes in the environment because they have more information and have it at an earlier stage. For instance, the whole organizational logic of the BAT companies (Baidu, Alibaba, and Tencent) is built on a network mindset—a business ecosystem of interdependent businesses. Both large organizations and underdogs display a network mindset. For instance, Weihua developed collaborations at an early stage of its product development and market entry.

Although we acknowledge that individually these six ways to innovate are not new to China, the ways that Chinese innovators combine them make for a unique approach. Figure 8.2 illustrates the six actions that represent the approaches that Chinese innovators take that allow them to thrive on uncertainty. Perhaps the most unique feature of the ways that Chinese companies innovate is that they thrive on uncertainty rather than manage or fight it. To some extent, they prefer a dynamic environment because they are better equipped to compete in such environment. If we take a more traditional perspective on innovation, we cannot explain why Chinese companies innovate and do it so well. For instance, perspectives such as stage gating and an innovation systems approach assume relatively stability and a reduction of complexity. In contrast, our research shows a different perspective on innovation and identified actions that allow organizations to thrive on uncertainty. These findings may prove useful not only for other emerging markets but also for Chinese companies competing in developed markets. Recent characterizations of the developed markets of Western Europe and the United States have started to include terms such as VUCA (volatility, uncertainty, complexity, and ambiguity) due to digital disruptions, and Chinese innovators may be well positioned—maybe even better positioned than European and American companies—to survive and thrive in such an environment.

The Chinese Innovators' Way Compared to Silicon Valley and the Asian Tigers

To compare China's approaches to innovation with other innovation ecosystems, we selected Silicon Valley and the Asian Tigers as two extreme cases. We compare the six ways of Chinese innovation as described earlier in this chapter and in chapter 6 with broad characterizations of innovation in Silicon Valley and the Asian Tigers. Both are successful stories of how regions were able to emerge quickly as global hot spots for innovation.

Silicon Valley is home to many of the world's largest high-tech corporations and includes the headquarters of thirty-nine businesses listed in the Fortune 100 and thousands of startup companies. Silicon Valley also accounts for a third of all of the venture capital investment in the United States, which has helped it to become a leading hub and startup ecosystem for high-tech innovations and scientific development.[2] Key ingredients include government support, the presence of rich people, and technology talent. The culture of Silicon Valley is often described as consisting of a particular entrepreneurial mindset that includes acceptance of failure, experimentation, hero entrepreneurs dreaming big, technology-driven product innovations, novel business models, strong labor mobility, and strong self-reinforcing feedback networks between investors, entrepreneurs, and customers.

Similar to Silicon Valley innovators, Chinese innovators like to tinker and network. Both have strong local ecosystems with company magnets, top universities, talent, and capital—that is, strong geographies of innovation. Overall, however, the Chinese innovators' way is rather different from the tradition in Silicon Valley. One key difference is that companies from Silicon Valley tend to compete on differentiation and strong technology, trying to be the unique disruptor. Chinese innovators, on the contrary, are often following the "swarm," which allows collective innovation to occur when one emerging opportunity attracts many entrepreneurs and companies in China. Second, Silicon Valley innovators often start with cutting-edge technology and then promote the new product to the market. They also have developed a strong culture and capability for marketing and promotion. Chinese innovators, on the other hand, are far more customer driven and listen to current market demands. This is not surprising given that that the Chinese market is still underdeveloped and overall consumer behavior is highly unpredictable. Third, Silicon Valley innovators compete fiercely on intellectual property (IP), whereas Chinese innovators are slowly adopting protection measures for IP. Fourth, Silicon Valley is more culturally diverse, and Silicon Valley innovators tend to be more globally oriented with strong international ambitions. Chinese innovators tend to be more local, even in the first-tier innovation ecosystems of Beijing, Guangzhou, Shanghai, and Shenzhen. A unique feature of Chinese innovators is that they almost always go local for local.

The Asian Tigers and their innovation economies are different from Silicon Valley and mainland China. Hong Kong (China), Singapore, South Korea, and Taiwan underwent rapid industrialization, technological innovation, and development and also maintained exceptionally high growth rates (in excess of 7 percent to 8 percent a year). These four countries and regions invested heavily in their infrastructure and in developing the intellectual abilities of their human resources, fostering and retaining talent to help further develop and improve their respective countries and regions. The Asian Tigers are mostly state-organized business systems where the state plays a significant role in aligning economic interests and allocating resources such as talent and capital. For instance, South Korea's business landscape is characterized by large *chaebol*, or business groups, that coordinate a variety of resources and are mostly self-sufficient in terms of the activities they control. These companies are highly centralized and grow by related diversification, often vertically integrating the value chain. With largely self-sufficient and integrated companies, they have limited external networks. A strong culture of paternalism and long-term employer and employee commitments is significantly different from Silicon Valley and China's fluid labor markets and quick decision making. The company leaders are closely connected to the political elite with well aligned interests and are highly dependent on state banks and agencies. The Asian Tigers' way is one of coordinated, state-led capitalism. Hong Kong, with its famous laissez-faire policies, seems an exception, but the role played by the British colonial government in creating infrastructure, the rule of law, and the rules of competition tends to be overlooked. The state too has played an essential role in the rise of the Hong Kong Tiger. Furthermore, Hong Kong also has its small number, a dozen or so, of dominant business families that operate sprawling business empires.

The Chinese innovator's way is similar to the Asian Tiger's way in several aspects. First, both follow a network and integrated ecosystem approach for organizing innovation. Both Asian Tigers and Chinese innovators strongly coordinate business activities. Second, both started at the low end of the market but quickly upgraded technology as well as market positioning, first competing on cost and process before competing on technology and knowledge. Third, the time lines are similar: it took the Asian Tigers and Chinese innovators roughly two to three decades to emerge. Fourth, both experience and experiment with renewing organizational and management models. Finally, similar to the Asian Tigers' governments, China's government plays an important role in supporting Chinese innovation by providing direct policy and subsidy support but also indirectly by shielding foreign competitors in certain sectors.

Nevertheless, Chinese innovators also differ markedly from the innovators among the Asian Tigers. First, the contextual differences are significant, including market size, global impact, political system, and nature of competition. Second, the Asian Tigers have much less entrepreneurial activity and far fewer entrepreneurs compared to China. Swarm innovation is not possible in such a context. Third, experimentation and tinkering are less accepted in the Asian Tigers because there is a strong coordination of business activities and less acceptance of failure. Even though in principle China's government is not democratic and is less favorable to a free-market economy, the reality is that the Chinese market is highly competitive with lots of room for experimentation. In fact, the Chinese government has encouraged experimentation in both its markets and its institutions, such as with special economic zones and free-trade areas. Finally, China's state banks and agencies are largely disconnected from the private sector. Although the government is certainly present in private-sector activities, the direct alignment, as in the case of the Asian Tigers, is less obvious.

Comparing the Chinese innovators' way to the Silicon Valley way and the way of the Asian Tigers, we find both similarities and differences. However, the differences stand out, and the Chinese approach to innovation is distinct. The following section deals with the important questions of whether and to what extent Chinese innovators can replicate their success abroad and which features are China specific and which ones can be exported.

Can China's Innovators Replicate Their Success outside China?

Chinese innovators are looking over the border and starting to develop business abroad (chapter 7). Although the pioneers and hidden champions

Table 8.3
Replicating the Chinese innovators' way abroad?

Market advantages	**Cannot find outside China**	**Can leverage outside China**
	Scale of the economy Speed of growth Protectionism Weak IP	Strong home base Capital availability Supportive government Sense of urgency
Innovation approaches	**Difficult to replicate**	**Possible to replicate**
	Swarm innovation A strong customer focus A network mindset	Tinkering Quick technology upgrades Rapid centralized decision making

Source: Authors' research.

have had more time to experience and adapt to foreign markets, the underdogs and changemakers are new to the game. To what extent have the incumbents replicated their approach to innovation outside China? And how likely is it that the newcomers will be able to achieve similar success abroad?

We propose that Chinese companies can certainly replicate parts of their success outside China. However, certain conditions and approaches are difficult to export to other markets. Table 8.3 summarizes the considerations and limitations of replicating the Chinese innovators' way abroad.

Some drivers of success of the Chinese innovators are clearly China specific. First, the scale of China's economy and large customer base cannot be compared to almost any other economy. India is the only other market that is as large as China's, but India is not yet seeing a booming consumer economy. Second, the growth speed of China's economy is not unprecedented (the Asian Tigers also saw rapid growth), but considering the size of the economy and its continuous expansion, there is not likely to be another large market that will be able to grow as rapidly as China. Growth speed and growth dynamics are key drivers for innovation, both in terms of creating a sense of urgency and creating a market that is more forgiving of failure (chapter 1). Third, the Chinese government has defined several industries as being of particular interest, including new energy, healthcare, the Internet, and aerospace. These industries receive preferential treatment, receive subsidies, and are often more difficult to enter for foreign companies. Although China's Internet economy certainly developed for reasons other than the Chinese firewall that limits foreign competitors, it is a prime example of protectionism that is also found in other industries. Finally, because China's regulatory system is still under development, enforcement of regulation is still relatively weak. For instance, the enforcement of IP regulation is still limited, and that creates less pressure for Chinese companies to have their IP in order. Xiaomi suffered from this when entering India in 2014 because at that time it did not have a strong IP base, violated multiple IP claims, and was sued by Ericsson immediately.

Some drivers of success are China specific but give Chinese innovators an advantage abroad. First, many Chinese companies have a strong home base. The large domestic market shields them from direct failure, and they can afford to lose the first step abroad to experiment and learn. Second, generally speaking, Chinese companies are not tight on capital and are willing to spend on venturing into new markets. The foreign market presence often gives them domestic reputation effects that go beyond revenues from foreign markets. Third, the support of the government and its facilitation of both innovation (such as in Made in China 2025 and the National Medium- and Long-Term Plan for the Development of Science and Technology for 2006 to 2020) and internationalization (such as the Go Abroad and One Belt One Road policies) at least do not create barriers. Finally, beyond the domestic reputation effects of going abroad, intense domestic competition is also forcing Chinese companies to go abroad. For the pioneers and hidden champions, the international markets have always been a necessity for expansion, but we also see this trend with the younger innovators like the underdogs and changemakers.

Three of the six ways of innovating elaborated on in chapter 6 and earlier in this chapter appear to be not difficult to replicate abroad. Tinkering is a way of experimenting and rapid iteration that is not uncommon abroad. The Silicon Valley way is also based largely on this way of innovating, and popular concepts such as lean startup, effectuation, and agile development are all accepted in European and American markets. Quickly upgrading technology and starting from a low or middle end are not difficult to implement abroad, particularly because Chinese companies can leverage their China advantages in terms of technology talent and labor costs in combination with government R&D support in some cases. Speed of decision making can be replicated abroad because this is mostly an internal process.

However, three of the innovators' ways are more difficult to replicate abroad. Although a highly customer-focused approach to new markets may help Chinese companies to gain initial market share quickly and create legitimacy, it will not be a long-term, sustainable advantage. The size of most overseas markets is too small to follow an approach that customizes too deeply or enters too many very small niche markets, so keeping this approach may be too costly. Moreover, swarm innovation will be unlikely to succeed outside China. The quantity of enterprises abroad is far too small, so local competitors, particularly in developed market economies, will compete mostly on differentiation rather than collectively pursue the same opportunity. One example in location-based services (LBS) is the dominance of one online food delivery platform, Thuisbezorgd, in Belgium, and Germany, and the Netherlands, with only a handful of competitors. Finally, a network mindset works anywhere in the world in general, but the Chinese way of quickly connecting and disconnecting will pose challenges with foreign partners. Developed market economies, in particular, already have well established local networks, and it will not be easy for new players to become part of, let alone lead, such networks and ecosystems.

The key difference between the large emerging economies and developed economies is scale and speed.[3] China is not unique in its large home base and speed of development. However, innovators in India face more stringent resource and technology constraints and more constrained affordability issues for Indian consumers. The innovation approach of Chinese companies may prove useful for Indian innovators as well. In particular, with limited resources, an approach of tinkering solutions, rather than building perfect products, may work well. Moreover, with limited resources and affordability issues for Indian consumers, a network or platform mindset may allow Indian innovators—and consumers—to mobilize better external resources and collectively build innovative products and services. Considering the significant presence of multinationals and possible spillover and joint R&D creation with Indian companies, a network mindset appears to apply. A focus on quick upgrading and increased speed of decision making (chapter 6) also may match well with the Indian reality. Finally, India is often considered the home of "frugal innovation," which in many ways translates into highly customer-focused approaches to innovation for large groups of consumers who could not consume a wide variety of products and services before. Such competition with nonconsumption is facilitated by the Chinese innovators' way.

It is not likely that Chinese innovators can follow the exact same approach in different markets where they face different customers and competitors. The question is whether Chinese companies can adapt to other approaches or whether they can find a competitive advantage by following a diverging approach to innovation. Just as in China, the advantages of MNCs include not being local and Chinese but being different and foreign. Competing on quality, technology, and foreign reputation still gives MNCs a clear advantage in the Chinese markets. So if Chinese companies abroad follow a different approach to innovation and business development than local companies do, maybe they will have a competitive advantage abroad. In fact, the Chinese innovators' capability to thrive on uncertainty and change may prove to be a key advantage. Their excellent learning capability (chapter 6) makes Chinese innovators more like a chameleon rather than a dragon.

What Are the Challenges for China's Innovators?

The challenges for innovation in China are widely discussed in academia and books.[4] Besides the challenges of protecting intellectual property (chapter 1), an important risk of innovation is failure. There is a large amount of evidence on the failure of innovation initiatives, and such failure is not uncommon in China. In other words, the largest risk of innovation for China's innovators is the failure of their innovation activities. Our interviews indicate that Chinese entrepreneurs have a significant sense of risk. In line with the outcomes of the Global Entrepreneurship Monitor, where the fear of failure by entrepreneurs is higher on average than the global and regional average, entrepreneurial activity brings large risks of failure.[5] This is not surprising considering the high levels of dynamism and uncertainty in China. To some extent, China's innovators have mitigated these risks by adopting approaches to innovation such as tinkering, a networked way of resource mobilization, and quick decision making. Although the first two approaches focus on the process of innovating, the third focuses on decision making based on the success or failure of the innovation. Our interviews suggest that entrepreneurs are quick decision makers and follow a principle of affordable loss rather than predictable revenues.

Here we focus on the challenges for the innovators, at the company level, as summarized in table 8.4, other than risks of imitation and failure. The challenges for the four types of Chinese innovators are different,

Table 8.4
Challenges for China's innovators

Pioneers	Talent development Overseas competition Building up fundamental technology capabilities Succession challenges
Hidden champions	Technology disruption New players from emerging markets Limited pressure of innovation Innovating the niche
Underdogs	Commercializing niche technology Under the radar Betting on one horse Limited legitimacy
Changemakers	Creating a sustainable competitive advantage Horizontal diversification An internal management system Too much capital Unpredictable regulations

Source: Authors' research.

and a deeper understanding of what challenges these innovators face will help us assess their sustainability.

The challenges for the pioneers include talent development, particularly global talent development. We have seen Alibaba's Global Leadership Academy and Haier's 360 Talent Engine as examples of how pioneers are trying to develop and mobilize global talents for their organizations. Second, competition in foreign markets is different (local rules must be followed), but regulatory challenges are not to be underestimated. Third, a clear challenge is to build up a real fundamental technology capability, especially because the pioneers grew up at a time when developing technology capability was less important than grasping the market. They are increasingly challenged by changemakers—digital disruptors. Finally, most of them are still first-generation founders, and their succession challenge should not be neglected. Ma Yun has retreated as CEO since 2013 but remains as the brain of Alibaba even today. Huawei's Ren Zhengfei is still the real boss next to his rotating CEO, keeping a veto right on any decisions made by the rotating CEO. Baidu's Li Yanhong is notorious for not being willing to let go of his CEO role.

The biggest challenge for the hidden champions is technology disruption, particularly because most of these hidden champions are not competing on high-end technology as the German hidden champions tend to do. Second, new players from other emerging economies such as India and Southeast Asia could repeat the history. Third, being an industry leader can come with arrogance and less pressure. Fourth, they need to keep innovating in the niche. For example, Hikvision is forced to become visible when diversifying into new businesses like family security solutions, logistic robotics, and industrial drones. But they lose their hidden status advantage by doing so.

The challenges for the underdogs include finding good business models for commercializing their innovations. Market validation and attracting capital and talent are key challenges given their low legitimacy and under-the-radar status. Moreover, underdogs find it difficult to pivot their businesses. Most of them are betting on one horse, and the importance of the market's acceptance of their technology is significant. However, due to swarm innovation patterns, they have a lot of competitors, and it will be difficult to differentiate themselves in the market. Finally, there are barriers to accessing knowledge due to language, Internet limitations, and overall limited legitimacy for attracting talent.

The challenges for the changemakers include creating a sustainable advantage. Growth and speed are not issues, and the changemakers excel at disrupting markets. But knowing when to monetize the business is always a challenge. We have seen in China a lot of winner-take-all competitions, such as the Didi/Kuaidi and Mobike/Ofo situations. Another challenge is knowing how to diversify after they win the competition. Many of these changemakers are in narrow verticals like food delivery, social ecommerce for young women, taxi hailing, and bike sharing. Diversification is inevitable in the long term. Third, a typical problem for companies that grow quickly is knowing how to build a mature internal managerial system. For instance, Ofo suffered from several news articles exposing its internal financial chaos in May 2017, and another internationally famous changemaker, Uber, experienced a similar drawback. Founder Travis Kalanick had to step down in June 2017 to respond to internal managerial disorder. Fourth, changemakers sometimes may attract too much capital, which pushes them to make more mistakes and lose their sense of urgency, which are valuable qualities for startups. Finally, they need to know how to deal with regulatory requirements and make the required changes. The changemakers are playing the game to disrupt traditional industries, such as public transportation, banking, and healthcare. Many of these traditional industries are state managed or controlled, and the government has often an emerging interest in monitoring these industries, which often cannot be predicted. For example, a regulatory change for the taxi-hailing market limited the service only to taxi drivers who had local household registrations in 2016, cutting over half of the original workforce overnight.

What Should Multinationals Do to Deal with China's Innovators?

Chinese innovators come in several forms, have certain unique advantages, and also face various challenges. They appear to thrive on uncertainty, and their successes may be replicated abroad in the middle or even long term. This begs the question of what current leading multinational corporations should do to deal with these Chinese innovators, especially the hidden champions, underdogs, and changemakers, which are difficult for them to spot and assess. Based on our research and frequent interactions with global executives, we have distilled six lessons for MNCs.

- *Challenge assumptions:* MNCs should benchmark the Chinese innovator's way to their own innovation practices. The six actions that all types of Chinese innovators take are distinct from the traditional practices of multinationals. At the very least, these innovation approaches may be a source of inspiration for innovating and exploring which approaches might work best for them in China. Moreover, they provide an opportunity to challenge the assumptions of the MNCs' innovation approaches.
- *Stop competing in the dark:* Our research shows that the competitive landscape of innovators in China goes well beyond the tip of the iceberg. The currently visible competitors within particular industries are easily identified. However, our research gives a clear warning that MNCs should be aware of the less visible opponents (such as underdogs) that may rise within the next decade to become hidden champions and the players outside their own industry (such as changemakers and digital pioneers) that are disrupting from within the MNCs' blind spots. The former situation is illustrated by Dongcheng and Positec power tools, which were clearly underdogs two decades ago but now outcompete Bosch power tools in terms of market share in China and, in the case of Positec, have captured

a large market share in the United States. The latter situation is illustrated by Baidu's smart chopsticks, clearly a health tech product of interest for Philips but one that is emerging from an unexpected corner.

- *Cast a wide net:* Although traditional strategy management and organization theory explains the advantages of having a focused strategy, particularly for mature companies, the Chinese innovators remind us that a broader approach may be still relevant as well, especially when a broader strategic approach is combined with an organizational model that goes beyond the traditional corporation. The more the organization functions as a business ecosystem, the better the company deals with emerging opportunities and sudden challenges. Here three requirements stand out—deep local autonomy, to overcome the "headquarters knows best" syndrome; flexibility in strategy, to overcome linear causal thinking traps; and organizational plurality, to overcome the "protect the corporate boundaries" mindset. Companies such as Bosch, a large multinational with over 300,000 employees worldwide and 60,000 in China, has slowly started to connect locally. Its recent investment in a Beijing tech venture producing Internet of things (IoT) network equipment is a good example. Bosch invested $15 million, together with Tsing Capital, a Chinese venture capital firm, in Sensoro, an IoT technology venture established in 2013. Similarly, DSM, a global specialty chemicals giant, started to diversify by first collaborating with and then acquiring a Chinese photovoltaic back sheet company in Suzhou that was founded only in 2011—an underdog. We have observed an increasing number of ecosystem and open innovation initiatives by multinationals in China. For instance, the medical giant Pfizer developed partnerships with insurer Pingan and Tencent to run business plan contests in healthcare for local ventures.
- *Embrace digital:* If there is one thing that most Chinese innovators remind us of, it is to think of digitizing a business process, strategy, and mindset. In many ways, Chinese innovators and China's markets have been quick to adopt new digital technologies. From digital payment and healthcare to data-driven talent analytics, China has embraced digital life. Although it has increasingly become a necessity for multinationals to survive in China, the rest of the world is also catching up with China in adopting the digital trend. Therefore, Chinese companies have a clear advantage abroad in terms of

digital mindset and the digital readiness of their organizations. Multinationals have to embrace and invest in digitalizing their business, whatever businesses they are in. For instance, Pfizer has started to realize the importance of being digital in its traditionally non-IT industry. During its China Medical Partnership Event in December 2015, Pfizer attracted 377 participants, about half of which were Internet healthcare companies. It discovered digital healthcare startups (such as Diabetes Doctor on the Palm) via these kinds of local contests. One of its global competitors, Sanofi, launched Sanofi Discovery, an innovation initiative to generate services, especially digital ones, to add value to its products' current and future portfolios. Moreover, it has started an employees' digital savviness index as part of its key performance indicators system.

- *Strengthen your home base:* There is no reason to assume that Chinese innovators will fail abroad (chapters 7 and 8). Therefore, even if some MNCs are not operating in China or are not very dependent on the Chinese market, Chinese innovators are coming after them. Even though a company may be a locally embedded organization abroad and have a long history of experience and expertise, its biggest mistake would be to feel superior and ignore the competitive threat. This means that MNCs need to understand how Chinese innovators operate and innovate and then to strengthen their home markets—by sustaining access to talent and knowledge, understanding the changing customer needs in the home market, digitalizing the business, and preparing for the seemingly strange business approaches that the Chinese innovators may bring. For instance, online payment (such as Alipay from Alibaba) could be a serious threat, considering that online payment development in some countries and regions, even in Western Europe, remains far behind China. For niche innovators such as the hidden champions and underdogs, their taking over can be very quiet and not easily noticed. For example, EbaoTech took a big share of the insurance policy software market in Western European countries such as France, the Netherlands, Russia, and Spain. Other examples are new market creation and disrupting existing markets. For instance, DJI, a Chinese company that focuses on drones for the consumer market, was founded in 2006 by Wang Tao in his college dormitory and now claims 70 percent of the consumer drone global market share. Finally, there is a new generation of born-globals, such as Yunmai Tech, which was founded in 2014 and launched a smart body fat scale internationally with initial success in countries such as South Korea. Founder Wang Yang is in his twenties and has an international mindset without geographic boundaries, even for nondigital or offline products.

- *Keep your company DNA:* The previous five lessons suggest changes that MNCs can make in how they organize and do business. However, one further important lesson is that they need to keep their company DNA. This means competing on their own terms and leveraging their own "unfair" advantages, such as strong implementation capability, a global IP and talent pool, and multinational operational experience. The more MNCs are aware of the specific challenges of Chinese innovator, the better they can design competitive countermeasures. In the end, multinationals should compete on their strengths and not become too local. They can never win the competitive game locally by being local.

Are China's Innovations Sustainable?

The sustainability of China's innovations depends on the innovation ecosystem conditions, entrepreneurial activity, and the relative independence of China's innovation capability.[6] First, the necessity for and capacity of innovation for Chinese companies is strong (chapter 1). Although there are plenty of challenges for China's innovators (this chapter), the overall framework is supportive and facilitative of innovation. The focus of this book, however, is not on assessing the necessity for and sufficiency of innovation conditions in China. Most other books on China's innovation have such a focus, and we refer to them for further insights. We have approached the question of the sustainability of China's innovation from a grassroots, bottom-up perspective—that of the entrepreneurs.

Second, we propose an entrepreneurial perspective on the sustainability of innovation in China. Our evidence and rich cases indicate that the sheer number of innovative companies would provide a sufficient basis of sustainability for innovation. Whether it is mass-market manufacturers with innovative products, science-driven niche innovators for the industrial sectors, or disruptive consumer-focused service ventures, the iceberg of China's innovators is significant. Our empirical research shows that the approach to innovation taken by China's innovators is unique and different from the approaches followed in Silicon Valley and by the Asian Tigers. This suggests that China's innovators have found an approach to building innovative companies successfully within the conditions of China's political-economic framework. Regardless of the disadvantages of and limitations on innovation in China, entrepreneurs have found effective innovation approaches. Thriving on uncertainty in China may become a global competitive advantage for China's innovators.

Third, from a perspective of learning and knowledge spillovers between China's innovators and Western multinationals, we can make several conclusions about the independence of China's innovation capability. It is clear that China's innovators have strong international ambitions, have built global innovation networks, and have invested overseas. International collaborations have provided complementary technology to China's innovators, as illustrated by the examples shown in table 8.5.

Our empirical research shows that the role played by learning and knowledge spillovers in the wide variety of cases we studied is mostly

Table 8.5
Illustrations of cooperation between Chinese innovators and international collaborators

Case	Type of innovator	International partner	Form	Outcome
Sany	Pioneer	Putzmeister	Acquisition	Complementary technology
Lenovo	Pioneer	NEC and EMC	Joint ventures	Innovation collaboration
Goldwind	Hidden champion	Vensys	R&D partnership	Joint R&D
Hikvision	Hidden champion	Secure Holdings	Acquisition	Complementary technology
Weihua Solar	Underdog	Merck	Partnership	Joint R&D
Malong Tech	Underdog	Microsoft	Accelerator program	Access to technology resources
Mobike	Changemaker	DowDuPont	R&D partnership	New materials development

Source: Authors' research.

complementary. Contrary to popular belief, our study also indicates that the amount of knowledge spillovers from Western multinationals to China's innovators is limited. Forced technology transfer to joint venture partners was prevalent in the 1990s but is no longer a requirement. This policy has been largely abandoned because it was not successful. For instance, even though a policy of forced technology transfer was in place in the automotive industry, China has largely missed traditional automotive opportunities. In other words, such technology transfers did not help Chinese companies much. China's innovators do have the potential to leapfrog to next-generation cars, not unlike what happened when they leapfrogged to green technology (such as the solar photovoltaic industry). The government supports developments in new energy vehicles, not by forced technology transfers but by supporting local companies and research institutes and by building international collaborations. Our interviews with automotive executives reveal their awareness of China's strong technology in connected cars, driverless cars, and electric cars. Companies such as Aston Martin, Ford, and Volkswagen have been acquiring and collaborating with leading Chinese technology companies such as Baidu and Mobvoi to explore next-generation cars. [7]

Finally, hidden champions and changemakers have made many overseas acquisitions. Changemakers are mostly looking for market access and branding. Driven by digital technology—one of China's advantages—they do not need to leverage foreign technology. Pioneers and hidden champions make overseas acquisitions to gain access to markets but also to acquire technology, such as in the examples of Sany and Lenovo. These acquisitions of technology are complementary to their own technologies. Without Sany and Lenovo's own strong R&D capability and technology, they would not have been able to absorb the complementary technology from overseas.

In conclusion, returning to the debate about the copycat view of China's innovation (chapter 1), our evidence suggests that the strong indigenous innovation competence of China's innovators is self-developed, relatively independent, sustainable, and globally competitive.

How Is China Changing the Global Innovation Arena?

An increasingly deeper involvement of Chinese innovators in global innovation is a foreseeable trend. In chapter 7, we outline the five approaches taken by Chinese innovators that go global—global digital ecosystems, global innovation networks, overseas innovation bases, technology outposts, and born-global ventures. The pioneers and hidden champions are currently global market players and increasingly integrate into the global innovation arena. The underdogs and changemakers, however, may be the future of China's integration into global innovation. Underdogs may become the innovation and technology suppliers of future industries, and changemakers may bring disruptive business models to international markets.[8]

The rise of Chinese innovators within global value chains is discussed at length by George S. Yip and Shameen Prashantham in "Innovation in Emerging Markets."[9] The authors discuss how local companies evolve from local assemblers, to component manufacturers, to in some cases value-adding innovators and partners to multinationals. As shown in this book, many of them have become innovating multinationals themselves. The consequences for global value chains are significant because the locus of innovation is changing from developed economies to emerging economies. Moreover, the underdogs and changemakers are entrepreneurial ventures with global ambitions. From the start, they have been not assemblers or component manufacturers but value-adding innovators that have sought a solid position in global value chains. In addition, the swarm of Chinese entrepreneurial ventures has had an important impact on the structure of global value chains. They provide a stronger innovation imperative on developed economy multinationals than the other way around.

With the increasing importance of digital innovation to companies all around the world, China may be well positioned to lead the global digital innovation arena. China's innovation pioneers are transforming their organizations to embrace digital technology and platform business models. Changemakers are driven by digital business models, and underdogs are developing core technologies such as AI and big data. We observe an increasingly active group of Chinese digital companies in Europe, where they are making investments and expanding services.[10] Moreover, China's government has clear ambitions to expand China's digital innovations abroad. For instance, in the context of the Belt Road Initiative (BRI), a March 2015 white paper calls for growth in digital trade and the expansion of communications networks to develop a so-called Digital Silk Road.[11] Initiatives are well under way. For instance, Huawei recently delivered fiber optic cables to Australia and Afghanistan, and the BAT companies have provided digital services. Alibaba's Ma Yun announced a partnership with the Malaysian government to establish the world's first digital free-trade zone to reduce trade barriers in ecommerce, which is an example of the digital era equivalents of the World Trade Organization.

All in all, the evidence—the large number of unknown innovative entrepreneurial ventures, a supportive home government with global ambitions, and a unique approach to innovation—suggests that China's innovators will change the global innovation arena. Our research suggests that foreign government, companies, and academics need to prepare for a shift in global innovation to the East.

Notes

Chapter 1: Introduction

1. Peter J. Williamson and Eden Yin, "Accelerated Innovation: The New Challenge from China," *MIT Sloan Management Review* 55, no. 4 (Summer 2014): 27–34.

2. Arie Y. Lewin, Martin Kenney, and Johann P. Murmann, *China's Innovation Challenge: Overcoming the Middle-Income Trap* (Cambridge, UK: Cambridge University Press, 2016); Yu Zhou, William Lazonick, and Yifei Sun, *China as an Innovation Nation* (Oxford: Oxford University Press, 2016); Xiaolan Fu, *China's Path to Innovation* (Cambridge, UK: Cambridge University Press, 2015).

3. George Haour and Maximilian von Zedtwitz, *Created in China: How China Is Becoming a Global Innovator* (London: Bloomsbury, 2016).

4. Douglas Fuller, *Paper Tigers, Hidden Dragons* (Oxford: Oxford University Press, 2016); Dan Breznitz and Michael Murphree, *Run of the Red Queen: Government, Innovation, Globalization, and Economic Growth in China* (New Haven: Yale University Press, 2011).

5. George S. Yip and Bruce McKern, *China's Next Strategic Advantage: From Imitation to Innovation* (Cambridge, MA: MIT Press, 2016); Ming Zeng and Peter J. Williamson, *Dragons at Your Door: How Chinese Cost Innovation Is Disrupting Global Competition* (Boston: Harvard Business School Press, 2007).

6. Shaun Rein, *The End of Copycat China: The Rise of Creativity, Innovation, and Individualism in Asia* (New York: Wiley, 2014); Yinglan Tan, *Chinnovation: How Chinese Innovators Are Changing the World* (Singapore: Wiley, 2011).

7. Mark J. Greeven and Wei Wei, *Business Ecosystems in China: Alibaba and Competing Baidu, Tencent, Xiaomi, and LeEco* (Abingdon, UK: Routledge, 2018).

8. We thank an anonymous MIT Press reviewer for suggesting that we include this section.

9. Regina M. Abrami, William C. Kirby, and F. Warren McFarlan, "Why China Can't Innovate," *Harvard Business Review* 92, no. 3 (March 2014): 107–111.

10. Yip and McKern, *China's Next Strategic Advantage*.

11. Williamson and Yin, "Accelerated Innovation."

12. "China Mobile Technology Innovation Beats Silicon Valley," *New York Times*, August 3, 2016, http://www.nytimes.com/2016/08/03/technology/china-mobile-tech-innovation-silicon-valley.html; "WeChat's World," *The Economist*, August 6, 2016, 10; "China's Tech Trailblazers," *The Economist*, August 6, 2016, 10.

13. Mark J. Greeven, "New Wave of Digital Entrepreneurs Rises in China," *Nikkei Asian Review*, June 5–11, 2017, 60.

14. Global Entrepreneurship Monitor, "Economy Profiles: China," Global Entrepreneurship Research Association, London, 2017, http://www.gemconsortium.org/country-profile/51.

15. "Doing Business in China," World Bank, 2017, http://www.doingbusiness.org/data/exploreeconomies/china.

16. Based on the authors' calculations using data from National Bureau of Statistics of China, *China Statistical Yearbook 2017*, http://www.stats.gov.cn/tjsj/ndsj/2017/indexeh.htm.

17. National Bureau of Statistics of China, *China Statistical Yearbook 2017*.

18. Jiaofeng Pan, "China's S&T Strategic Options" (presentation, Oxford Sino-UK Innovation and Development Forum, November 10, 2016).

19. Center for Strategic and International Studies, "Made in China 2025," last modified June 1, 2015, https://www.csis.org/analysis/made-china-2025.

20. David Beier and George Baeder, "China Set to Accelerate Life Science Innovation," *Forbes*, July 6, 2017, https://www.forbes.com/sites/realspin/2017/07/06/china-set-to-accelerate-life-science-innovation/#2a9f28b4e73b.

21. Global Entrepreneurship Monitor, "Economy Profiles: China."

22. Haour and von Zedtwitz, *Created in China*, 45.

23. Fuller, *Paper Tigers, Hidden Dragons*.

24. Andrew Tylecote, "Twin Innovation Systems, Intermediate Technology and Economic Development: History and Prospect for China," *Innovation* 8, no. 1–2 (2006): 62–83.

25. Organisation for Economic Co-operation and Development, "Main Science and Technology Indicators," last modified March 2018, http://www.oecd.org/sti/msti.htm.

26. We thank an anonymous MIT Press reviewer for suggesting that we include this section.

27. Matthew Bey, "In China, Innovation Cuts Both Ways," *Forbes*, October 24, 2017, https://www.forbes.com/sites/stratfor/2017/10/24/in-china-innovation-cuts-both-ways/#4ec21b8d79e8.

28. For detailed discussions of the role played by the government and the Communist Party in private business, see Lewin, Kenney, and Murmann, *China's Innovation Challenge*, and Fuller, *Paper Tigers, Hidden Dragons*.

29. Steven Veldhoen, Bill Peng, Anna Mansson, George Yip, and Jian Han, "China's Innovation's Going Global: 2014 China Innovation Survey," Strategy& and China Europe International Business School Center on China Innovation, 2014.

30. Menita Cheng Liu and Can Huang, "Transforming China's IP System to Stimulate Innovation," in *China's Innovation Challenge*, ed. Arie Y. Lewin, Martin Kenney, and Johann P. Murmann, 152–188 (Cambridge, UK: Cambridge University Press, 2016).

31. For an in-depth treatment of managing intellectual property rights in China, see Oliver Gassmann, Angela Beckenbauer, and Sascha Friesike, *Profiting from Innovation in China* (Berlin: Springer, 2012); Andrew C. Mertha, *The Politics of Piracy: Intellectual Property in Contemporary China* (Ithaca, NY: Cornell University Press, 2007); Yip and McKern, *China's Next Strategic Advantage*.

32. Global Entrepreneurship Monitor, "Economy Profiles: China."

33. Based on the authors' discussions with experts and various CCTV news reports.

34. China Innovation and Entrepreneurship Competition Committee, "China Innovation and Entrepreneurship Competition," Beijing, accessed May 1, 2018, http://www.cxcyds.com.

35. Fuller, *Paper Tigers, Hidden Dragons*.

36. Global Entrepreneurship Monitor, "Economy Profiles: China."

37. "Comparison of Private Equity Fund Data between China and the US" (in Chinese), *PEStreet*, December 1, 2015, http://www.pestreet.cn/article/2015000000058943.html.

38. Yip and McKern, *China's Next Strategic Advantage*, 8.

39. Greeven and Wei, *Business Ecosystems in China*, 8.

Chapter 2: Pioneers

1. Based on an estimation by the authors and an assessment of various lists of the most innovative companies published by the Boston Consulting Group, the China European International Business School (CEIBS), *Fast Company*, *Forbes*, *MIT Technology Review*, Strategy&, and others.

2. "China Mobile Technology Innovation Beats Silicon Valley," *New York Times*, August 3, 2016, http://www.nytimes.com/2016/08/03/technology/china-mobile-tech-innovation-silicon-valley.html; "China's Tech Trailblazers," *The Economist*, August 6, 2016, 10.

3. "Who's Afraid of Huawei?," *The Economist*, August 4, 2012, http://www.economist.com/node/21559922.

4. Kathy Hu, "Good Signals: Huawei Pushes Further Forward," *CKGSB Magazine* 25, March 27, 2017, http://knowledge.ckgsb.edu.cn/2017/03/27/china-business-strategy/huawei-strategy-push-forward.

5. Geerten van de Kaa and Mark J. Greeven, "LED Standardization in China and South East Asia: Stakeholders, Infrastructure and Institutional Regimes," *Renewable and Sustainable Energy Reviews* 72 (2017): 863–870.

6. The following section draws on insights from the sources in notes 3, 4, and 5 in particular; interviews done by the second author with a Huawei manager; public information from the Huawei website (https://www.huawei.com/cn/press-events/annual-report); and a variety of news publications on Huawei in the *Financial Times*, *Caijing* (Chinese), Sina (Chinese), Baijiahao (Chinese), and ifeng (Chinese) among others; and insight on the Huawei culture from Tao Tian, David De Cremer, and Chunbo Wu, *Huawei: Leadership, Culture, and Connectivity* (Thousand Oaks, CA: Sage, 2017).

7. "Zhang Ruimin," *Fortune*, accessed May 1, 2018, http://fortune.com/worlds-greatest-leaders/zhang-ruimin-24.

8. "HOPE-Open Innovation Platform," Haier, accessed May 1, 2018, http://hope.haier.com/?lang=en.

9. Geert Duysters, Jojo Jacob, Charmianne Lemmens, and Jintian Yu, "Internationalization and Technological Catching Up of Emerging Multinationals: A Comparative Case Study of China's Haier Group," *Industrial and Corporate Change* 18, no. 2 (2009): 325–349.

10. Bill Fisher, "Unlock Employee Innovation That Fits with Your Strategy," *Harvard Business Review*, October 27, 2014, https://hbr.org/2014/10/unlock-employee-innovation-that-fits-with-your-strategy.

11. George S. Yip and Bruce McKern, *China's Next Strategic Advantage: From Imitation to Innovation* (Cambridge, MA: MIT Press, 2016), 51.

12. "Sany Gets Innovation Ranking from Forbes," *Construction Equipment*, September 20, 2012, https://www.constructionequipment.com/sany-gets-innovation-ranking-forbes.

13. "Sany Named Innovative Company by *Fortune China*," *Construction Equipment*, August 28, 2012, https://www.constructionequipment.com/sany-named-innovative-company-fortune-china.

14. "Sany Wang Xiaofeng: IoT as Service, Data as Value, Company Should Focus on IoT Construction" (in Chinese), hc360.com, November 28, 2016, http://info.cm.hc360.com/2016/11/281606646914.shtml.

15. "Lenovo to Buy Google's Motorola Mobility for $2.91 Billion," *TechNode*, January 30, 2014, http://technode.com/2014/01/30/lenovo-to-buy-googles-motorola-mobility-for-2-91-billion.

16. "Lenovo Launches $500M Start-up Fund Aimed at Robotics, AI, and Cloud Computing," *TechNode*, May 5, 2016, http://technode.com/2016/05/05/lenovo-launches-500m-start-up-fund-aimed-at-robotics-ai-cloud-computing.

17. "Lenovo Plans to Invest over $1Bn in AI and IoT," *TechNode*, April 19, 2017, http://technode.com/2017/04/19/lenovo-plans-to-invest-over-1bn-in-ai-and-iot.

18. "IT Juzi Wen Feixiang: Only 1% of Startups Can Be Listed, Half of Unicorns Have BAT Blood Relationship" (in Chinese), *Lieyun Net*, accessed December 30, 2016, http://www.lieyunwang.com/archives/159641.

19. "*Fast Company* Most Innovative Companies," *Fast Company*, accessed May 1, 2018, https://www.fastcompany.com/section/most-innovative-companies.

20. Mark J. Greeven, Shenyun Yang, Tao Yue, Eric van Heck, and Barbara Krug, "How Taobao Bested eBay in China," *Financial Times*, March 12, 2012, https://www.ft.com/content/52670084-6c2c-11e1-b00f-00144feab49a.

21. Mark J. Greeven and Wei Wei, *Business Ecosystems in China: Alibaba and Competing Baidu, Tencent, Xiaomi and LeEco* (Abingdon, UK: Routledge, 2018).

22. Greeven and Wei, *Business Ecosystems in China*, 5.

23. Feng Wan, Peter J. Williamson, and Eden Yin, "Antecedents and Implications of Disruptive Innovation: Evidence from China," *Technovation* 39–40 (May–June 2015): 94–104.

24. Greeven and Wei, *Business Ecosystems in China*.

25. "How about Strict Regulation? Ant Financial and Tencent Finance Valuation Reaches 1 Trillion RMB," *Sina*, April 24, 2018, http://finance.sina.com.cn/money/bank/bank_hydt/2018-04-24/doc-ifzqvvsa2605102.shtml.

26. Greeven and Wei, *Business Ecosystems in China*.

Chapter 3: Hidden Champions

1. "2016 Chinese Manufacturing Hidden Champion List" (in Chinese), *Sino Manager*, accessed December 12, 2016, http://www.sino-manager.com/?p=22140.

2. Lun Feng, *Barbaric Growth* (in Chinese) (Guangzhou: Guangdong People's Press, 2014).

3. David Barboza, "How a Chinese Billionaire Built Her Fortune," *New York Times*, August 2, 2015, https://www.nytimes.com/2015/08/02/business/international/how-zhou-qunfei-a-chinese-billionaire-built-her-fortune.html.

4. Hermann Simon, *Hidden Champions of the Twenty-First Century: Success Strategies of Unknown World Market Leaders* (Berlin: Springer, 2009).

5. "National Company Innovation Survey 2014," National Bureau of Statistics of the People's Republic of China, 2014.

6. "2016 Chinese Manufacturing Hidden Champion List."

7. Jianwei Zhang, *The Why of Hidden Champions: The Ultimately Focused, Practical and Persistent Business Approach* (in Chinese) (Beijing: Beijing University of Posts and Telecommunications Press, 2015).

8. Steven Veldhoen, Bill Peng, Anna Mansson, George Yip, and Jian Han, "China's Innovation Is Going Global: 2014 China Innovation Survey,"

Strategy& and China Europe International Business School Center on China Innovation, 2014.

9. "UNCTAD FDI Data," UNCTAD, accessed July 1, 2017, http://unctadstat.unctad.org/wds/ReportFolders/reportFolders.aspx?sCS_referer=&sCS_ChosenLang=en; "FDI Data MOFCOM," Ministry of Commerce, People's Republic of China, accessed May 1, 2018, http://english.mofcom.gov.cn/article/statistic/foreigninvestment/201301/20130100012618.shtml.

10. Veldhoen, Mansson, Peng, Yip, and Han, "China's Innovation Going Global."

11. Simon, *Hidden Champions of the Twenty-First Century.*

Chapter 4: Underdogs

1. Arthur Yeung, Katherine Xin, Waldemar Pfoertsch, and Shengjun Liu, *The Globalization of Chinese Companies: Strategies for Conquering International Markets* (Singapore: Wiley, 2011).

2. "China Sees Biggest Overseas Returning Wave in Recent Years," *China Daily*, February 24, 2017, http://europe.chinadaily.com.cn/china/2017-02/24/content_28330296.htm.

3. Marina Peter, "From an Empa Laboratory to a Start-up in China," Swiss Federal Laboratories for Materials Science and Technology, September 23, 2011, https://www.empa.ch/web/s604/weihua-solar?inheritRedirect=true.

4. John Child and Susana Rodrigues, "The Internationalization of Chinese Firms: a Case for Theoretical Extension," *Management and Organization Review* 1, no. 3 (2005): 381–410; Peter J. Buckley, Jeremy L. Clegg, Adam R. Cross, Xin Liu, Hinrich Voss, and Ping Zheng, "The Determinants of Chinese Outward Foreign Direct Investment," *Journal of International Business Studies* 38, no. 4 (July 2007): 499–518.

5. Anat Keinan, Jill Avery, and Neeru Paharia, "Capitalizing on the Underdog Effect," *Harvard Business Review* (November 2010), https://hbr.org/2010/11/capitalizing-on-the-underdog-effect.

6. Based on the authors' calculations with data from National Bureau of Statistics of China, *China Statistical Yearbook 2017*, accessed February 1, 2018, http://www.stats.gov.cn/tjsj/ndsj/2017/indexeh.htm.

7. "China Innovation and Entrepreneurship Competition," China Innovation and Entrepreneurship Competition Committee, Beijing, accessed May 1, 2018, http://www.cxcyds.com.

8. *China Statistical Yearbook 2017.*

9. "About Advanced Solar Power," Advanced Solar Power, accessed February 1, 2018, http://www.advsolarpower.com/en/index.php/about.

10. Ewen Callaway, "Second Chinese Team Reports Gene Editing in Human Embryos," *Nature*, April 8, 2016, http://www.nature.com/news/second-chinese-team-reports-gene-editing-in-human-embryos-1.19718?WT.mc_id=TWT_NatureNews.

11. "A Study to Assess CD19-Targeted Immunotherapy T Cells in Patients with Relapsed or Refractory CD19+ B Cell Leukemia," *ClinicalTrials*, accessed September 8, 2018, https://clinicaltrials.gov/ct2/show/NCT02672501.

12. Charlie Campbell, "The Innovator: Baidu's Robin Li Takes on the Titans of Silicon Valley," *Time*, January 29, 2018, 21–23.

13. "MIIT Layout China USD 200$ Billion New Material Industry," JEC Composites, accessed September 14, 2016, http://www.jeccomposites.com/knowledge/international-composites-news/miit-layout-china-usd-200-billion-new-material-industry.

14. "Self-Innovation to Promote Market Development of Thermal Insulation Materials" (in Chinese), *51Sole*, May 20, 2015, http://news.51sole.com/article/5753.html.

15. One *mu* in the Chinese metric system equals approximately 0.066 hectares.

16. Emma Lee, "This ex-NASA Scientist Is Using Big Data to Raise Yields on China's Small Farmlands," *TechNode*, July 14, 2016, http://technode.com/2016/07/14/gago-agri-tech.

17. National Bureau of Statistics of the People's Republic of China, "National Company Innovation Survey 2014," 2014.

18. "Uninano: Save One Third to One Tenth Product Cost" (in Chinese), *Sina*, September 4, 2014, http://finance.sina.com.cn/hy/20140904/112120211867.shtml.

19. Gong Zhang, "Continuous Refreshing Data, Gago Wants to Enter the Trillion RMB Agriculture Market by Means of Big Data" (in Chinese), *Toutiao*, August 7, 2016, http://www.toutiao.com/i6315993963849318913.

20. "China's Infrared Imaging Moving to Civilian Market, It May Boom Together with Smart Home" (in Chinese), *Asmag*, April 2016, http://www.asmag.com.cn/news/201604/86666.html.

21. "Easy Power Disrupts the Traditional Digital Power Chip Technology and leads Power Management to Enter 2.0 era" (in Chinese), *EEFOCUS*, September 24, 2016, http://www.eefocus.com/analog-power/329911.

22. "Chinese Scientists Created 3D Bio-printed Organs," *TechNode*, August 8, 2013, http://technode.com/2013/08/08/chinese-scientists-developed-a3d-bio-printer-bringing-artificial-organs-into-scope.

Chapter 5: Changemakers

1. Youchi Kuo, "Three Great Forces Changing China's Consumer Market," World Economic Forum, January 4, 2016, https://www.weforum.org/agenda/2016/01/3-great-forces-changing-chinas-consumer-market.

2. Youchi Kuo, Jeff Walters, Hongbing Gao, Angela Wang, Veronique Yang, Jian Yang, Zhibin Lyu, and Hongjie Wan, "The New China Play Book: Young, Affluent, E-Savvy Consumers Will Fuel Growth," Boston Consulting Group, December 21, 2015, https://www.bcgperspectives.com/content/articles/globalization-growth-new-china-playbook-young-affluent-e-savvy-consumers.aspx.

3. "Internet Live Stats," Internet Live Stats, accessed February 1, 2018, http://www.internetlivestats.com.

4. "Internet Statistics," China Internet Network Information Center, accessed February 1, 2018, http://www.cnnic.net.cn.

5. Don Weinland and Sherry Fei Ju, "China's Ant Financial Shows Cashless Is King," *Financial Times*, April 4, 2018, https://www.ft.com/content/5033b53a-3eff-11e8-b9f9-de94fa33a81e.

6. "Mobike Accelerates European Expansion with Second Stop in Italy," *TechNode*, July 26, 2017, http://technode.com/2017/07/26/mobike-accelerates-european-expansion-with-second-stop-in-italy.

7. "Mobike Teams Up with China's Largest Thin-Film Solar Cell Manufacturer," *TechNode*, May 3, 2017, http://technode.com/2017/05/03/mobike-teams-up-with-chinas-largest-thin-film-solar-cell-manufacturer.

Chapter 6: The Chinese Innovators' Way

1. "Every Day Fifteen Thousand New Company Registered" (in Chinese), *Finance World*, January 20, 2017, http://finance.jrj.com.cn/2017/01/20102021992277.shtml.

2. Global Entrepreneurship Monitor, "Economy Profile: China," Global Entrepreneurship Research Association, 2017, http://www.gemconsortium.org/country-profile/51.

3. "China Innovation and Entrepreneurship Competition," China Innovation and Entrepreneurship Competition Committee, Beijing, People's Republic of China, accessed May 1, 2018, http://www.cxcyds.com.

4. Hugo van Driel and Mark J. Greeven, "Coping with Institutional Voids: Identity Shaping and Resource Tapping by Zhejiang Entrepreneurs in the Chinese Reform Era in a Historical Perspective," paper prepared for the European Business History Association conference, Uppsala University, Uppsala, Sweden, August 2013.

5. S. H. Sheng and Y. W. Zheng, *Competitive Advantage: Zhejiang Industry Collective Transformation and Development Research* (in Chinese) (Hangzhou: Zhejiang University Press, 2009).

6. Zhejiang Provincial Bureau of Statistics, *Zhejiang Statistical Yearbook 2014*, accessed February 1, 2018, http://tjj.zj.gov.cn/tjsj/tjnj.

7. Jiang Wei, Minfei Zhou, Mark J. Greeven, and Hongyan Qu, "Governance Mechanisms, Dual Networks and Innovative Learning of Industrial Clusters: Multiple-Case Study in China," *Asia Pacific Journal of Management* 33, no. 4 (December 2016): 1037–1074.

8. "Fourth China Innovation and Entrepreneurship Contest New Energy and Energy-Saving Environmental Protection Industry Finalists Recommended Shortlist of Enterprises and Teams" (in Chinese), *East Money*, accessed December 3, 2017, http://cyds.shtic.com/wx/contest/topic/1049.html.

9. Mark J. Greeven, "New Wave of Digital Entrepreneurs Rises in China," *Nikkei Asian Review*, June 5–11, 2017, 60.

10. "Reshuffle of Construction Machinery Industry, Only over Twenty Companies Left from 110 Excavator Companies" (in Chinese), *CEWeekly*, accessed June 20, 2017, http://www.ceweekly.cn/2016/1121/171434.shtml.

11. "Tongwei Acquired LDK with Large Investment, Bottom Fishing Photovoltaic Industry" (in Chinese), *Ifeng Finance*, accessed May 23, 2017, http://finance.ifeng.com/a/20131123/11145610_0.shtml.

12. Karl E. Weick, *Making Sense of the Organization* (Hoboken, NJ: Wiley-Blackwell, 2001).

13. Mark J. Greeven and Wei Wei, *Business Ecosystems in China: Alibaba and Competing Baidu, Tencent, Xiaomi, and LeEco* (Abingdon, UK: Routledge, 2018).

14. Orit Gadiesh, Philip Leung, and Till Vestring, "The Battle for China's Good-Enough Market," *Harvard Business Review* 85 (September 2007), https://hbr.org/2007/09/the-battle-for-chinas-good-enough-market.

15. Marcus M. Keupp, Angela Beckenbauer, and Oliver Gassmann, "How Managers Protect Intellectual Property Rights in China Using De Facto Strategies," *R&D Management* 39, no. 2 (March 2009): 211–224.

16. Helen Perks, Kenneth Khan, and Cong Zhang, "An Empirical Evaluation of R&D-Marketing NPD Integration in Chinese Firms: The Guanxi Effect," *Journal of Product Innovation Management* 26, no. 6 (2009): 640–651; Wai-sum Siu and Qiong Bao, "Network Strategies of Small Chinese High-Technology Firms: A Quantitative Study," *Journal of Product Innovation Management* 25, no. 1 (2007): 79–102.

17. Mark J. Greeven, "Sources of Institutional Capability for Innovation in China's Catching Up Economy: An Explorative Study," in *Quality Innovation: Knowledge, Theory, and Practices*, ed. Chen Jin and Latif Al-hakim, 406–417 (Hersey, PA: IGI Global, 2014).

18. Steven Veldhoen, Bill Peng, Anna Mansson, George Yip, and Jian Han, "China's Innovation Is Going Global: 2014 China Innovation Survey," Strategy& and China Europe International Business School Center on China Innovation, 2014.

Chapter 7: China's Innovators Going Global

1. Steven Veldhoen, Bill Peng, Anna Mansson, George Yip, and Jian Han, "China's Innovation Is Going Global: 2014 China Innovation Survey," Strategy& and China Europe International Business School Centre on China Innovation, 2014.

2. Piter de Jong, Mark J. Greeven, and Haico Ebbers, "Getting the Numbers Right on China's Actual Overseas Investment: The Case of the Netherlands," *Journal of Current Chinese Affairs* 46, no. 1 (2017): 187–209.

3. Alberto Di Minin, Jieyin Zhang, and Peter Gammeltoft, "Chinese Foreign Direct Investment in R&D in Europe: A New Model of R&D Internationalization?," *European Management Journal* 30, no. 3 (2012): 189–203.

4. Héctor Hernández, Fernando Hervás, Alexander Tübke, Antonio Vezzani, Mafini Dosso, Sara Amoroso, Nicola Grassano, Alexander Coad, and Petros Gkotsis, "2015 EU Industrial R&D Investment Scoreboard," Joint Research Centre–Institute for Prospective Technological Studies, European Commission, Luxembourg, 2015, http://iri.jrc.ec.europa.eu/scoreboard15.html.

5. Mark J. Greeven and Wei Wei, *Business Ecosystems in China: Alibaba and Competing Baidu, Tencent, Xiaomi, and LeEco* (Abingdon, UK: Routledge, 2018).

6. "Huawei 'Iron Triangle': Lessons from Big Failures" (in Chinese), Geonol Graduate School of Business, March 29, 2017, http://www.geonol.com/news/shownews.php?lang=cn&id=59.

7. "Disclose Huawei's Strategic Collaborations with Global Leaders: Thirty-six Joint Innovation Centers" (in Chinese), *C114*, accessed July 8, 2017, http://www.c114.net/news/126/a974506.html.

8. Yong Hu, Yazhou Hao, and Des Dearlove, *Haier Purpose: The Real Story of China's First Global Super Company* (London: Infinite Ideas, 2017).

9. Ye Wang, Donghui Teng, Cheng Huang, Jianguo Wang, and Xinming Wan, "Haier: Pioneering Innovation in the Digital World," *WIPO Magazine*, August 2015, http://www.wipo.int/wipo_magazine/en/2015/04/article_0006.html.

10. "Hikvision to Establish R&D Center in Montreal and Research Institute in Silicon Valley," *SDM Magazine*, accessed August 8, 2017, http://www.sdmmag.com/articles/93556-hikvision-to-establish-rd-center-in-montreal-and-research-institute-in-silicon-valley.

11. "Like Kong Ming's Strategy Planning, Envision Smart Wind Power Products Ally with Dozens of Electric Power Groups" (in Chinese), *Science China*, October 21, 2016, http://science.china.com.cn/2016-10/21/content_9104330.htm.

12. "Envision: Super Conductive Wind Turbine Does Not Compete in the Same Dimension with Traditional Wind Turbine" (in Chinese), *Energy Observer*, September 25, 2015.

13. "Yili Still Has the No. One Market Share But with a Decreased Milk Powder Income" (in Chinese), *Sina Finance*, March 31, 2017, http://finance.sina.com.cn/stock/s/2017-03-31/doc-ifycwunr8323637.shtml.

14. See more at http://www.foodvalley.nl.

15. Marina Peter, "From an Empa Laboratory to a Start-Up in China," Swiss Federal Laboratories for Materials Science and Technology, September 23, 2011, https://www.empa.ch/web/s604/weihua-solar?inheritRedirect=true.

16. Mark J. Greeven, Ona P. Akemu, Tom Hoorn, and Marcel Kleijn, "Chinese Investments Strengthen the Dutch Innovation Systems" (in Dutch), Dutch Advisory Council for Science and Technology Policy, 2012.

17. "About Cheetah Mobile" (in Chinese), Cheetah Mobile, accessed August 8, 2017, http://www.cmcm.com/zh-cn/about.

18. Information based on reporting by *TechNode*, accessed May 5, 2017, http://technode.com/2017/05/05/china-funding-daily-may-4th-and-5th-power-banks-wearable-devices-and-mobile-iot.

19. "The Life-or-Death Battle of Startups, Where Is the Next Right Thing for musical.ly," *Jiemian*, August 20, 2017, http://www.jiemian.com/article/1220817.html.

20. "Papaya Mobile Announces IPO on NEEQ for International Expansion," *TechNode*, May 24, 2016, http://technode.com/2016/05/24/papayamobile-announces-ipo-neeq-international-expansion.

Chapter 8: China's Emerging Innovators

1. Dan Breznitz and Michael Murphree, *Run of the Red Queen: Government, Innovation, Globalization, and Economic Growth in China* (New Haven: Yale University Press, 2011).

2. Although not all ventures in the Silicon Valley region follow one specific way of innovating, the following books provide insightful accounts: Elton B. Sherwin Jr., *The Silicon Valley Way: Discover Forty-five Secrets for Successful Start-Ups*, 2nd ed. (Energy House Publishing, September 9, 2010); AnnaLee Saxenian, *Regional Advantage: Culture and Competition in Silicon Valley and Route 128* (Cambridge, MA: Harvard University Press, 1996); William Draper III, *The Startup Game: Inside the Partnership between Venture Capitalists and Entrepreneurs* (New York: St. Martin's Griffin, 2012).

3. We thank an anonymous MIT Press reviewer for suggesting this section.

4. For instance, Yu Zhou, William Lazonick, and Yifei Sun, *China as an Innovation Nation* (Oxford: Oxford University Press, 2016).

5. Global Entrepreneurship Monitor, "Economy Profiles: China," Global Entrepreneurship Research Association, 2017, http://www.gemconsortium.org/country-profile/51.

6. We thank an anonymous MIT Press reviewer for suggesting this section.

7. Excellent discussions on the role played by competition and collaboration with Western multinationals and the role of international joint venture portfolios are found in George S. Yip and Bruce McKern, *China's Next Strategic Advantage: From Imitation to Innovation* (Cambridge, MA: MIT Press, 2016); Ming Zeng and Peter J. Williamson, *Dragons at Your Door: How Chinese Cost Innovation Is Disrupting Global Competition* (Boston: Harvard Business School Press, 2007); Sunny L. Sun and Ruby P. Lee, "Enhancing Innovation through International Joint Venture Portfolios: From the Emerging Firm Perspective," *Journal of International Marketing* 21, no. 3 (2013): 1–21; Regina M. Abrami, William C. Kirby, and F. Warren McFarlan, "Why China Can't Innovate," *Harvard Business Review* 92, no. 3 (March 2014): 107–111; George S. Yip and Shameen Prashantham, "Innovation in Emerging Markets," in *Oxford*

Handbook on Management in Emerging Markets, ed. Karl Meyer and Rob Grosse (Oxford: Oxford University Press, 2018).

8. We thank an anonymous MIT Press reviewer for suggesting this section.

9. Yip and Prashantham, "Innovation in Emerging Markets."

10. Mark J. Greeven and Paolo Cervini, "Digital China Is Coming to Europe," *LSE Business Review*, April 24, 2018, http://blogs.lse.ac.uk/businessreview/2018/04/24/digital-china-is-coming-to-europe.

11. Mark J. Greeven, "Chinese Innovation and OBOR," in *Reflections on the Challenges of the One Belt One Road Initiative*, ed. David De Cremer, Xiang Zhang, and Bruce McKern (Thousand Oaks, CA: Sage, 2018), chap. 13.

Selected Bibliography

Abrami, Regina M., William C. Kirby, and F. Warren McFarlan. "Why China Can't Innovate." *Harvard Business Review* 92 (3) (March 2014): 107–111.

Breznitz, Dan, and Michael Murphree. *Run of the Red Queen: Government, Innovation, Globalization, and Economic Growth in China*. New Haven: Yale University Press, 2011.

Buckley, Peter J., Jeremy L. Clegg, Adam R. Cross, Xin Liu, Hinrich Voss, and Ping Zheng. "The Determinants of Chinese Outward Foreign Direct Investment." *Journal of International Business Studies* 38 (4) (July 2007): 499–518.

Callaway, Ewen. "Second Chinese Team Reports Gene Editing in Human Embryos." *Nature* (April 2016). http://www.nature.com/news/second-chinese-team-reports-gene-editing-in-human-embryos-1.19718?WT.mc_id=TWT_NatureNews.

Child, John, and Susana Rodrigues. "The Internationalization of Chinese Firms: A Case for Theoretical Extension." *Management and Organization Review* 1 (3) (2005): 381–410.

De Jong, Piter, Mark J. Greeven, and Haico Ebbers. "Getting the Numbers Right on China's Actual Overseas Investment: The Case of the Netherlands." *Journal of Current Chinese Affairs* 46 (1) (2017): 187–209.

Di Minin, Alberto, Jieyin Zhang, and Peter Gammeltoft. "Chinese Foreign Direct Investment in R&D in Europe: A New Model of R&D Internationalization?" *European Management Journal* 30 (3) (2012): 189–203.

Draper, I. I. I. *William. The Startup Game: Inside the Partnership between Venture Capitalists and Entrepreneurs*. New York: St. Martin's Griffin, 2012.

Duysters, Geert, Jojo Jacob, Charmianne Lemmens, and Jintian Yu. "Internationalization and Technological Catching Up of Emerging Multinationals: A Comparative Case Study of China's Haier Group." *Industrial and Corporate Change* 18 (2) (2009): 325–349.

Economist. "China's Tech Trailblazers." August 6, 2016, 10.

Economist. "WeChat's World." August 6, 2016, 10.

Economist. "Who's Afraid of Huawei?" August 4, 2012. http://www.economist.com/node/21559922.

Feng, Lun. *Barbaric Growth* [in Chinese]. Guangzhou: Guangdong People's Press, 2014.

Fisher, Bill. "Unlock Employee Innovation That Fits with Your Strategy." *Harvard Business Review* (October 2014). https://hbr.org/2014/10/unlock-employee-innovation-that-fits-with-your-strategy.

Fisher, Bill, Umberto Lago, and Fang Liu. *Reinventing Giants: How Chinese Global Competitor Haier Has Changed the Way Big Companies Transform*. San Francisco: Jossey-Bass, 2013.

Fu, Xiaolan. *China's Path to Innovation*. Cambridge, UK: Cambridge University Press, 2015.

Fuller, Douglas. *Paper Tigers, Hidden Dragons*. Oxford: Oxford University Press, 2016.

Gadiesh, Orit, Philip Leung, and Till Vestring. "The Battle for China's Good-Enough Market." *Harvard Business Review* 85 (September 2007). https://hbr.org/2007/09/the-battle-for-chinas-good-enough-market.

Gassmann, Oliver, Angela Beckenbauer, and Sascha Friesike. *Profiting from Innovation in China*. Berlin: Springer, 2012.

Greeven, Mark J. Chinese Innovation and OBOR. In *Reflections on the Challenges of the One Belt One Road Initiative*, ed. David De Cremer, Xiang Zhang and Bruce McKern. Thousand Oaks, CA: Sage, 2018.

Greeven, Mark J. "New Wave of Digital Entrepreneurs Rises in China." *Nikkei Asian Review*, June 5–11, 2017, 60.

Greeven, Mark J. Sources of Institutional Capability for Innovation in China's Catching Up Economy: An Explorative Study. In *Quality Innovation: Knowledge, Theory, and Practices*, ed. Chen Jin and Latif Al-hakim. 406–417. Hersey, PA: IGI Global, 2014.

Greeven, Mark J., and Wei Wei. *Business Ecosystems in China: Alibaba and Competing Baidu, Tencent, Xiaomi, and LeEco*. Abingdon, UK: Routledge, 2018.

Greeven, Mark J., Shenyun Yang, Tao Yue, Eric van Heck, and Barbara Krug. "How Taobao Bested eBay in China." *Financial Times*, March 12, 2012. https://www.ft.com/content/52670084-6c2c-11e1-b00f-00144feab49a.

Haour, George, and Maximilian von Zedtwitz. *Created in China: How China Is Becoming a Global Innovator*. London: Bloomsbury, 2016.

Hu, Yong, Yazhou Hao, and Des Dearlove. *Haier Purpose: The Real Story of China's First Global Super Company*. London: Infinite Ideas, 2017.

Keinan, Anat, Jill Avery, and Neeru Paharia. "Capitalizing on the Underdog Effect." *Harvard Business Review* (November 2010). https://hbr.org/2010/11/capitalizing-on-the-underdog-effect.

Keupp, Marcus M., Angela Beckenbauer, and Oliver Gassmann. "How Managers Protect Intellectual Property Rights in China Using De Facto Strategies." *R & D Management* 39 (2) (March 2009): 211–224.

Lewin, Arie Y., Martin Kenney, and Johann P. Murmann. *China's Innovation Challenge: Overcoming the Middle-Income Trap*. Cambridge, UK: Cambridge University Press, 2016.

Liu, Menita Cheng, and Can Huang. Transforming China's IP System to Stimulate Innovation. In *China's Innovation Challenge*, ed. Arie Y. Lewin, Martin Kenney and Johann P. Murmann. 152–188. Cambridge, UK: Cambridge University Press, 2016.

Mertha, Andrew C. *The Politics of Piracy: Intellectual Property in Contemporary China*. Ithaca, NY: Cornell University Press, 2007.

Perks, Helen, Kenneth Khan, and Cong Zhang. "An Empirical Evaluation of R&D-Marketing NPD Integration in Chinese Firms: The Guanxi Effect." *Journal of Product Innovation Management* 26 (6) (2009): 640–651.

Rein, Shaun. *The End of Copycat China: The Rise of Creativity, Innovation, and Individualism in Asia*. New York: Wiley, 2014.

Saxenian, AnnaLee. *Regional Advantage: Culture and Competition in Silicon Valley and Route 128*. Cambridge, MA: Harvard University Press, 1996.

Sheng, S. H., and Y. W. Zheng. *Competitive Advantage: Zhejiang Industry Collective Transformation and Development Research* [in Chinese]. Hangzhou: Zhejiang University Press, 2009.

Sherwin, Elton B. Jr. *The Silicon Valley Way: Discover Forty-five Secrets for Successful Start-Ups*. 2nd ed. Knoxville, TN: Energy House Publishing, 2010.

Simon, Hermann. *Hidden Champions of the Twenty-First Century: Success Strategies of Unknown World Market Leaders*. Berlin: Springer, 2009.

Siu, Wai-sum, and Qiong Bao. "Network Strategies of Small Chinese High-Technology Firms: A Quantitative Study." *Journal of Product Innovation Management* 25 (1) (2007): 79–102.

Sun, Sunny L., and Ruby P. Lee. "Enhancing Innovation through International Joint Venture Portfolios: From the Emerging Firm Perspective." *Journal of International Marketing* 21 (3) (2013): 1–21.

Tan, Yinglan. *Chinnovation: How Chinese Innovators Are Changing the World*. Singapore: Wiley, 2011.

Tian, Tao, David De Cremer, and Chunbo Wu. *Huawei: Leadership, Culture, and Connectivity*. Thousand Oaks, CA: Sage, 2017.

Tylecote, Andrew. "Twin Innovation Systems, Intermediate Technology and Economic Development: History and Prospect for China." *Innovation* 8 (1–2) (2006): 62–83.

Van de Kaa, Geerten, and Mark J. Greeven. "LED Standardization in China and South East Asia: Stakeholders, Infrastructure and Institutional Regimes." *Renewable & Sustainable Energy Reviews* 72 (2017): 863–870.

Wan, Feng, Peter J. Williamson, and Eden Yin. "Antecedents and Implications of Disruptive Innovation: Evidence from China." *Technovation* 39–40 (May–June 2015): 94–104.

Wei, Jiang, Minfei Zhou, Mark J. Greeven, and Hongyan Qu. "Governance Mechanisms, Dual Networks and Innovative Learning of Industrial Clusters: Multiple-Case Study in China." *Asia Pacific Journal of Management* 33 (4) (December 2016): 1037–1074.

Weick, Karl E. *Making Sense of the Organization*. Hoboken, NJ: Wiley-Blackwell, 2001.

Weinland, Don, and Sherry Fei Ju. "China's Ant Financial Shows Cashless Is King." *Financial Times*, April 4, 2018. https://www.ft.com/content/5033b53a-3eff-11e8-b9f9-de94fa33a81e.

Williamson, Peter J., and Eden Yin. "Accelerated Innovation: The New Challenge from China." *MIT Sloan Management Review* 55 (4) (Summer 2014): 27–34.

Yeung, Arthur, Katherine Xin, Waldemar Pfoertsch, and Shengjun Liu. *The Globalization of Chinese Companies: Strategies for Conquering International Markets*. Singapore: Wiley, 2011.

Yip, George S., and Bruce McKern. *China's Next Strategic Advantage: From Imitation to Innovation*. Cambridge, MA: MIT Press, 2016.

Yip, George S., and Shameen Prashantham. Innovation in Emerging Markets. In *Oxford Handbook on Management in Emerging Markets*, ed. Karl Meyer and Rob Grosse. Oxford: Oxford University Press, 2018.

Zeng, Ming, and Peter J. Williamson. *Dragons at Your Door: How Chinese Cost Innovation Is Disrupting Global Competition*. Boston: Harvard Business School Press, 2007.

Zhang, Jianwei. *The Why of Hidden Champions: The Ultimately Focused, Practical and Persistent Business Approach* [in Chinese]. Beijing: Beijing University of Posts and Telecommunications Press, 2015.

Zhou, Yu, William Lazonick, and Yifei Sun. *China as an Innovation Nation*. Oxford: Oxford University Press, 2016.

Index

Note: Figures and tables are denoted by *f* and *t*, respectively, following page numbers.

Printed in the United States
by Baker & Taylor Publisher Services